USING OCLC UNDER PRISM

A How-To-Do-It Manual

Robert T. Warwick
Kenneth Carlborg

HOW-TO-DO-IT MANUALS
FOR LIBRARIANS

NUMBER 61

NEAL-SCHUMAN PUBLISHERS, INC.
New York, London

Published by Neal-Schuman Publishers, Inc.
100 Varick Street
New York, NY 10013

Library of Congress Cataloging-in-Publication Data

Warwick, Robert T.
   Using OCLC under PRISM / Robert T. Warwick and Kenneth Carlborg.
     p. cm.—(How-to-do-it manuals for libraries ; no. 61)
   Includes bibliographical references and index.
   ISBN 1-55570-179-5
   1. OCLC PRISM (Informational retrieval system) 2. Cataloging—Data
processing. I. Carlborg, Kenneth. II. Title. III. Series.
Z699.4.029W34   1996
025.3'32—dc21   96-44332

CONTENTS

FIGURES

PREFACE

OCLC's history is a story of explosive growth and innovation. It started with the Ohio College Association, a small organization limited to college libraries in Ohio. This association generated customized cataloging cards for its small group of member college libraries. In 1974 this arrangement was renamed the Ohio College Library Consortium (the origin of the acronym OCLC) when this arrangement became more cooperative and expanded both the scope of its services and the number of libraries it served.

Today OCLC stands for Online Computer Library Center, Inc. Over 20,000 libraries throughout the world use a range of services available from OCLC including cataloging, interlibrary loan, end-user searching, and reference verification. In mid-1996, OCLC's Online Union Catalog contained over 35 *million* bibliographic records!

How did OCLC grow so rapidly? By continuously evolving with changing technology and user expectations. OCLC's introduction of PRISM in the early 1990s was one such step in this evolutionary cycle. PRISM brought many changes to everyday operations which help save OCLC users time, money, and unnecessary keystrokes (with their accompanying inevitable errors).

USING THIS MANUAL

Using OCLC Under PRISM: A How-To-Do-It Manual is designed to introduce library science students, librarians, and library paraprofessionals to PRISM's technical processing applications. It updates Neal-Schuman's earlier *Using OCLC: A How-To-Do-It Manual* by incorporating the changes and enhancements—such as keyword searching—OCLC introduced with the PRISM system. As OCLC continues to evolve, new ways of using the system and performing operations will be introduced. We expect, though, that these changes will augment rather than replace the basic operations we describe.

We have designed this manual so that its organization follows the typical order of technical services processing in today's libraries:

- Part I discusses connecting to OCLC, including step-by-step instructions for logging on to and off of PRISM.
- Part II is a detailed guide to utilizing PRISM's many kinds

of searches. Four chapters cover using the system's indexes and entering searches; maximizing the accuracy of available search formats; displaying search results; and qualifying searches for maximum efficiency and cost savings. Part II concludes with three exercises which reinforce these principles.

- Part III shows you how to catalog library materials once you've either located records for them or determined that an appropriate record does not exist in OCLC's database. The manual uses detailed instructions and a myriad of actual OCLC screens to show you how to edit and create records; utilize PRISM's cut, copy, and paste functions; enter entirely new records; save and validate records; and update and produce records for your library's collection. A final two exercises—one on field content, the other on tagging—reinforce concepts introduced in this part of the book.
- Four appendices, a glossary, and an index are included to make this manual "user-friendly" and facilitate its use at your workstation.

We have designed the exercises to be completed while connected to OCLC. Completing them will help you understand and internalize the main points covered in Parts II and III. The supplemental material in the appendices—such as descriptions of selected MARC fields and summary tables of commonly used commands and search keys—will make using OCLC easier until you have memorized these commands through everyday use.

Calculating the numbers of hours and dollars OCLC's PRISM service saves libraries everyday would require a supercomputer. We hope you'll find *OCLC Under PRISM: A How-To-Do-It Manual* a practical, easy-to-follow guide to make your cataloging even easier and more cost-efficient.

CONVENTIONS

The following conventions for input data and commands will be used in this manual:

- Character strings enclosed by angle brackets indicate either specific keys or commands for which you must use the assigned function key or key equivalent. They cannot be entered as text (e.g., press <Alt><a> to get a list of automatic scripts);
- Symbols or letters enclosed by single quotation marks indicate data that should be entered into the computer, without the quotes (e.g., enter 'gre,ho,' and press <SEND>);
- Capitalized character strings used alone indicate commands that can be entered either as text or by using the assigned function key or key equivalent. The text need not be capitalized when you enter it (e.g., enter PDN to see the next page of the record).

1 GETTING STARTED

CONNECTING THROUGH PASSPORT

You must first establish a telecommunications connection before you can log on to the PRISM service. The recommended connection method is through PASSPORT, which is a software package available from OCLC that is expressly designed to provide access to a variety of OCLC online services, including PRISM. You install PASSPORT software on your local computer or on a local area network (LAN) before connecting to OCLC. PASSPORT manages many important functions for you. It stores the specific communications parameters necessary for successful connection to OCLC through leased telephone lines, dial access, or the Internet. Its terminal emulation features store default function key definition files for individual services and applications—such as PRISM cataloging—as well as customized files for individual users should you so desire. It can store automatic logon/logoff scripts for each OCLC service you may access. It stores information about the kind of printer, keyboard, and monitor you are using and where downloaded records and files should be routed or stored. These features facilitate online editing, printing, and record export. In short, PASSPORT effectively handles the underlying mechanics necessary to connect to a desired OCLC service properly, thereby allowing you to communicate and work efficiently within that service.

Some infrequent users of the PRISM service may choose to connect through another commercial telecommunications software package such as ProComm. Those users will lose many important PASSPORT benefits, such as support for diacritics and special characters, special function keys, full screen editing, automatic logon/logoff, and record export. Their capabilities will be more limited. This manual describes PRISM service functionality from the perspective of a user connected through PASSPORT.

As very briefly mentioned above, PASSPORT offers many options that facilitate efficient work processes but it is beyond the scope of this manual to describe them in more detail. Full information can be found in the current edition of OCLC's *PASSPORT Software User Guide*.

COMMAND NOTATION

This manual generally uses the character string that can be entered into the system as a command rather than the corresponding function key(s) or key equivalents that accomplish the same thing. For example, the character string "PDN" is used to indicate the action "page down" rather than its corresponding function key <F4>. Commands with no character string equivalent are placed in angle brackets to show what action is being performed. Function keys are still not used. For example, "send" has no character string equivalent and is noted as <SEND>. Its corresponding function key, <F10>, is not used. While function keys are highly recommended for routine work, using them in a manual makes it harder for the beginner to understand exactly what action is suggested at a given point. Also, since PASSPORT allows individual users or institutions to assign or reassign command sequences to function keys, some key assignments may vary slightly from site to site. However, the underlying command sequence will always remain the same. Maximize efficient system use in your work environment by using the standard function keys and any customized key mapping that may have been installed at your institution.

LOG ON

After PASSPORT has established your telecommunications link to the PRISM service, you are ready to log on to PRISM. To do this, you must enter an authorization number which has been assigned by OCLC to your particular institution followed by a password associated with that number. Each authorization number is valid for some set of PRISM applications, such as cataloging and/or interlibrary loan. Within each valid application, an authorization number has an associated set of activities, or "modes," which define the range of operations, or level of work, a person using that number can perform. For example, in the cataloging application, one mode allows the user to search the database only; another mode allows the user to create new records but not add them to the master database; another mode allows the user both to create and add new records to the database. Yet another mode allows the user to add information and enhance existing full records in the database.

The recommended PRISM service log-on method is to use the PASSPORT automatic log-on/log-off feature. Select a logon/logoff script matching your connection option in PASSPORT for DOS (or use the session guide in PASSPORT for Windows), enter your authorization information into it, and store it for future use. Then to log on at some later point, press <Alt><a> to get a list of available automatic scripts in PASSPORT for DOS, select the correct one, and press <Enter>. If you are using PASSPORT for Windows, click on Open in the pull-down menu under Session. The system displays the available sessions. Click on the one you want. The software will establish the telecommunications link and complete the logon process in a single operation. Should you choose to log on manually, you must still press <Alt><a> in PASSPORT for DOS to get a list of telecommunications scripts. Select the appropriate one and press <Enter>. Similarly, in PASSPORT for Windows, you must still open a session. However, after the software establishes the telecommunications link, you will be presented with an initial PRISM service screen on which the system will first request your authorization number (enter it and press <SEND>) followed by your password (enter it and press <SEND>).

PASSPORT provides some other configuration options that make logging on even easier for many users. For example, suppose a computer workstation is on one staffmember's desk and suppose this staffmember is the only person who uses the computer and always logs on to the same PRISM application using the same connection method and the same authorization number. In such cases the entire log-on process can be fully automated and could be completed merely by selecting an "OCLC PRISM" menu option from some menu on the computer. There is no need to stop at any point in the process to request information (like connection script or authorization number) because that information never changes.

Following a successful logon (either automatic or manual), the PRISM service will respond with a greeting personalized to the name to which that authorization has been assigned, tell you the default application and mode that is in effect for that session (unless you change it), and display any general message of the day. For example, your response may look like one of these:

```
Hello SEARCHER
You will be using the CATALOGING system
in the SEARCH mode.

<Message of the day>

Hello TRACEY
```

```
You will be using the CATALOGING system
in the FULL mode.

<Message of the day>
```

Below the greetings and system/mode statement, you will usually see some message of the day. This message will vary regularly and includes such things as announcements of installed system enhancements, changes in hours of availability of some service, OCLC job announcements, conference announcements, system problem notices, or product announcements. You may be referred to PRISM News for fuller information. You should always read the message for its impact (if any) on your work session that day and as a reminder of relevant upcoming system activities (like a holiday closing reminder).

An authorization number can always be set to a lower mode of operation in a particular session than the default mode for which it is authorized. The lowest mode in the Cataloging system is "Search" and the next higher mode is "Limited." Search mode will only allow you to search for cataloging and authority records and to export records. While learning to use the system, you may want to use the Limited mode which will allow you to search for cataloging and authority records, practice editing existing records for local use, practice creating new records when no record exists for the item in hand, and enter your practice records into a temporary *Cataloging Save* file for later review. Limited mode will not let you add anything permanently to the database or order any output products, like catalog cards or tape records. This can save you from creating database problems or getting accidental product requests while you are learning to use the system.

To change temporarily to a lower mode for a given session, as part of a manual logon process, enter the three character abbreviation for the desired mode following the authorization number and a comma at the time you log on. For example, enter '<authorization number>,sch' for Search mode or '<authorization number>,ltd' for Limited mode. Then press <SEND>. The initial greeting message will show your selected mode rather than the usual default mode.

```
Hello TRACEY
You will be using the CATALOGING system
in the LIMITED mode.

<Message of the day>
```

To change temporarily to a lower mode for a given session following an automatic logon or after a manual logon has been completed, enter 'tem sch' for Search mode or 'tem ltd' for Limited mode in the home position and press <SEND>. The system will respond with the message:

```
Authorization mode changed.
```

The system will not allow you to request a mode for which your authorization number is not valid.

THE PRISM SCREEN

The PRISM service maintains a standard screen layout throughout a session. Across the top of the screen is a status line, generally in reverse video. The information displayed at the beginning of the line varies with the method used to establish a particular connection and remains constant throughout the session. Figure 1-1 shows two sample status lines, one for an Internet connection and one for a CompuServe connection. The empty space in the middle of the line is used during certain operations to indicate a system or record status. For example, the indications "LCK" and "SENT" appear temporarily after you send the system a search request and while your screen is locked, waiting for the response. The status line is not included on other screen display figures later in this manual although it does appear at the top of every screen.

The left corner of the line immediately below the status line is referred to as the "home position." When you first log on, the cursor will be in the home position ready for you to enter some command. The cursor indicates the place on the screen where keystrokes will be recorded and generally appears as a blinking square (similar to the ■ character used to indicate the cursor in Figure 1-1) or a blinking underscore, although other options are possible. After executing most requests the system returns the cursor to the home position, ready for another command. Most instructions to the system (such as search requests) are entered at the home position. Sometimes the cursor must be returned to the home position from elsewhere on the screen before taking an action. The keyboard has a <HOME> key which, when pressed, performs this move quickly. Unless otherwise specified, all system requests and commands in this manual are entered and executed from the home position.

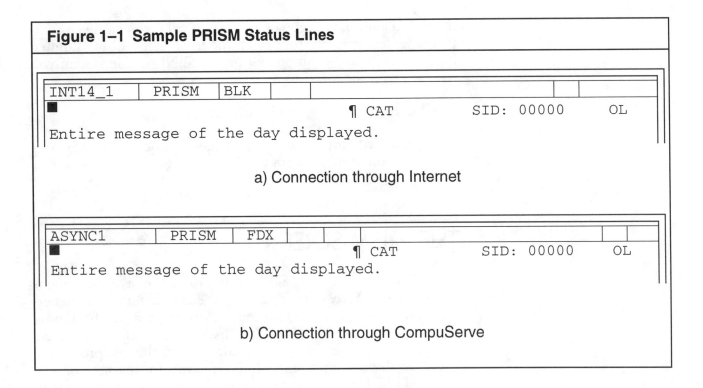

Figure 1–1 Sample PRISM Status Lines

```
INT14_1     PRISM   BLK
                                ¶ CAT        SID: 00000       OL
Entire message of the day displayed.
```

a) Connection through Internet

```
ASYNC1      PRISM   FDX
                                ¶ CAT        SID: 00000       OL
Entire message of the day displayed.
```

b) Connection through CompuServe

An end-of-message symbol (the ¶ symbol in this manual) appears next, near the center of the line. Whenever you press <SEND>, the system attempts to process everything from the previous start-of-message (the symbol ▶ in this manual) relative to the cursor position until the next end-of-message. This line begins with an implicit start-of-message. When you enter an instruction and press <SEND>, the system processes the entire line from the beginning up to the end-of-message. Occasionally, you may want the system to stop processing at your cursor position and ignore extra characters beyond the cursor but before the next end-of-message. If you press the <¶SEND> key instead of the <SEND> key, the system will place an end-of-message symbol at the cursor position before processing your request. This stops the system from processing those extra characters. The same technique (pressing <¶SEND> rather than <SEND>) can be used elsewhere in the record with a similar result.

A three-character code indicating which system you are logged into appears next. These examples both show "CAT" (cataloging); other possibilities include "ILL" (interlibrary loan) and "ULS" (union listing). Further along the line is the session ID ("SID") which is a number assigned to this specific session at logon. Each separate session will have its own unique ID for the duration of that session. OCLC technical support personnel will ask for this session ID if you have problems while online and contact them for assistance; you should note this number before calling OCLC. The final piece of information on this line is a two-character code indicating the database in which you are currently working. These examples both show "OL" (Online Union Catalog); other possibilities include "AF" (authority file) fnd "IL" (interlibrary loan transaction file). This code will change during your session if you change databases.

The next line is reserved for system messages, or prompts, which you sometimes get in response to an action. These examples both show the message "Entire message of the day displayed." which appeared at logon. Other possibilities include such messages as:

```
Beginning of record displayed.
End of holdings displayed.
Please complete marking.
Unrecognized command.
```

Not every action returns a message and this line could be empty.

The rest of the PRISM screen varies during a session depending on your current activities. You could be displaying the system message of the day, a bibliographic record, a title index display, an authority record, or a help screen. Other figures later in this manual show some of these display possibilities.

LOG OFF

The log-off process has two steps that perform different functions and must be done in the proper order to be successful. You may choose to do the first step but not the second. However, you should not do the second step without completing the first step.

First you must disconnect from the PRISM service itself. To disconnect manually from PRISM, enter 'logoff' in the home position and press <SEND>. To use an automatic log-off script, in PASSPORT for DOS, press <Alt><o> and the system will execute the log-off portion of the automatic log-on/log-off script that you selected at logon. In PASSPORT for Windows, click on Disconnect in the pull-down menu under Session. This step closes your connection with PRISM; however, your PASSPORT software is still open. You may wish to stop at this point and leave PASSPORT open. Perhaps you know that the next user at this computer will also connect to an OCLC service using her or his own authorization number. Or perhaps this particular computer has been dedicated exclusively to OCLC use in your environment and you are instructed to exit PASSPORT only at the end of the work day.

The second step is to close the PASSPORT software itself when you wish to return the computer to other uses or to a menu screen. Press <Alt><x> to initiate this step in PASSPORT for DOS. The system responds by displaying a warning message screen with a reminder that closing the PASSPORT software does not disconnect your PRISM session as part of the process. Press <Enter> to exit PASSPORT and return your computer to other uses; press <Esc> to leave PASSPORT open. In PASSPORT for Windows, click on Close under the Session pull-down menu to close your session and Exit to exit the software altogether. Closing PASSPORT without first disconnecting from PRISM may have unwanted consequences. For example, you may continue to tie up ports or incur connection charges (which could get expensive over time) until such time as you get disconnected due to inactivity. Remember to disconnect from your service provider *before* closing PASSPORT in order to avoid such complications.

2 INDEXES AND ENTERING SEARCHES

This chapter presents a basic overview of the available index types, instructions for entering searches in the Online Union Catalog and Authority File, and strategies for selecting various index options. Specific instructions for formatting many of the searches will be covered in the next chapter.

INDEXES

Each master record in the Online Union Catalog or Authority File is indexed at the time it is added to the database and reindexed any time it is subsequently corrected or enhanced. (Keyword indexing can take up to 24 hours; other indexes are generally built immediately.) During the indexing process, information is extracted from specified fields or portions of fields (called subfields) in each record and stored in corresponding index files along with similar information from other records in the database. Your search requests are processed against these index files, not the database records themselves.

The extracted information could be full words (such as for a subject keyword index) or only some characters from words (such as for a derived title index). For example, the system will pull some of the characters from an author's last, first, and middle names to create an author key and store it in the personal name index file along with author keys from other records in the database.

Similarly named indexes exist within several index types but they do not always include information from exactly the same fields or subfields. For example, both the derived title search key and title keyword indexes extract information from the main title for their respective indexes. However, the derived title search key index extracts only from the main title itself, not from any subtitle. The title keyword index extracts from both the main title and subtitle. As another example, the derived title search key index includes a series title while the title phrase index does not. These differences lead to different search results from similarly named indexes. The Appendix lists the fields and subfields from which information is extracted for each index.

Records can be retrieved using any search for which matching index keys were created at the time of indexing. There are three general index categories from the perspective of how keys are built and how search requests are processed:

- Search key indexes (where parts of words are combined and indexed);
- Keyword indexes (where whole words are individually indexed); and
- Phrase indexes (where whole words in a sequence are indexed).

SEARCH KEY SEARCHES

Search keys are the oldest search type and follow very strict formats. Because of technological and economic constraints when the OCLC database was first developed, the initial indexes were designed to store only small parts of words in a short, fixed format rather than entire, long words. OCLC still builds search keys using those early designs along with building the newer full word indexes introduced under PRISM. There are two types of search keys: numeric search keys from standard numbers in the record and derived search keys from author's names or words in titles. Numeric search keys include such indexes as LCCN (Library of Congress control number), ISBN (International Standard Book Number), and ISSN (International Standard Serial Number). Derived search keys include personal and corporate names, titles, and a name/title combination. In addition, each record also may be recalled by an internally-assigned OCLC control number.

Each search key follows a different specific format which is one way the system identifies which database and index file to search with a particular key. A search key format is a combination of punctuation (or lack of punctuation) and length of data. For example, a derived title search key for the Online Union Catalog uses the first three letters of the first word in the title, followed by a comma, followed by the first two letters of the second word, followed by another comma, followed by the first two letters of the third word, followed by another comma, and ending with the first letter of the fourth word in the title. Thus, the derived title search key contains four data elements of several lengths and three commas. A search key with exactly the same structure but beginning with an open bracket ([) signals the system that this derived title search key should be processed in the Authority File instead of the Online Union Catalog. The unique identifiable structure of each search key provided sufficient information for the pre-PRISM OCLC system to process your request and continues to be recognized in PRISM. A search request in the Online Union Catalog using search keys might look like one of these examples.

```
81-40411            [recognized as an LCCN search request]
0719543320          [recognized as an ISBN search request]
for,wh,th,b         [recognized as a derived title search request]
coop,jam,f          [recognized as a derived personal name search request]
```

A search request in the Authority File using search keys might look like one of these examples.

```
[81-40411           [recognized as an LCCN search request]
[lec,no,in,m        [recognized as a derived title search request]
[coop,jam,f         [recognized as a derived name search request]
```

With the introduction of the PRISM service, OCLC implemented a newer search method using commands and index labels to structure a search request. Indexes that have been newly implemented since PRISM was introduced (such as the keyword indexes) have no old form and, therefore, always use commands and index labels. The old search key indexes from the pre-PRISM system discussed here can continue to be entered the old way shown above or they can be entered the new way using commands and index labels shown below. Each index has two possibilities:

```
fin ln 81-40411     [recognized as an LCCN search request]
fin bn 0719543320   [recognized as an ISBN search request]
fin dt for,wh,th,b  [recognized as a derived title search request]
fin dp coop,jam,f   [recognized as a derived personal name search request]
```

Notice that the search key structure following the command and index label remains exactly the same in these examples as in the pre-PRISM search key examples shown earlier. Due to fewer required key strokes or simply from habit, many users still enter search keys without commands or index labels. Search keys all use the 'Find' command which can be abbreviated 'fin' as in the above examples. The other search command that is currently implemented in PRISM is the 'Scan' command which is used in the phrase searches discussed. Each index label is a unique two-character code that identifies one index to the system. Figure 2-1 lists search key index labels for the Online Union Catalog and the Authority File.

Figure 2–1 Search keys and corresponding index labels	
SEARCH KEY	INDEX LABEL
Online Union Catalog	
OCLC control number	an
Numeric keys	
CODEN	cd
Government document number	gn
International Standard Book Number (ISBN)	bn
International Standard Serial Number (ISSN)	sn
Library of Congress control number (LCCN)	ln
Music publisher number	mn
Derived keys	
Corporate or conference name	dc
Name/title	da
Personal name	dp
Title	dt
Authority File	
OCLC control number	an
Numeric keys	
International Standard Book Number (ISBN)	bn
International Standard Serial Number (ISSN)	sn
Library of Congress control number (LCCN)	ln
Derived keys	
Personal/corporate/conference/geographic name	dn
Title	dt

A new search capability using search keys has been introduced with PRISM. Two search keys connected with an 'and' can be combined into a single search. Because this is a new capability introduced only since PRISM has been implemented, you must use the 'fin' command and an appropriate index label for each search key. There is no "old" form that can be used. A combined search key request will look something like this.

```
fin dp hemi,ern, and dt for,wh,th,b
```
[recognized as a combined derived personal name and derived title search request]

KEYWORD SEARCHES

Keyword searching is a new search type introduced with PRISM. Keyword indexes include individual words from many additional parts of a record than just the author and title fields used to construct the derived search key indexes. Keywords are pulled from such other fields as subjects, notes, and publishers. You can combine up to eight separate keywords in a single search (each with its own index label) although it is rare in practice to include that many. This makes keyword searching very flexible and powerful for problem records since you have an opportunity to use the most distinctive words found almost anywhere in a record. However, it also uses more system resources than do the older and more constrained search key searches (and is priced higher as a result) and does not necessarily produce better search results for the average record.

Keyword indexes have been introduced so far only in the Online Union Catalog, not the Authority File. They always use the 'fin' command and index labels. Figure 2-2 lists the current keyword index labels. The only connector currently available between index terms is 'and' and every term must be preceded by its own index label, even when a term takes the same label as the previous one. The keyword index does not offer the full range of boolean connectors like "or" and "not" and has not implemented term nesting and parentheses which are unnecessary with 'and' as the only available connector.

```
fin au christie and ti poirot
fin ti sawyer and ti finn and au twain
```

Figure 2–2 Keywords and corresponding index labels	
KEYWORD	**INDEX LABEL**
Online Union Catalog	
Author	au
includes personal, corporate, and conference names	
Frequency	fq
Language	la
Notes	nt
Publisher name	pb
Publisher place	pl
Report number	rn
Series	se
Subject	su
Subject/Title/Contents	st
includes words from subject, title, or contents note	
Title	ti
Uniform title	ut

PHRASE INDEXES

The phrase index search is another search type introduced in PRISM. Unlike search keys or keyword indexes, the phrase indexes don't actually return a set of records that match your search request. Instead, you are placed into the area of an index where your search phrase or its closest match would be located. As a result, you always get some response from the system, although you still may not find a useful title in the area of the index where you are placed.

The phrase indexes use the 'Scan' command (abbreviated 'sca') rather than the 'Find' command used by the other search types. Using a different command reinforces the basic differences between the phrase indexes and the other indexes. Phrase searches don't retrieve matching records directly. They merely browse a list of index entries instead. Phrase indexes are the only ones that include multiple words following a single index label. They treat all of the words in the order they are entered as if they were a single character string and match them as such. Matching is only done from the beginning of an entry in the index, not from the middle or the end of entries. The only phrase index that has been implemented so far in the Online Union Catalog is the title phrase index, but others are being considered as future enhancements. Several phrase indexes are currently available in the Authority File. Current phrase index labels are listed in Figure 2-3. Since these are also new indexes they are always entered using commands and index labels.

```
sca ti homemade houses
sca au christie
```

ENTERING YOUR SEARCH REQUEST

To enter a search request, return your cursor to the home position, type in your selected entry as discussed above, and press <SEND> (or <¶SEND> if you need to add an end-of-message symbol after your search string). For example, to search for the record

Figure 2–3 Phrase searches and corresponding index labels	
PHRASE	INDEX LABEL
Online Union Catalog Title	ti
Authority File Conference name Corporate name Personal name Title Subject	cn co pn ti su

for *Handmade Houses* by Art Boericke using the LCCN search key, enter '73-78445' and press <SEND>. Depending on the search type you selected, there may be some additional considerations when entering your request.

You may need to specify a different database in which to execute the search. Explicitly changing databases is not required when using search keys without commands and labels since the structure of the search key itself already includes the database as part of every request. A search request either begins with '[' for an Authority File search or does not begin with '[' for an Online Union Catalog search. However, command and index label searches do not have the database built in as do the older search key searches. You must explicitly change databases when necessary. If the system recognizes your search type as valid for your current database it will try to process it. If your search type is not valid for that database the system message line will display an error message similar to the following example.

```
Search label dp isn't valid for this database.
```

Some index labels are valid in both the Online Union Catalog and the Authority File and some are valid in only one of them. For example, in Figure 2-1 notice that 'an,' 'ln,' and 'dt' are in both the Online Union Catalog and the Authority File while 'dc,' and 'da' are only in the Online Union Catalog and 'dn' and 'ds' are only in the Authority File. Suppose that after viewing a record in the Authority File you wish to search for a bibliographic record using a derived title search key. Since the command and index label 'fin dt . . . ' is valid in the Authority file and your current database is 'AF,' the system will process your new search request in the Authority File. In order to have the system process your request in the Online Union Catalog you must explicitly select that database before entering the new search.

You select a different database with the 'Choose' command, which can be shortened to 'cho.' You can change databases and enter your search request in one step by chaining the two commands together. First you choose a new database (e.g., 'cho ol'), then enter a semicolon, and then enter your search key. The semicolon is recognized by the system as a separator between commands. Each command is processed in turn and you are only presented on screen with the result of the final command. Intermediate steps are not shown unless one of them produces an error, in which case the system stops at that command for you to resolve the error. Chaining a search request with changing the database will look something like this:

```
cho ol;fin dt for,wh,th,b
cho af;fin an 1128759
```

Some numeric search key searches can be misinterpreted by the system when a single record or a list of records is already displayed on screen. For example, you enter a numeric search key that includes a dash (e.g., an LCCN or ISSN search) but the system interprets the request as an attempt to edit a field or select a record range and responds with an error message. Either you need to reenter your search using a command and index label which will not be misinterpreted or you need to clear the current display from your screen before entering the search. The current display is cleared by the RET (return) command. If you choose to press the function key for RET then all you need to do subsequently is enter your search key. You can also enter 'ret' and chain it with your search key as in the following example.

```
ret;87-35710
```

SELECTING A SEARCH STRATEGY

You should always try to select an efficient search strategy based on the quality of the information available to you. Numeric search keys are more efficient to use when they are available because they tend to be relatively unique, retrieving a single record or only a few records. Derived search keys, on the other hand, often represent many records and could result in time consuming searches with a large number of records retrieved. When a given search retrieves more than the maximum records allowed by the system, the result is a dead-end search. (The maximum number of bibliographic records currently retrieved in a search is 1,500; the number of authority records is 600.) Records cannot be retrieved by that search the way it is formulated. Either modify the search request, perhaps by adding a qualifier as discussed in a later chapter, or use a different search.

Begin with the most unique search request that you can construct from the information you have. However, it may be necessary to use many or all available search techniques when trying to retrieve a bibliographic record. For example, a record in the database may not contain an ISBN or an LCCN, even though one or both may appear in the item or citation you have. Those search keys would not retrieve that record. Similarly, the apparent main or added entry or title proper of a work in hand may vary somewhat from the entry or title proper appearing on a database record for that work. If you are a cataloger, finding a record in the database can save you the task of cataloging the work yourself and will prevent you from duplicating a record already in the Online Union Catalog. OCLC strongly discourages the knowing addition of duplicate records and has an active program to clean up the ones that already exist or are newly discovered. Once you find a desirable record, always note its OCLC control number to facilitate easy and immediate retrieval later.

When searching the online catalog, it is a good habit to use a strategy that is likely to retrieve the fewest records the soonest. This will save you both time and resources. Your search strategy should start out with number search keys (when available) followed by other search types. Scan title has become increasingly popular as an early strategy, often used after numbers and before derived search keys. The following order of preference is one example of such a strategy:

```
OCLC number (when known)
ISBN
LCCN
Scan title
Derived title
Combined derived author and derived title
Derived name/title
Derived name
```

The use of search qualifiers (discussed in a later chapter) can make some of these searches even more specific. Keyword searches are rarely used as part of a routine early search strategy, although they are often an excellent approach for certain classes of problem items with very common or generic names and titles. One of the exercises following Chapter 5 will demonstrate a range of results from using different search strategies to locate the same item.

3 SEARCH FORMATS

SOME NUMERIC SEARCH KEYS

This section describes the three most commonly used numeric search keys available in the Online Union Catalog and the Authority File: OCLC control number, ISBN, and LCCN. It also discusses two search keys (government document number and music publisher number) that are constructed quite differently than the other numeric search keys and are only available in the Online Union Catalog. The structures for all the numeric search keys can be found in the Appendix.

OCLC CONTROL NUMBER

Each record in the database is assigned a unique OCLC control number which appears with the label 'OCLC:' in various bibliographic record displays and with the label 'ARN:' in various authority record displays. This is the most specific search and the fastest way to retrieve a single record from a database. Only one record will be retrieved from the selected database using the OCLC control number. The search key in the Online Union Catalog consists of the number sign (#) or the asterisk (*) followed by a number. The search key in the Authority File consists of an open bracket ([) followed by the number sign or asterisk followed by a number. The system will interpret this structure as a request to search the OCLC control number index file in the appropriate database. When using index labels, you do not need to enter the number sign or asterisk before the control number. However, you may need to choose a database before entering your request.

CONTROL NUMBER	SEARCH KEY	OR	INDEX LABEL
754622	#754622		fin an 754622
27976571	*27976571		fin an 27976571
376340	[#376340		fin an 376340
3351657	[*3351657		fin an 3351657

This search key is particularly useful when you want to call up a specific record that you already know about, especially if the initial search for that record involved a time-consuming, extended search.

If you happen to include the number sign or asterisk with the number as part of an index label search request, the system will still process your request properly in your current database. If your current database is AF, you can even include the open bracket and have the request processed properly. However, you get an error message if your current database is OL and you include an open bracket with the index label.

ISBN

An International Standard Book Number (ISBN) can be found in most recently published books. It consists of 10 digits, usually separated by hyphens or spaces when printed. In some books published in the late 1960s you will find a 9 digit SBN (prior to the internationalization of this number) which is also indexed in this index file. The ISBN search key consists of the 9 or 10 digits, with no spaces or hyphens. The system interprets that structure as a request to search the ISBN index file. The number is entered exactly the same way when using index labels.

Since an SBN is converted to an ISBN by adding a leading zero to the 9 digit number, the system is programmed to allow you to either include or exclude any leading zero in your search key. When the final check "digit" in an ISBN is an "X," include it in your search key. The "x" can be entered either in upper or lower case.

ISBN		SEARCH KEY	OR	INDEX LABEL
0–7195–4332–0		0719543320		fin bn 0719543320
	or	719543320		fin bn719543320
2–03–505302–1		2035053021		fin bn 2035053021
0–85229–493–X		085229493x		fin bn 085229493
	or	85229493x		fin bn 85229493x

LCCN

The Library of Congress control number (formerly called the Library of Congress card number) often appears in a book as 1 or 2 digits, followed by a hyphen, followed by 1 to 6 digits. The LCCN search key in the Online Union Catalog consists of the 1 or 2 digits, a hyphen, and the 1 to 6 digits. This key must contain a hyphen after the first or second digit. The search key in the Authority File begins with an open bracket and follows the same format. The system will interpret this structure as a request to search the LCCN index file in the appropriate database.

The hyphen is not necessary when using the index label. You can either enter it or leave it out. However, if you leave it out, you will need to add a lead fill zero to any number that has fewer than two digits before the hyphen.

LCCN		SEARCH KEY	OR	INDEX LABEL
92–39374		92-39374		fin ln 9239374
	or			fin ln 92-39374
3–22517		3-22517		fin ln 0322517
	or			fin ln 3-22517
79–40104		[79-40104		fin ln 79-40104
	or			fin ln 7940104

The LCCNs in many bibliographic and authority records have an alphabetic prefix (e.g., "gb86–16790" or "n 92106882"). When you do not include the prefix as part of your search key, the system will return matching records both with and without the prefix. However, if you do enter a prefix as part of your search string, the system will only return matches that have the prefix. Similarly, you can enter a circumflex (^) before a number to have the system only return matches that have no prefix. Close up any spaces between the prefix and the number when constructing a search key.

LCCN	SEARCH KEY	OR	INDEX LABEL
gb86–16790	gb86-16790		fin ln gb86-16790
86–16790	^86-16790		fin ln ^86-16790
n 92106882	[n92106882		fin ln n92106882

GOVERNMENT DOCUMENT NUMBER

Government document numbers are not structured as uniformly as the ISBNs and LCCNs described above. They vary considerably in length and can contain different combinations of letters, numbers, punctuation, and spaces in any order.

A search key for this index is constructed from parts of the number based on the following design. The basic search key begins with a two character prefix code and colon ('gn:') which tells the system which index to search. This code is followed by zero, one, or two letters and one to ten numerals. For the letters, select as many as the first two letters that appear before the first numeral. This could be zero (when the number begins with a numeral), one, or two. Ignore all letters thereafter. For the numerals, take all numerals in order from the first up to the tenth, ignoring all intervening spaces, punctuation, or letters. When using index labels you do not need to enter the 'gn:' prefix.

NUMBER	SEARCH KEY	OR	INDEX LABEL
HED11/620.2/OC1/1988	gn:he1162021198	fin gn he1162021198
HE 1.18/4:Ad 7/3	gn:he118473	fin gn he118473
HED11.4/Y2	gn:he1142	fin gn he1142
He 1 St.1/2:F 3/1985	gn:he11231985	fin gn he11231985
HED1/10.2/P69/1987/Sum.	gn:he1102691987	fin gn he1102691987

One special feature of this index is its implicit truncation of the search key. You do not need to include the entire numeral portion in your search key in order to match a record. If you enter just a few beginning numerals, the system will retrieve records with matching numbers that are at least that long or longer. For example, notice that all of the above examples begin with "he11" before anything is different. They could all be retrieved with the same shorter search key 'gn:he11' provided the key retrieves fewer records than the maximum the system will return. A problem with short search keys is that they frequently retrieve too many records while a problem with long search keys is that they are more prone to transcription errors. You can balance your entry of long numbers by perhaps including only four or five numerals rather than all eight or ten. Experiment and see what works in your own environment with the kinds of numbers you regularly search.

A corollary problem is how to retrieve a record with a government document number that indeed is short when that short number retrieves more records than the system will display. You do not want records with longer numbers returned as part of the search result set. The system allows you to enter a circumflex (^) following the numerals to override the implicit truncation feature. Such keys will not return any records with longer numbers which limits the size of the result set.

NUMBER	SEARCH KEY	OR	INDEX LABEL
HES 1.1	gn:he11^	fin gn he11^
HEO/Se1.1	gn:he11^	fin gn he11^
HED11.4/Y2	gn:he1142^	fin gn he1142^

Decisions on what to include, what not to include, how long to make the search key, and so forth, can get confusing. There is yet another option. You can enter all the letters, numerals, and punctuation in the entire number (with two exceptions) and let the system construct a search key for you. The two exceptions are spaces which cannot be understood and slashes which are interpreted as an attempt to qualify the search (qualifiers are discussed in Chapter 5). Therefore both must be excluded from the number. However, you can still include them with the index label search method if you surround the number with quotation marks.

NUMBER	SEARCH KEY	OR	INDEX LABEL
HE 1.18/4:Ad 7/3	gn:he1.184:ad73		fin gn he1.184:ad73
or			fin gn "he 1.18/4:ad 7/3"
He 1 St.1M:1980	gn:he1st.1m:1980		fin gn he1st.1m:1980
or			fin gn "he 1 st.1m:1980"

MUSIC PUBLISHER NUMBER

Music publisher numbers can be just as varied as government document numbers. From the perspective of index building in OCLC, music publisher numbers are similar enough to government document numbers that all of the features and options described above apply to these numbers as well. Read the government document number section above for fuller information which is not repeated here.

Music numbers also begin with a two character code and colon (in this case 'mn:') which is followed by up to two letters and ten numbers. Punctuation and spaces are ignored. Implicit truncation is in place unless explicitly overwritten with an ending circumflex. You have the option of entering everything and letting the system create the search key (with the restriction about surrounding entries containing spaces or slashes with parentheses). All of this is exactly like the government document number search key described above.

MUSIC NUMBER	SEARCH KEY	OR	INDEX LABEL
GES.1118	mn:ge1118		fin mn ge1118
GE–15001	mn:ge15001		fin mn ge15001
Gesellschaft 102216	mn:ge102216		fin mn ge102216
GEF/1	mn:ge1^		fin mn ge1^
GE 17	mn:ge17^		fin mn ge17^
GESD–1	mn:ge1^		fin mn ge1^
GEMA US12/L48	mn:gemaus12148		fin mn gemaus12148
or			fin mn "gema us12/148"
GEMA 18–7770–2	mn:gema18-7770-2		fin mn gema18-7770-2
or			fin mn "gema 18-7770-2"

However, music numbers offer an additional collection of capabilities for constructing search keys because, unlike government document numbers, multiple music numbers can appear in the same field. The system identifies candidates for multiple number processing by the presence of certain character strings: a double dash ('--'), a comma space (', '), and/or parentheses.

The double dash is interpreted as a range of numbers when the number following the double dash is higher than the number before it and the first two alphabetic characters before both numbers are the same. Every number in that range is indexed separately (up to 20 numbers).

MUSIC NUMBER	SEARCH KEY	OR	INDEX LABEL
GE–116–1—GE–116–12	`mn:ge1161`		`fin mn ge1161`
	`mn:ge1162`		`fin mn ge1162`
	`etc.`		`etc.`
	`mn:ge11611`		`fin mn ge11611`
	`mn:ge11612`		`fin mn ge11612`
GEM 110—116	`mn:ge110`		`fin mn ge110`
	`mn:ge111`		`fin mn ge111`
	`etc.`		`etc.`
	`mn:ge115`		`fin mn ge115`
	`mn:ge116`		`fin mn ge116`

This range of numbers rule only applies to double dashes. single dashes are interpreted as one number (e.g., GEM 110–116 is one number, not a range of numbers).

The comma space is interpreted as separating discrete numbers, each of which is indexed separately.

MUSIC NUMBER	SEARCH KEY	OR	INDEX LABEL
GRC 112, 114	`mn:gr112^`		`fin mn gr112^`
	`mn:114^`		`fin mn 114^`
GRC–1001, D1000	`mn:gr1001`		`fin mn gr1001`
	`mn:d1000^`		`fin mn d1000^`

This only applies to comma space. A comma without a following space is interpreted as one number (e.g., GRC 115,116 is one number).

Numbers enclosed within parentheses are also interpreted as separate numbers. You could have a double dash or comma space within a set of parentheses. In that case they follow the rules for double dash and comma space as well as the rules for parentheses.

MUSIC NUMBER	SEARCH KEY	OR	INDEX LABEL
7–LL (RCA DEK1–0061-DEK1–0069)	`mn:7^`		`fin mn 7^`
	`mn:rc1006110069`		`fin mn rc1006110069`
1004 (GRC–1001, D1000)	`mn:1004`		`fin mn 1004`
	`mn:gr1001`		`fin mn gr1001`
	`mn:d1000^`		`fin mn d1000^`

SOME DERIVED SEARCH KEYS

This section describes basic guidelines for constructing the four most common derived search keys: title, personal name, corporate/meeting name, and name/title. The title and the name search keys are available in both the Online Union Catalog and the Authority File. The name/title search key is available only in the Online Union Catalog. The structures for all derived search keys can be found in the Appendix.

DERIVED TITLE

The derived title search key is used to search main titles (titles proper), uniform titles, various types of added entry titles, and traced series titles in the Online Union Catalog and uniform titles and series titles in the Authority File. The search key contains some characters from each of the first four "significant" words of the title that is being searched. The structure of the search key is often expressed as '3, 2, 2, 1'—the first 3 characters of the first significant word of the title, a comma, the first 2 characters of the second word of the title, a comma, the first 2 characters of the third word of the title, a comma, and the first character of the fourth word of the title. The system will interpret this structure as a request to search the title index file in the Online Union Catalog. The derived title search key in the Authority File begins with an open bracket and then follows the same format. When using index labels you must still structure the search request following the label in exactly the same way. The same index label is used in both the Online Union Catalog and the Authority File.

TITLE	SEARCH KEY	OR	INDEX LABEL
For Whom the Bell Tolls	for,wh,th,b		fin dt for,wh,th,b
Murder on the Orient Express	mur,on,th,o		fin dt mur,on,th,o
War of 1812 Index of Soldiers	war,of,18,i		fin dt war,of,18,i
Anatomy of an Illness	ana,of,an,i		fin dt ana,of,an,i
Lecture noted in mathematics	[lec,no,in,m		fin dt lec,no,in,m

You need not capitalize any letters in the search key. Use only letters, numerals, or the seven special symbols (& $ £ * % @ ♭) in your search key. Do not include any other punctuation or diacritics. Remember, you must be aware of how internal punctuation may affect a given search key.

In a title, the definition of a word is a character or group of characters between two blank spaces. It is the blank space that separates words, not other punctuation. This has implications for the way you search the system for a title when a cataloger may or may not have included spaces with internal punctuation. For instance, "U.S." is a single title word (us), whereas "U. S." is two title words (u and s) since the cataloger inserted a space. You may need to search an ambiguous title several ways before discovering an existing bibliographic record in the database. For example:

TITLE	SEARCH KEY	OR	INDEX LABEL
U.S.–Soviet Relations in Europe	uss,re,in,e		fin dt uss,re,in,e
U.S. – Soviet Relations in Europe	us,so,re,i		fin dt us,so,re,i
U. S.–Soviet Relations in Europe	u,ss,re,i		fin dt u,ss,re,i
U. S. – Soviet Relations in Europe	u,s,so,r		fin dt u,s,so,r

While we have come a long way in our quest for cataloging standardization and guidelines for computer data entry, many areas are still open to interpretation and many older records remain in the database that were created years ago under earlier practices. You may need to account for variant interpretations by different catalogers over a period of time when constructing a search.

You arrive at the first "significant" word in a title by eliminating any initial articles in any language that has them. Once you start your search key, include any internal articles; you only eliminate the initial articles. For example:

TITLE	SEARCH KEY	OR	INDEX LABEL
The Red Badge of Courage	red,ba,of,c		fin dt red,ba,of,c
Les Rayons et les Ombres	ray,et,le,o		fin dt ray,et,le,o
The War of 1812 in the Northwest	war,of,18,i		fin dt war,of,18,i

The proper indexing of title fields depends upon accurate data entry and coding of those titles within the machine readable record. For title fields that contain a filing indicator (such as field 245), the system uses the filing indicator value to determine whether there is a need to eliminate an initial article prior to indexing. If this value is incorrect, the system will not properly eliminate the initial article or may eliminate a word that should be indexed. For title fields that do not contain a filing indicator (such as field 246) the system relies on the cataloger having eliminated any initial article from a title during the cataloging process. You may need to search a title several ways if your initial search method retrieves no matching records. OCLC is a dynamic database built by many people over many years and contains a certain number of errors. Users are highly encouraged to report any inaccurate indexing to OCLC so that those records can be fixed.

When constructing a derived title search key, ignore any subtitle or other title information. Use only the main title. This is different than the title phrase search key and keyword search key which are discussed later. They both include the subtitle as part of their indexing.

The derived title search keys that have been demonstrated thus far all contain at least four words and have all had three commas. However, it is important to remember that the structure of the title search key requires three commas, even when there are less than four words in the title proper. For example:

TITLE	SEARCH KEY	OR	INDEX LABEL
Les Miserables	`mis,,,`		`fin dt mis,,,`
Les Miserables : a Musical in Two Acts	`mis,,,`		`fin dt mis,,,`
Planet News	`pla,ne,,`		`fin dt pla,ne,,`
Handmade Houses : A Guide to the Woodbutcher's Art	`han,ho,,`		`fin dt han,ho,,`
The Hunchback of Notre-Dame	`hun,of,no,`		`fin dt hun,of,no,`
The Hunchback of Notre Dame	`hun,of,no,d`		`fin dt hun,of,no,d`
Star Trek	`[sta,tr,,`		`fin dt sta,tr,,`
Baby-sitters Club	`[bab,cl,,`		`fin dt bab,cl,,`

Again you must rely on the correct coding of the automated record by the cataloger for proper indexing. If the subtitle is not coded as a subtitle but is entered as part of the title proper instead, it will be indexed even though it shouldn't be. Also, the typography and layout of some items leave title fragments open to interpretation as to whether they are subtitles or part of the title proper. Two catalogers could easily interpret such title fragments differently leading to two different titles proper. If you don't find a matching record in the database and there is some question as to where a title ends and a subtitle begins, you may need to do an additional search to cover both options.

DERIVED PERSONAL NAME

The derived personal name search key may be used for searching personal names in the Authority File or personal names found as main entries or added entries in the Online Union Catalog. The structure of the derived personal name search key may be thought of as "4, 3, 1"—the first four letters of the last name, a comma, the first three letters of the first name, a comma, and the middle initial. The derived personal name search key must contain two commas. The system will interpret this structure as a request to search the derived personal name index file in the Online Union

Catalog. The derived personal name search key in the Authority File begins with an open bracket and then follows the same format. When using index labels you must still structure the search request following the label in exactly the same way. Different index labels are used in the Online Union Catalog and the Authority File. For example:

PERSONAL NAME	SEARCH KEY	OR	INDEX LABEL
Harry S. Truman	trum,har,s		fin dp trum,har,s
Katherine Hepburn	hepb,kat,		fin dp hepb,kat,
James Fenimore Cooper	coop,jam,f		fin dp coop,jam,f
Victor Hugo	hugo,vic,		fin dp hugo,vic,
James Fenimore Cooper	[coop,jam,f		fin dn coop,jam,f
Victor Hugo	[hugo,vic,		fin dn hugo,vic,

Do not worry about including a middle initial in your search key. Because the information available to the searcher may be incomplete, the system has been programmed to retrieve matching names that contain a middle name or initial even if you do not include one in your search key. (In Chapter 5, we will discuss how to override this feature by using a circumflex.) However, using a middle initial when you know one creates a more specific search key and retrieves fewer matching records. For example, the search key "trum,har,s" above might retrieve 1,404 records while the more general search key "trum,har," might retrieve 1,418 records. Those additional 14 records retrieved in the more general search represent headings containing a middle name or initial beginning with something other than "s." Using the more specific search is recommended.

Similarly, you do not need to use all of the first three letters of the first name in your search. If you use only the first initial the system will retrieve every surname which has a forename that begins with that letter. Thus, in the above search for Katherine Hepburn, "hepb,k," will also retrieve the desired records. Again, remember that the less information the system is given, the more matches will result.

To retrieve personal names that consist of only one significant element use the search key "4,,". For example:

PERSONAL NAME	SEARCH KEY	OR	INDEX LABEL
Madonna	mado,,		fin dp mado,,
Aristotle	aris,,		fin dp aris,,
Anne, of France, 1461–1522	anne,,		fin dp anne,,
Josquin, des Prez, d. 1521	josq,,		fin dp josq,,

If no second element is present in the search key the system will not retrieve all surnames that begin with that string regardless of forename. At least one letter must be present following the first comma for the system to retrieve names made up of multiple elements.

Since names in the derived personal name index in the Online Union Catalog are taken from bibliographic records, they reflect the generally inverted form of name heading used by the cataloger rather than the generally direct form of name as it appears on a work. Many names are straightforward and a bibliographic form for the derived search key can be easily constructed from the work. However, several types of names can present problems.

Constructing a search key based on the authorized bibliographic form of a name can lead to uncertainty as to the correct name form when your author has a compound surname or an article as part of the name. In such cases, the Authority File can help you determine the correct bibliographic form of an uncertain name since both the authorized form of the name as well as other forms found in the cross references are indexed in the Authority File. When you search the Online Union Catalog you should use only the authorized form that you found in the Authority File. If you have a name that is not in the Authority File, you may need to search the name several ways in the Online Union Catalog to ensure that you have retrieved any desired bibliographic records. For example:

PERSONAL NAME	CORRECT SEARCH KEY	INCORRECT SEARCH KEY
Erich von Stroheim	`vons,eri,`	`stro,eri,v`
Lope de Vega	`vega,lop,d`	`deve,lop,`
Barbara E. Harrell-Bond	`harr,bar,e`	`bond,bar,e`

BUT

Erich von Stroheim		`[vons,eri,`	
	or	`[stro,eri,v`	matches a cross reference
Lope de Vega		`[vega,lop,d`	
	or	`[deve,lop,`	matches a cross reference

The above examples also illustrate another principle for constructing derived personal name search keys. The first element of the search key that you enter is the "surname," which generally consists of everything before the first comma in the heading. The "surname" may actually be several names or elements separated by spaces or hyphens (e.g., Harrell-Bond) or may include a preposition or article (e.g., von Stroheim). Eliminate any punctuation and close up all spaces in the surname when constructing your search key. For example:

BIBLIOGRAPHIC FORM OF PERSONAL NAME	SEARCH KEY	OR	INDEX LABEL
De la Mare, Walter	`dela,wal,`		`fin dp dela,wal,`
Le Carre, John	`leca,joh,`		`fin dp leca,joh,`
Van Buren, Abigail	`vanb,abi,`		`fin dp vanb,abi,`
Van Buren, Abigail	`[vanb,abi,`		`fin dn vanb,abi,`

You also need to be aware of any nicknames that an author may use in a work. Those nicknames may or may not be used in the bibliographic form of the name. Under current cataloging rules, the nickname will be used if that is the predominant form in the author's published works. This is another situation where searching the Authority File can lead you to the correct name form to use in the Online Union Catalog. Again, if you do not find the name in the Authority File you may need to search several ways in the Online Union Catalog to discover existing bibliographic records. For example:

PERSONAL NAME ON PIECE	OFFICIAL NAME HEADING		SEARCH KEY
Bobby Kennedy		not	`kenn,bob,`
	Kennedy, Robert F.	but	`ken,rob,f`
Edward Van Halen		not	`vanh,edw,`
	Van Halen, Eddie	but	`vanh,edd,`

BUT

Kennedy, Robert F.		`[kenn,rob,f`
Kennedy, Bobby	matches a cross reference	`[kenn,bob,`
Van Halen, Eddie		`[vanh,edd,`
Van Halen, Edward	matches a cross reference	`[vanh,edw,`

OCLC has made an exception in the derived personal name index processing for surnames, beginning with the prefix "Mc" or "Mac." If either of these prefixes is followed by a capital letter, the first part of the search key consists of the letter "m" followed by the letter that was capitalized and the two subsequent letters. However, when these prefixes are not followed by a capital letter, this rule does not apply. For example:

PERSONAL NAME	SEARCH KEY	OR	INDEX LABEL
Robert A. MacDonald	`mdon,rob,a`		`fin dp mdon,rob,a`
Andrew McGuire	`mgui,and,`		`fin dp mgui,and,`
Maureen A. MacKenzie	`mken,mau,a`		`fin dp mken,mau,a`
Robert A. MacDonald	`[mdon,rob,a`		`fin dn mdon,rob,a`
Maureen A. MacKenzie	`[mken,mau,a`		`fin dn mken,mau,a`

BUT

James Macdonald	`macd,jam,`		`fin dp macd,jam,`
Barbara Mackey	`mack,bar,`		`fin dp mack,bar,`
Ann Macfarlane	`macf,ann,`		`fin dp macf,ann,`
James Macdonald	`[macd,jam,`		`fin dn macd,jam,`
Ann Macfarlane	`[macf,ann,`		`fin dn macf,ann,`

If you are unsure whether the bibliographic form of a name has an internal capital letter or not, you may need to search the Online Union Catalog both ways to find any existing records in the database. The Authority File does not help you in this case because authority records rarely provide a cross reference from one capitalization to the other (e.g., from Macdonald to MacDonald). The rules for cross references in authority records do not routinely dictate such cross references for capitalization.

DERIVED CORPORATE AND MEETING NAME

The derived corporate/meeting name search key may be used for searching corporate or meeting names in the Authority File or those appearing as main entries or added entries in the Online Union Catalog. Corporate names include such things as schools, companies, and government agencies. Meeting names include such things as conferences, seminars, workshops, and other meetings. The structure of the search key is the same as the derived personal name search key, except that it is preceded by an "equals sign." When the OCLC first developed search keys in the Online Union Catalog, there was only one derived name index which included personal names, meeting names, and corporate names. This index was subsequently split into two indexes with this nearly identical structure—one containing personal names and the other containing corporate and meeting names. However, the derived name index in the Authority File never underwent such a split. All names remain in the same index and have the same structure.

The derived corporate/meeting name search key in the Online Union Catalog may be thought of as "=4,3,1"—an equals sign, the first 4 characters of the first significant word of the name, a comma, the first 3 characters of the second word of the name, a comma, and the first character of the third word of the name. The system will interpret this structure as a request to search the corporate/meeting name index file in the Online Union Catalog. The derived name search key structure in the Authority File is exactly the same as in the Online Union Catalog except that a search key begins with an open bracket and does not include the equals sign. This is the same structure described earlier under the personal name search key and uses the same index label ("dn"), since all derived names are in the same index in the Authority File. When using index labels you do not need to include the equals sign or the open bracket. The label itself indicates which index file to search. For example:

CORPORATE/MEETING NAME	SEARCH KEY	OR	INDEX LABEL
Mobil Oil Corporation	=mobi,oil,c		fin dc mobi,oil,c
Public Broadcasting Service (U.S.)	=publ,bro,s		fin dc publ,bro,s
Rutgers University	=rutg,uni,		fin dc rutg,uni,
Educational Testing Service	[educ,tes,s		fin dn educ,tes,s
Ford Foundation	[ford,fou,		fin dn ford,fou,
UNESCO	[unes,,		fin dn unes,,

Notice that the structure of the derived corporate/meeting name search key requires two commas even when your heading has fewer than three words (e.g., Rutgers University, UNESCO).

With corporate/meeting names, the definition of a word is the same as it is for titles: a character or group of characters between two blank spaces. Therefore you must again be aware of variant punctuation and spacing conventions within corporate/meeting names that different catalogers may have used at different points in time. You may need to search a heading several ways to verify whether or not a record exists in the Online Union Catalog with that heading. The Authority File may not help much since very few authority records contain cross references for variant spacing conventions. For example:

CORPORATE/MEETING NAME	SEARCH KEY	OR	INDEX LABEL
U.S.–Japan Conference on Sewage ...	=usja,con,o		fin dc usja,con,o
U. S.–Japan Conference on Sewage ...	=u,sja,c		fin dc u,sja,c
U.S.–Canadian Northern Civil ...	=usca,nor,c		fin dc usca,nor,c
U. S.–Canadian Northern Civil ...	=u,sca,n		fin dc u,sca,n

We again need to determine the first "significant" word in the heading just as we needed to do with titles, but here it is a little more complex. To begin with, you should eliminate from your search key any initial articles in any language that has them. The system generally eliminates initial articles before indexing the heading based on the language code in the bibliographic record. Next, you need to eliminate certain very common words that frequently appear at the beginning of the name heading. Derived search keys using these common words nearly always retrieved too many records which made large segments of the index useless. OCLC decided to improve access in this index by ignoring specific common words that caused the most problems when constructing the corporate/meeting name index keys. Since they were ignored when creating the index file, they must also be ignored when constructing a derived search key to search the index file.

OCLC lists the ignored words in a "stoplist" which should be consulted when constructing your search key. The current corporate/meeting name stoplist is shown in Figure 3–1. A copy is also available in the PRISM online help. To use the stoplist, check the first word of your heading against the stoplist. If the first word of your heading appears on the stoplist, skip it and check the second word, the third word, and so on until you find the first word that is not on the stoplist. Beginning with that word, construct your search key. Once you start to construct your search key, ignore the stoplist and use every word in your heading; the stoplist only applies to words at the beginning of the heading. The same stoplist is used for constructing corporate/meeting name search keys in both the Online Union Catalog and the Authority File. For example:

CORPORATE/MEETING NAME	SEARCH KEY	OR	INDEX LABEL
California Natural Disaster Assistance Program.	=natu,dis,a		fin dc natu,dis,a
United States. Dept. of the Interior. Bureau of Public Affairs.	=inte,bur,o		fin dc inte,bur,o
University of Rhode Island. Graduate School of Oceanography.	=grad,sch,o		fin dc grad,sch,o
United States. Dept. of the Interior. Bureau of Public Affairs.	[inte,bur,o		fin dn inte,bur,o

In the second heading, notice that you use "bureau" and "of" in constructing your search key even though they are both on the stoplist. Once you start to construct your search key with the first significant word (in this case, "interior"), you ignore the stoplist and use every following word.

Figure 3–1   Corporate and Meeting Name Stoplist

The names of ALL THE STATES plus:

a	East	Seminar
A.	for	Senate
American	France	Society
an	Great Britain	South
Association	Gt. Brit.	State
Australia	Gt.Brit.	Subcommittee
Bureau	House	Symposium
Canada	India	the
Colloquium	Institute	U. N.
Commission	Institution	U. S.
Committee	International	U.N.
Conference	Joint	United Nations
Congress	National	United States
Council	North	University
Department	of	U.S.
Dept.	on	West

DERIVED NAME/TITLE

The derived name/title search key contains elements from both the name and the title and is only defined in the Online Union Catalog, not the Authority File. The structure of the derived name/title search key is "4,4"—the first four characters of the last name or first significant word of the author, a comma, and the first four characters of the first significant word of the title. There is only one comma in the name/title search key. The system will interpret this structure as a request to search the name/title index file in the Online Union Catalog. When using index labels you must still structure the search request following the label in exactly the same way.

The name element of the derived name/title search key can be either a personal, corporate, or meeting name. The title element can be either a title proper, a uniform title, or a title added entry. Apply the same structure guidelines described above under the other derived search keys when constructing the appropriate element of this search key. Follow the personal and corporate/meeting name guidelines when constructing the name portion of the search key (for example, use the corporate name stoplist for a corporate name, use the "Mc/Mac" guidelines for a personal name). Follow the title guidelines when constructing the title portion of the search key (for example, ignore an initial article). For example:

NAME/TITLE	SEARCH KEY	OR	INDEX LABEL
Wise Blood, by Flannery O'Connor	ocon,wise		fin da ocon,wise
The Sun Also Rises, by Ernest Hemingway	hemi,sun		fin da hemi,sun
As I Lay Dying, by William Faulkner	faul,as		fin da faul,as
Cape Fear, by John D. MacDonald	mdon,cape		fin da mdon,cape
Pennsylvania. Bureau of Motor Vehicles. Forms Manual.	moto,form		fin da moto,form
New Jersey. Commission on Environmental Education. Report.	envi,repo		fin da envi,repo

Notice that in the derived name/title search key you do not precede a corporate/meeting name with an equals sign. There is no punctuation distinction in the "name" portion of this index between personal and corporate/meeting names.

You can also use a version of the derived name/title search key with records in which the title is the main entry. In such a construction, the name portion before the comma is empty. Your search key begins with a comma followed by the first four letters of the first word of the title (using the same title guidelines mentioned above). This construction may be a useful search key for some titles (especially short titles) where using the fourth letter of the first word increases specificity more than would be provided by using the first three letters of the first word in a derived title search. For example, a search on 'poc,,,' might retrieve 542 records while a search on ',poca' might retrieve only 113 records. One category of items for which this is sometimes a useful search technique is motion pictures or videorecordings which are nearly always cataloged as title main entries. For example:

NAME/TITLE	SEARCH KEY	OR	INDEX LABEL
The Birds	,bird		fin da ,bird
Pocahontas	,poca		fin da ,poca

COMBINING TWO SEARCH KEYS

Any two of the above numeric or derived search keys (except for the OCLC control number) can be combined in a single search statement using 'and' in the Online Union Catalog. This capability is not available at this time in the Authority File. You must always enter a combined search using the 'fin' command and index labels and each search key must have its own index label, even when they are the same label. All of the rules and guidelines discussed above for constructing a specific numeric or derived search key apply here if you use that search key as one of the elements of your combined search.

The combined search is most frequently used in place of the name/title search key. This often results in greater specificity. The system generally returns a smaller result set when the full derived name and derived title search keys are used than when only part of the name and part of the title are used as in the name/title derived search key. For example, 'dura,age' might retrieve 27 records whereas 'fin dp dura,wil, and dt age,of,vo,' might retrieve only 5 records. This search is also sometimes used to combine two titles (such as, one for the series and one for the specific work) or two personal names (such as, for co-authors).

SEARCH ELEMENTS	INDEX LABEL
The Age of Voltaire, by Will and Ariel Durant	`fin dp dura,wil, and dt age,of,vo,`
Wise Blood, by Flannery O'Connor	`fin dt wis,bl,, and dp ocon,fla,`
The Sun Also Rises, by Ernest Hemingway	`fin dt sun,als,ri, and dp hemi,ern,`
Cape Fear, by John D. MacDonald	`fin dp mdon,joh,d and dt cap,fe,,`

KEYWORD SEARCHING

As mentioned in Chapter 1, keyword searching is one of the new search strategies that only became available after the PRISM service was introduced. Therefore, all keyword search keys are entered using commands and index labels. There is no "old" form that can be used as there is with the derived search keys. Keyword searching is currently available only in the Online Union Catalog, not the Authority File. Unlike the search keys described above, which use only parts of words in a specific order to form a search key, keyword searches use full words and in any order. Generally searchers select several of the most unique keywords available to help narrow the search to a reasonable result set.

You can combine up to eight keywords from many different areas of the record in a single search. As with the combined search key described above, each separate keyword gets its own index label (even when several keywords are from the same index) and the only connector currently available is 'and.' Keywords can be combined in any order. One of the principal advantages of keyword searching is the ability to specify terms from areas of the bibliographic record other than the traditional numeric, author, and title indexes described above. For example, you may be looking for a classic title by a specific publisher. Keyword searching gives you the ability to retrieve only books by that publisher. A complete listing of all indexed fields and subfields for each keyword index is found in the Appendix.

SEARCH ELEMENTS	INDEX LABEL
The Age of Voltaire, by Will and Ariel Durant	`fin au durant and ti voltaire`
For Whom the Bell Tolls, by Ernest Hemingway, published by Hall	`fin au hemingway and pb hall and ti bell`
Romeo and Juliet, by William Shakespeare, published by Macmillan	`fin ti juliet and ti romeo and pb macmillan`

Just as with the derived corporate/meeting name search key, some very common words have been excluded from indexing in the keyword index and therefore should not be used as a keyword search term. These words are listed in a keyword stoplist shown in Figure 3–2. They are also available online through PRISM help. The stoplist consists primarily of common English prepositions, pronouns, verbs, and conjunctions. The stoplist is not language specific, however. Any of these letter combinations appearing in any language should be ignored. For example, the German pronoun "was" should be ignored along with the English verb "was."

Keyword searching offers two masking characters which allow the system to match multiple words from a single search term. Each of the masking characters operates slightly differently. One character is the question mark ("?"), which you place at the end of a search term. The system will retrieve records with words that exactly match the search term you entered plus longer words that begin with that character string. You must enter at least three characters of your search term before the question mark. For example:

Figure 3–2	Keyword stoplist

a	be	have	it	the
an	but	he	not	this
and	by	her	of	to
are	for	his	on	was
as	from	in	or	which
at	had	is	that	with
				you

MASKED SEARCH TERM	MATCHED WORDS
`fin st artist?`	artist
	artistic
	artistically
	artistry
	artists
`fin st sport?`	sport
	sporting
	sports
	sportscast
	sportsman
	sporty

When you enter only a few characters before the question mark, you run the risk of matching too many words, in which case you will get an error message. (The current system limit is 300 matching words.) For instance, truncating either of the above examples after the first three characters (i.e., 'art?' or 'spo?'), while technically legal, would match more than the current system limit and return an error message.

The other masking character is the pound sign ("#") which can be used either in the middle of a word or at the end of a word. Unlike the question mark, which can match many characters, the pound sign only matches zero or one character. You must have at least three characters at the beginning of your search term before using a pound sign. For example:

MASKED SEARCH TERM	MATCHED WORDS
`fin au labo#r`	labor labour
`fin ti sport#`	sport sports sporty

You can use up to five masking characters in a single word although that is rarely done. The above examples for each of the masking characters show only a single word for demonstration purposes, but in practice, additional terms would be included when searching the database. Used alone, each example would likely retrieve more than the maximum number of records that the system will return for a search.

Keyword searching does not necessarily result in better retrieval than search keys for most items for which you have good author and title information. Most authors and titles have relatively few matches using search keys. Even for prolific works, search key searches using qualifiers (a technique that will be introduced in Chapter 5) can sometimes return a result set as narrow as a corresponding keyword result set. Using an earlier example, suppose you are looking for a record for an edition of Ernest Hemingway's *For Whom the Bell Tolls* that was published by G.K. Hall in 1994. Perhaps the keyword search 'fin au hemingway and ti bell and pb hall' retrieves only 2 records. However, the derived name/title search 'hemi,for' limited to only a 1994 publication date may also retrieve only 2 records. Even when not limited to a 1994 publication date, 'hemi,for' may still retrieve only 197 records.

On the other hand, keyword searching can be quite advantageous when looking for items with only incomplete or suspect information in hand. Perhaps you only have an author's last name and a few significant words of a title but are uncertain of their order or which additional "insignificant" words are also in the title. It is difficult or impossible to construct a reasonable search key under such circumstances and keyword searching achieves a better result. Keyword searching is also useful for access to information in fields of the record that are not included in the traditional search key indexes, such as subjects or contents notes. Perhaps you are looking for one particular story or play within a collection of stories or plays and the title proper of the collection can be anything. Keyword access to the contents note can retrieve a desired record where the search key indexes would be useless. Keyword searching is very powerful but it is not necessarily the best or most efficient approach to finding a desired record in the database. It all depends on the nature of the information you have at hand when conducting the search.

PHRASE SEARCHING

Phrase searching is the final category of search techniques currently available in PRISM. As mentioned in Chapter 2, phrase searches are entered using the 'Scan' command (rather than the 'Find' command used by search key and keyword searches) and index labels. Title phrase is the only phrase index that has been introduced thus far in the Online Union Catalog. Other phrase indexes are being considered as future enhancements. The Authority File has a full complement of title, name, and subject phrase searching available. A full listing of the indexed fields and subfields can be found in the Appendix.

TITLE PHRASE

The title phrase index is built from all words in the title in the order they appear, beginning with the first word following an initial article. Your title phrase search key is constructed similarly. Begin your search key with the first word following an initial article and include everything up until you stop your search key. You can include as much or as little of the title in your search key as you think necessary and can stop at any point, even in the middle of a word. For example:

TITLE		SEARCH PHRASE
For Whom the Bell Tolls		`sca ti for whom the bell tolls`
	or	`sca ti for whom the bell tol`
	or	`sca ti for whom the bel`
The Sound and the Fury		`sca ti sound and the fury`
	or	`sca ti sound and the fu`
	or	`sca ti sound and the`

In response to a title phrase search, the system always displays the area of the index closest to where a title matching your search string would appear, regardless of whether or not the database actually has a title matching that character string. You never receive a "No matching records." message in response to a phrase search. Although you can enter as little of the title as you choose and always get a result, you may be many screens away from your title if you enter too little of the title in the search request. Ideally, you want to enter enough of the title in the search request so that your title displays on the first result screen. For most titles it is sufficient to use only the first three or four words to result in a display close to your entry in the index. For example, if you enter 'sca ti sound and' as a search for *The Sound and the Fury*, the system will respond by displaying the area of the index near titles beginning with "sound and a . . . " You may need to scroll through twelve screens before arriving at the index area containing "sound and t . . . " However, a search using 'sca ti sound and the' may be sufficient to place you in the area of the index such that your title is on the initial display screen without having had to enter "fury" as part of the search string.

Phrase searching always adds an additional step to the search process that is not shared by the other search types. The phrase search result only places you in an area of the index near your title. You still must select a matching entry in order to retrieve the corresponding record or set of records, even when that index entry lists only one record. The other search types retrieve a matching record or set of records directly from the search.

For many titles a derived title search is an extremely effective first search strategy, directly returning only one or a few matching records without going through several steps. On the other hand, title phrase searching is a very effective approach for titles which begin with a string of very common words before any distinctive words. Derived title search keys usually match more than the system limit for such titles since the search key only uses the first four words of the title. For instance, the derived search key for *The Proceedings of the International Conference on Neural Networks* would be 'fin dt pro,of,th,i'—which has no distinctive words at all and would result in a record set that exceeds the system limit. A title phrase search for the same title (such as 'sca ti proceedings of the international conference on neura') allows you to enter enough words so that your search string includes some of the distinctive words in the title. This search would return a display in the proper area of the index for this title.

Another advantage of the phrase indexes is that they are forgiving of typographical errors later in the search entry. The system still displays the same area of the index as it would for a search without a typographical error. This lessens the need to re-enter searches because of misspellings. For example, suppose you misspelled "neura" as "neuar" in the above search phrase. The system would still most likely return the same screen because the phrase with the misspelled word is still very close to the phrase with the correct spelling. Both titles would wind up on the same index screen were they both in the system. Of course, if you misspell an early word in the phrase (e.g., "praceedings" or "proceeding" instead of "proceedings" in the above example), you usually wind up in an entirely different area of the index and need to reenter your search.

INDEXED FIELDS AND SEARCH FORMATS

The search formats described above operate on several indexes with similar names that include similar information. For example, there is a derived title index, a title keyword index, and a title phrase index. However, these indexes do not include exactly the same information even though they share a similar name. This is important to keep in mind as you move back and forth among the various search strategies and use a variety of search formats. A field or subfield that is included in one index may not be included in another when you expect it should because of their similar names. This can lead to confusion when records retrieved through one search strategy are unavailable through a similar strategy that the searcher anticipated would index the same information. For instance, while you might reasonably expect that an author and a title index contain different information, you might also reasonably expect that two title indexes contain the same information.

Differences among similar indexes occur at two levels: fields and subfields. At the field level, some fields are included in one index but not in another. This difference is demonstrated in Figure 3–3 which compares the handling of selected title fields across the three title indexes that have been discussed. Figure 3–3 shows, for example, that traced series titles (fields 440 and 830) are indexed in both the derived title and title keyword indexes, but not in the title phrase index. It also shows that untraced series titles (field 490) are indexed in the title keyword index, but not in the derived title and title phrase indexes. If you are searching for a series title then these differences have a significant effect on which index you should choose to search. Since series titles are not included in some title indexes, those indexes should not be used to search for a series title.

Figure 3–3 Comparison of Selected Indexed Fields Across Index Formats								
Index	Is Field Included							
	240	245	246	440	490	730	780	830
Derived Title	yes	yes	yes	yes	no	yes	yes	yes
Title Keyword	yes	yes	yes	yes	yes	yes	yes	yes
Title Phrase	yes	yes	yes	no	no	yes	no	no

Even when two indexes include the same field they sometimes index a different set of subfields within that field. Figure 3–4 lists which subfields from field 245 are indexed by the three title indexes discussed above. For example, the derived title index includes only the main title (‡a), while the title keyword and title phrase indexes include both the main title and the subtitle (‡a ‡b). This difference can influence your search strategy, especially when you have a very short main title with a subtitle. For example, including the subtitle in a derived title search will not retrieve a matching record with that main title while including the subtitle in a title phrase search will retrieve that matching record.

The Appendix contains a complete listing of indexed fields and subfields for each of the indexes discussed in this chapter.

Figure 3–4 Tag 245 Indexing Comparison	
INDEX	245 INDEXED SUBFIELDS
Derived Title	‡a
Title Keyword	‡a ‡b ‡n ‡p
Title Phrase	‡a ‡b ‡n ‡p ‡f ‡g ‡k

SOME COMMON ERROR MESSAGES

The following system messages represent some of the most common entry errors associated with search requests when the system recognizes that you are trying to enter a search. The system displays these messages on the system message line.

When the system interprets your command as an attempt to initiate a search, it moves the problem search request to the middle of the screen between start-of-message and end-of-message symbols, with the cursor at the first letter of the command. You can then revise your search and reenter it by pressing <SEND>. However, you can always choose to ignore this revise search prompt and enter a new search at the home position instead. Figure 3–5 demonstrates a revise search screen. When moving your search request the system processes it in two ways. First, the command is always written out in full with the first letter capitalized ("Find" or "Scan") regardless of how it was actually entered. Second, if you entered a search key the old way without commands and index labels (e.g., "for,who,th,b"), the system will transcribe it here

---

Figure 3–5   Revise search screen

```
                              ¶ CAT                        SID: 00000    OL
Too many characters in DP key.




                              REVISE

▶ Find dp monta,ann,r                                                    ¶


```

---

in the new way (e.g., "Find dt for,who,th,b").

When the system does not interpret your command as an attempt to initiate a search, it leaves the problem search request in the home position without moving it or processing it in any way. For example, the system may interpret your command as an attempt to edit the record on display rather than a search for a new record, thereby leaving the command in the home position.

```
Improper character ["["] in AN key.
Improper character ["."] in DA key.
```

A character in your search key cannot be processed by the system. Perhaps you are in the OL database and enter a search key search using an index label but you also include the open bracket associated with a search in the AF database (e.g., "fin an [37294"). This search is processed properly if you are already in the AF database but cannot be processed in the OL database.

Generally, all you need to do is remove or replace the offending character and resubmit your search. You may also need to change databases.

```
Too many characters in DP key.
Too many characters in DA key.
```

One or more segments of a derived search key has too many characters. This could result from one of two situations. First, you truly entered too many characters in a segment. For example, with "for,who,th,b" you intended to enter a derived title search but included too many characters in the second segment. Second, you left out a comma and the system interpreted your search key differently than you intended. For example, with "cri,an,pu" you intended to enter a derived title search but left out the final comma and the system interpreted your request as a derived author search with too many characters in the third segment.

You may need to correct the number of characters in one or more search key segments, add punctuation, and/or correct the system supplied index label.

```
Not authorized for Field Edit command.
Invalid line number or invalid range specified.
```

You had either a single or multiple record display on screen and entered a search key search beginning with a number without using a command and index label. Perhaps you entered an ISBN or LCCN search or a derived title search where the first word was a number. The system interpreted your request as an attempt either to edit a field in the single record or to request a record or range of records from the multiple record display.

You could either enter RET to clear the screen before entering your search key or use the command and index label.

```
Search label dp isn't valid for this database.
Invalid parameter for Scan command.
```

You used an index label that is not recognized in your current database. Perhaps you forgot to change databases before issuing your new search or you accidentally used an index label from another database (e.g., you are in the AF and used "fin dp" instead of "fin dn" for a derived name search); perhaps you entered an incorrect index label that is not valid anywhere (e.g., you used "sca tu" instead of "sca ti" for a title phrase search).

You could either choose the appropriate database or correct your index label.

```
These search keys may not be combined on this database.
```

You either used index labels for two search keys that cannot be combined or you were in the wrong database. Perhaps you were in the AF and forgot to change to the OL before issuing your combined search key request. Perhaps you were in the OL and accidentally used the wrong index label for one of your combined keys (e.g., you used the index label 'dn' instead of 'dp' for the derived personal name search key).

You need to change databases or replace one of your combined search keys or its index label.

```
Unrecognized command.
```

The system was unable to interpret the command that you entered. This could have any number of causes. Perhaps you mistyped a command (e.g., 'fni' instead of 'fin'); perhaps you forgot a space between the command and index label (e.g., 'findp' instead of 'fin dp'); perhaps you were entering a derived search key and accidentally used a wrong character instead of the commas (e.g., 'for.wh.th.b' instead of 'for,wh,th,b'). The common factor in all these problems is that the system was unable to determine what you were trying to do. With the other problems listed above, the system was able to determine some action that you were trying to take (although it could have made a wrong determination), but that you were doing so incorrectly. With this error message, the system was unable to determine what you were trying to do in the first place.

4 DISPLAYING SEARCH RESULTS

ONLINE UNION CATALOG DISPLAYS

PRISM currently offers four basic record display formats in the Online Union Catalog. Without specific instructions to the contrary, the system displays a set of records in a default format determined by how many records are in the set.

Group display	for a set of 100–1500 records
Truncated display	for a set of 6–99 records
Brief display	for a set of 2–5 records
Single record display	for a set of 1 record

The four options form a display hierarchy based on set size. An initial record set consists of all the records that matched the search request—which could be anywhere from 1 to 1,500 records. The initial display format is based on the number of records in this initial set. If you subsequently select and display a subset of records from the initial set, the system will also display them in a format based on the size of the subset. For example, if you select four records from a truncated display of 35 records, the system will present them in a brief display. If you select one record from that truncated display, the system will present it in a single record display. You can specifically request any display format if you prefer something other than the default. For example, you may prefer to view a set of 10 records in the brief display even though the default for that set would be the truncated display. The group display is the only one with restrictions. You will get the message "Not enough records for Group Display" if you request that format for fewer than 100 records. Each of these display formats is discussed below.

COMMON INFORMATION IN ALL DISPLAYS

Information on the first few lines of all displays is consistent. The system message line is used to provide information about which screen in a particular display you are currently viewing. The example group display in Figure 4–1 shows the message:

```
Entire list displayed.
```

This indicates that the entire display fits on this one screen. When a particular display takes up more than one screen, the system message line generally displays a beginning indication on the first screen and an ending indication on the last screen; middle screens show no indication. Examples of messages include:

```
Entire record displayed.
Beginning of list displayed.
Beginning of record displayed.
End of list displayed.
End of record displayed.
```

Below the system message line (and a blank line) is a header line containing several pieces of information that provide some context for the particular search result display you are viewing. The first element in this line indicates the database in which the search was conducted. A restatement of your original index label and search strategy appears next. For most searches, the end of the line shows either the total record count or the position of this record in relation to all records retrieved in the set. The specific information on this line will vary depending on your original search strategy, the size of the initial result set, and any intervening steps you may have taken since getting the initial display. The example in Figure 4–1 shows:

```
OLUC dt bul,,,/1985-              Records: 1159
```

indicating that this search was conducted in the Online Union Catalog ("OLUC"), that a derived title search was done using the search key "bul,,," and the date qualifier "1985-", and that the resulting set includes a total of 1,159 records. Other example context lines from later figures in this chapter are:

```
OLUC dt gre,ho,,               Records: 278
OLUC dp goul,ste,j             Record 25 of 155
OLUC da stee,wing              Records: 4
OLUC ti sound and the fury
AUTH dt lec,no,in,m            Records: 3
```

Information on the rest of the screen will vary with each display format.

GROUP DISPLAY

Group is the default display format for a search result matching between 100 and 1,500 records. Figure 4–1 shows an example of a group display. The group display provides the least infor-

---

Figure 4–1   Group display

```
                                    ¶ CAT              SID: 00000   OL
Entire list displayed.

OLUC   dt bul,,,/1985-                                Records: 1159
   Group#    Format              Dates          Records
▶     G1¶     Books               1985-1987         78
▶     G2¶     Books               1988-1989         70
▶     G3¶     Books               1990-1992         85
▶     G4¶     Books               1993-1995         65
▶     G5¶     Print Serials       1985              89
▶     G6¶     Print Serials       1986              99
▶     G7¶     Print Serials       1986               7
▶     G8¶     Print Serials       1987              83
▶     G9¶     Print Serials       1988              87
▶    G10¶     Print Serials       1989              83
▶    G11¶     Print Serials       1990              90
▶    G12¶     Print Serials       1991              85
▶    G13¶     Print Serials       1992              40
▶    G14¶     Print Serials       1993-9999         93
▶    G15¶     Visual Materials    1985-1995         57
▶    G16¶     Maps                1985-1994         13
▶    G17¶     Mixed Materials     1989               2
▶    G18¶     Sound Recordings    1985-1995         32
▶    G19¶     Computer Files      1986               1
```

---

mation about your search results. For example, no information is provided about the specific authors or titles that matched your search request. Only a very general categorization of the matching records is provided. Each entry in a group display only shows the format of the records grouped there, the range of their publication dates, and the total number of records under that entry. Entry numbers are sequential beginning with "G1" and have no meaning themselves. They merely provide a way to label a subset of records for retrieval from the system.

Matching records are first clustered together by format (Books, Print Serials, etc.) and then by publication date within that format. Record clusters from consecutive publication dates within one format are combined into a single entry until adding the next date cluster would make the entry larger than 99 records, at which point a new entry is started instead of continuing to add new years to the existing entry. Notice that entries G1 through G4 in Figure 4–1 all include multiple years. There is no limit to the range of years that can be included in a single entry provided the total number of records does not exceed 99. You can have as many entries as needed for a given record format. Notice that the Print Serials format has 10 entries while the Visual Materials format only has one entry. When there are multiple entries for the same format, the groups are arranged chronologically from earliest to latest dates.

The number of records collected into one entry can vary from one (entry G19) to 99 (entry G6), but no single entry can contain more than 99 records. This presents a problem when there are more than 99 matching records in a single format in a single year since a year is the smallest date unit used to divide records into clusters. When one year has more than 99 records, the system stops adding records to the first entry after record 99 and begins a new entry having the same format and year. Notice that entries G6 and G7 both contain Print Serials format records in the year 1986. Records are not sorted by author, title, and other parameters before the new entry is begun, however. Therefore, if the year in which you are interested spans several groups, you will need to look through all groups of records that have that year to find a potential bibliographic record because it could be in any one of them.

Some records lack a publication date entirely, either because the item that was cataloged lacked a publication date or because of an error in the data entry process. In those cases, the system can not find a usable date for clustering in the appropriate field in the record. It groups all such records within a given format into a single entry which displays as the last entry for that format and shows the value "NO DATE" in the Dates column. For example, a search for the book *Greenwood House* (using the derived title search key 'gre,ho,,') could result in a group display in which three of the entries have "NO DATE," one each in the Print Serials, Visual Materials, and Sound Recordings formats. This search result is demonstrated in Figure 4–2.

Navigation and selection commands

To view the matching records for one entry, enter its corresponding group number and press <SEND>. Your request can either include or exclude the beginning 'G' in the group number which can be in upper or lower case (e.g., 'g' or 'G'). You can also precede your number with the 'dis' command. However, when you

---

Figure 4–2   Derived title search for the title *Greenwood House*

```
                              ¶ CAT             SID: 00000      OL
Entire list displayed.

OLUCdt gre,ho,,                               Records: 278
  Group#        Format            Dates        Records
▶   G1¶         Books             1826-1982        99
▶   G2¶         Books             1983-1995        43
▶   G3¶         Print Serials     1883-1994        10
▶   G4¶         Print Serials     NO DATE           9
▶   G5¶         Visual Materials  1865-1994        19
▶   G6¶         Visual Materials  NO DATE           2
▶   G7¶         Mixed Materials   1966-1981         3
▶   G8¶         Sound Recordings  1900-1992        88
▶   G9¶         Sound Recordings  NO DATE           2
▶  G10¶         Music Scores      1929-1985         2
▶  G11¶         Computer Files    1990              1
```

use the 'dis' command you must include the 'G.' The system will respond to any of those requests with either a truncated display, a brief display, or a single bibliographic record depending on the number of records grouped under the selected entry. For example, if you select entry G2 in Figure 4–2 (enter '2' or 'g2' or 'dis g2' and press <SEND>), the system will respond with a truncated display of those 43 records. If you select entry G7 (enter '7' or 'g7' or 'dis g7' and press <SEND>), the system will respond with a brief display of those three records. If you select entry G11 (enter '11' or 'g11' or 'dis g11' and press <SEND>), the system will respond with a single record display of that one bibliographic record.

There is another way to view the records from one entry in a list. Notice that every group entry number in Figure 4–2 is preceded by a start-of-message symbol (▶) and followed by an end-of-message symbol (¶). You can move your cursor onto the line with the entry that you want to select, place it somewhere between the two symbols on that line, and press <SEND>. The system will respond the same way it responds to input at the home position (i.e., it will read the data between the two symbols and process the message accordingly). For example, to select entry G2 in Figure 4–2, you could move your cursor somewhere between the start-of-message and end-of-message symbols that contain 'G2' and press <SEND>. The system will respond with the same truncated display of 43 records that you got earlier by entering '2' or 'g2' or 'dis g2' in the home position. In practice, it is usually easier to type an entry number in the home position than it is to move the cursor to the proper line, but both methods achieve the same result. Also, you can only use this method to select one entry at a time, not with the multiple entry selection methods discussed next.

You can also simultaneously request multiple entries. Perhaps you are unsure of the publication date of the work for which you are trying to find a bibliographic record. It will be necessary in that case to search all candidate groups, one date range at a time, until you find a matching record or exhaust the possibilities. For example, suppose you do not know when *Greenwood House* was published but you do know that it is a book, not a print serial or sound recording. You would then need to look through the records in both entries G1 and G2 of Figure 4–2 since they are both for Books records.

There are several ways to select multiple entries at one time. You can list discrete entry numbers with commas and consecutive entries with a dash (e.g., '2,4–7,9'). Alternately, you can individually list all the consecutive entries separated with commas as well (e.g., '2,4,5,6,7,9'). The entries selected must be listed in ascending order or you will get an error message. As when requesting a single entry, you can either include or exclude the beginning "G" in any of the numbers. For example, the system will process 'g2,g4–g7,g9' and 'g2,4–g7,9' and '2,g4–7,g9' in exactly the same way. When you use the 'dis' command the first number must be preceded with the "G". For all later numbers the 'G' is optional as above. For example, the system will process 'dis g2,g4–g7,g9' and 'dis g2,4–g7,9' exactly the same way. However, 'dis 2,g4–g7,g9' will generate an error message.

The system will first display all records from the first group you selected in a display format appropriate for the number of records at that entry—either a truncated, brief, or single record display. If you wish to see the records from the second group you selected, enter 'for g' (for "forward group") and press <SEND>. The system will display all records from the next selected group entry in the same format as it displayed the records from the first group. To return to the first group you can enter 'bac g' (for "backward group") and press <SEND>. You can move forward and backward in this same manner through all of the group entries you selected.

Each subsequent group will use the same default display format as the first group regardless of how many records each contains. For example, suppose you selected multiple entries G8 with 27 records and G9 with three records from some group display. The 27 records from G8 will display in a truncated format. The three records from G9 will also display in a truncated format. Now suppose instead that you selected multiple entries G10 with two records and G11 with 89 records. The two records from G10 will display in a brief format. The 89 records from G11 will also display in a brief format. You can change this default display format by specifically requesting a different one using the 'dis' command. This can be done either initially when selecting all groups or later when viewing one of the selected groups. For example, in the above case you could have entered 'dis g10–11 tr' ("display G10 and G11 in a truncated format") when making your initial selection or you could have viewed G10 in the default brief format, entered 'for g' to go to G11, and then entered 'dis g11 tr' to view G11 in a truncated format. The other codes you can use are 'br' for the brief format and 'fu' ("full") for the single record format. If you change to a different display format, all subsequent group displays will use that new format until you request another change.

Returning to the *Greenwood House* example in Figure 4–2, you could enter '1–2' or 'g1–g2'; 'dis g1–g2'; '1,2'; or 'g1,g2'; or 'dis g1,g2' (among several options) and press <SEND> to select the two "Books" groups. All of those requests have the same result. The system will display the 99 records from entry G1 in a truncated display. If you do not find *Greenwood House* in this group and wish to see the second group of records, you would enter 'for g' and press <SEND>. The system will display the 43 records from entry G2 also in a truncated display. To return to the first group, you can enter 'bac g' and press <SEND>.

You can also view records from a group entry without having selected that entry initially (and without using the 'for g' and 'bac g' commands) by simply requesting the entry with the 'dis' command. For example, while viewing the records from entry G4 you can request to see the records from entry G8 by entering 'dis g8' and pressing <SEND>. This request only works using the 'dis' command. You cannot merely enter '8' or 'g8' at this point. When requesting group entries one at a time in this manner, each entry displays in a default format appropriate for the number of records at that entry. They don't all necessarily use the same format as the entries did above. Of course, to use this approach effectively you must always remember which entries you wish to see and keep requesting them specifically. Selecting entries all at once generally makes moving back and forth among the selected groups easier and more convenient.

You can return to the initial group display from the display of one of its entries with the 'GOB' ("go back") command. The 'GOB' command moves up one level higher in the display hierarchy from your current display (unlike the 'bac g' command mentioned earlier which goes back to an earlier entry at the same level). For example, perhaps you initially selected only entry G8 from a group display and, after viewing those records, decide that you need to view records from a different entry but don't remember which number it is. You can enter 'GOB' to return to the original group display and find the new entry number.

TRUNCATED DISPLAY

Truncated is the default display format for a search result matching between six and 99 records. It is also the default display format for an entry within that same size range selected from a group display. Figure 4–3 shows a truncated display of seven records that could result from a derived name/title search for *Lana: The Lady, the Legend, the Truth*, by Lana Turner (using the key 'turn,lana'). Figure 4–4 shows a truncated display of 19 records from entry G3 from an initial group display that could result from a derived personal name search for Stephen Jay Gould (using the key 'goul,ste,j').

A truncated display has a series of one-line entries, each with selected information from one record in the search result set. Each entry is uniquely identified by a sequential number that indicates its order in the list of records retrieved in the initial search. When the original search results in a truncated display, the numbering will begin with "1" (see in Figure 4–3). However, when the truncated display resulted from selecting an entry from a group display, the numbering will begin with whatever number is appropriate to show those record positions relative to all records retrieved in the initial group. The 19 records in Figure 4–4 are numbered in the range 114–132. The same number will be associated with one record throughout a search result set no matter which display format is selected.

The basic components of a truncated display entry include: name (or more properly, main entry), title, publisher, and date. Each component is displayed within a limited number of characters. The length varies slightly depending on the search. An entry fills as many characters for each component as it can. However, some components are blank when there is no information in the corresponding record that can be extracted to display in that area. For example, notice in Figure 4–3 that entries four and five have no publisher. Some entries may also lack a

Figure 4–3 Truncated display

```
                                    ¶ CAT              SID: 00000              OL
Entire list displayed.

OLUC    da turn,lana                              Records: 7
  Rec#  Name                 Title                    Publisher        Date  L
▶ 1¶    Turner, Lana,        Lana : the lady, the legend,     Dutton,          1982
▶ 2¶    Turner, Lana,        Lana : the lady, the legend,     New English Li   1983  U
▶ 3¶    Turner, Lana,        Lana : the lady, the legend,     G.K. Hall,       1983  D
▶ 4¶    Turner, Lana,        [Lana Turner is interviewed i                     1982
▶ 5¶    Turner, Lana,        [Lana Turner talks about Tyro                     1975
▶ 6¶    Turner, Lana,        Lana--the lady, the legend, t    Dutton,          1982  D
▶ 7¶    Turner, Lana,        Lana--the lady, the legend, t    Pocket Books,    1983
```

name or a date. Title is the only component that always contains information.

The first display element in an entry will vary with your search type. For instance, if you searched by title, the matching title element will display first with a corresponding main entry from the record as the second element. If you searched by name, the matching name element will display first with the corresponding title proper from the record as the second element. In Figure 4–3, the search type was a derived name/title search key and the entries display with the matching name first and the matching title second. In Figure 4–4, the search type was a derived personal name search key and the entries display with the matching name first and the title proper second. For searches which do not depend specifically on matching names or titles (like keyword searches), the display order is main entry (other than title proper) as the first element followed by title proper as the second. Entries from a government document number search or a music publisher's number search display an additional element, the matching number, before the main entry or title proper. The remaining components of an entry always display in the same order (publisher followed by date) regardless of search type. A final element appearing at the end of some entries is a one-character code indicating a record that was cataloged by one of a small group of national libraries whose records are loaded into the OCLC database. In Figure 4–3, records three and six were cataloged by the Library of Congress (code "D") and record two by the British Library (code "U"). Knowing which records in a

---

Figure 4–4   Truncated display from a group display entry

```
                              ¶ CAT                    SID: 00000        OL
Beginning of list displayed.

OLUC   dp goul,ste,j        G3: 114-135 vis 1975-1995       Records: 156
   Rec#    Name               Title                    Publisher      Date L
 ► 114¶   Gould, Stephen Jay. Barnes & Gould a conversation  AETN,         1991
 ► 115¶   Gould, Stephen Jay. [Basic pattern of life's hist                1990
 ► 116¶   Gould, Stephen Jay. Central role of the earth sci  National Scie 1980
 ► 117¶   Gould, Stephen Jay. A conversation with Stephen J  Cabisco Telep 1987
 ► 118¶   Gould, Stephen Jay. Darwin's revolution in though  Into the Clas 1995
 ► 119¶   Gould, Stephen Jay. Darwin's revolution in though  Into the Clas 1995
 ► 120¶   Gould, Stephen Jay. Darwin's revolution in though  Into the Clas 1995
 ► 121¶   Gould, Stephen Jay. Darwin's revolution in though  Into the Clas 1995
 ► 122¶   Gould, Stephen Jay. Evolution and human equality   Insight Video 1987
 ► 123¶   Gould, Stephen Jay. Evolution and human equality   Insight Video 1987
 ► 124¶   Gould, Stephen Jay. A glorious accident understan  Vpro ; Films  1992
 ► 125¶   Gould, Stephen Jay. A glorious accident : underst  Films for the 1994
 ► 126¶   Gould, Stephen Jay. A glorious accident : underst  Films for the 1994
 ► 127¶   Gould, Stephen Jay. How scientists know about pun  University of 1991
 ► 128¶   Gould, Stephen Jay. How scientists know about pun  National Cent 1991
 ► 129¶   Gould, Stephen Jay. Human insignificance and geol  s.n.],        1994
 ► 130¶   Gould, Stephen Jay. Prospects for life, then and  Science Cente 1993
 ► 131¶   Gould, Stephen Jay. Punctuated evolution the slen                1990
 ► 132¶   Gould, Stephen Jay. Size and shape or why the moo  Science Cente 1975
```

---

list were cataloged by a national library can be useful when selecting from among similar records.

Entries in a truncated list are arranged alphabetically by the first element, then alphabetically by the second element, and then chronologically by the date element. When all three of these elements are the same, entries are arranged by OCLC control number (which is not shown in a truncated display). However, an initial government number or music number element is ignored by the system for sorting purposes. Those entries are still arranged as described above but by the elements that follow the number. Unlike in a group display, entries for all record formats and publication years can appear in a single truncated display and are interfiled by name, title, and date—regardless of format when they appear together. There is no specific information in an entry that alerts you to its format, although some formats may be obvious because of information that does get used in an entry element. For example, you can be fairly confident that an entry with the title "Cats complete original Broadw" and the publisher "Geffen Records" is a sound recording (although you can not tell in a truncated display whether it's a music CD, a cassette, or a vinyl record). However, truncated displays that were selected from group displays will already be separated in some way by format and years, since that is how the original group display was organized. These truncated displays include additional information in the header line (following the index label and search strategy) showing the format and date range of the records included. For example, Figure 4–4 shows that the displayed records are all "vis" format from the years "1975–1995."

Navigation and selection commands

Several new navigational commands are introduced with truncated displays. A truncated display shows a maximum of 19 records on one screen (since a screen can have 19 lines of data) although you can have as many as 99 records returned in the default truncated display (and you can have even more when you specifically request the truncated display). When a truncated display list contains more records than fit on a single screen, you can display successive screens of entries by using successive PDN ("page down") or FOR ("forward") commands until the end of the list is reached. Successive PUP ("page up") or BAC ("backward") commands browse backward in a similar manner. For example, notice that Figure 4–4 shows only 19 records from the beginning of a list of 22 records (records 114–132 from a list that goes up to record 135). To see the additional three records in this list, enter either the PDN command or the FOR command. The remaining records from the list will display along with the message "End of list displayed." To return to this first screen, enter the PUP command or the BAC command. The top of the list will display along with the message "Beginning of list displayed." While the "beginning" and "end" messages display on the first and last screens of a multiple screen list, no message displays on any middle screens when there are three or more screens to display.

There is frequently enough information displayed for you to make a decision about whether any of the matching records may indeed be relevant for your needs. To view the single bibliographic record for one of the listed entries, enter its corresponding sequence number and press <SEND>. Alternately, you could enter the sequence number following the 'dis' command. For example, to view the record in Figure 4–3 for the 1983 edition of *Lana*, published by G.K. Hall, enter '3' or 'dis 3' and press <SEND>. The system will display the full bibliographic record for that publication. As with the group display, you can also move your cursor to the line with the entry that you desire, place the cursor anywhere between the start-of message (▶) and end-of-message (¶) symbols on that line, and press <SEND>. This method still has the same drawbacks, namely, that it usually requires more cursor movement to accomplish and that you can only select one entry at a time rather than multiple entries.

You can simultaneously select multiple entries in a similar way as selecting multiple entries from a group display. List discrete entry numbers separated with commas and consecutive entry numbers separated with a dash (e.g., '1–3,6–7' or 'dis 1–3,6–7') or list all numbers separated with commas (e.g., '1,2,3,6,7' or 'dis 1,2,3,6,7') and press <SEND>. Entries must be listed in ascending numerical order. For example, to display the two records in Figure 4–3 for *Lana* published by Dutton, enter '1,6' or 'dis 1,6' and press <SEND>. You will get an error message if you enter '6,1' or 'dis 6,1' instead. The system will display your selected multiple entries in a brief display format.

Since truncated displays can cover several screens, the system provides a related multiple record selection capability (called "marking" records) that allows you to select records from several screens before displaying them all together as a group. To select and mark records, begin exactly as above but without using the 'dis' command. That is, select one or more records from your current screen (e.g., '1–4,15'). However, follow your final selection with a comma (e.g., '1–4,15,') and press <SEND>. The system responds with the message "Please complete marking." Now you can go to your next screen ('PDN' or 'FOR') or previous screen ('PUP' or 'BAC'), select additional records from that screen (e.g., '21–23,30,32'), and press <SEND>. After the first screen, you need not end your selection list with a comma. The ending comma is only required on the first selection screen to initiate the marking process. Continue in this manner until you have visited all the relevant screens in your search result set. You can visit screens in any order but you must still select records from your current screen in ascending numerical order just as above. If you return to a screen that contains previously selected entries, they will appear highlighted. You can select additional items from a previously visited screen on a return visit and the system will incorporate them into the record subset you are building. Once you have finished examining all the screens and selecting all the records that you want, enter 'dis' and press <SEND>

to display the subset of records that you have selected. The system will display your selected multiple entries in a brief display format. You can specifically request a different format for this subset in the same way that was described above under the group display (e.g., 'dis tr' or 'dis fu').

To return to the original truncated display from an individual record or brief display, enter the 'GOB' ("go back") command. This is the same command introduced earlier to return to a group display from one of its entries. This command is used throughout the system to move you up one level higher in the display hierarchy from your current position.

Sometimes you may wish to skip an intermediate display level when returning to a higher level. For example, suppose you are viewing a single record that was selected from a brief display that was created from a subset of records that were selected from a truncated display. Entering 'GOB' from the single record returns you to the brief display; entering 'GOB' again returns you to the truncated display. To return directly to the truncated display from the single record, enter 'gob tr' and press <SEND>. This works throughout the system to skip intermediate steps. You can enter 'gob br,' 'gob tr,' or 'gob gr' as appropriate depending on what your initial search result was and how you arrived at your current display.

BRIEF DISPLAY

When two to five records in the database match a search request, the system will display the matching records in a brief format. Figure 4–5 is an example of a brief display. Unlike the one-line displays in a truncated list, each entry in a brief display typically covers several lines since it contains complete information from selected record fields rather than only a limited number of characters from those fields. The first part of the display includes information from some basic bibliographic description fields (when they exist in a given record) including main entry, uniform title, title proper, edition, and imprint. Some nonprint formats also include physical description fields as well (demonstrated in entry one). Information is laid out in an order similar to the order on a catalog card which makes it easily recognizable to many users.

Additionally, a brief display extracts selected information from other fields in the record and displays it following the basic bibliographic data. For example, several entries in Figure 4–5 show information from different fixed field elements. We find type of record for nonprint materials ("[MUSICAL RECORDING]" in

```
┌─────────────────────────────────────────────────────────────────────┐
│ Figure 4–5   Brief display                                          │
├─────────────────────────────────────────────────────────────────────┤
│                          ¶ CAT              SID: 00000        OL     │
│ Entire list displayed.                                              │
│                                                                     │
│ OLUC  da stee,wing                          Records: 4              │
│  Rec#  Description                                                  │
│ ▶ 1¶   Steel and Brass Band. Steel & brass sound recording / The   │
│        Steel and Brass Band. Los Angeles : United Artists, [1970]   │
│        1 sound disc (34 min.) : 33 1/3 rpm, stereo. ; 12 in.        │
│        [MUSICAL RECORDING]  OCLC: 13167755                          │
│ ▶ 2¶   Steel, Danielle. Wings / Danielle Steel. Large print ed.    │
│        New York : Delacorte Press, 1994.  [LARGE PRINT]  OCLC:      │
│        31416109   In XXX                                            │
│ ▶ 3¶   Steel, Danielle. Wings / Danielle Steel. New York, N.Y. :   │
│        Delacorte Press, 1994.  DLC  OCLC: 29669118                  │
│ ▶ 4¶   Steenblik, Jan W. The wingtip-to-wingtip waltz : ALPA       │
│        intensifies its opposition to flight procedures that        │
│        reduce the margins of safety on closely spaced parallel     │
│        approaches / by Jan W. Steenblik.  [ANALYTIC] OCLC:         │
│        19893347                                                    │
└─────────────────────────────────────────────────────────────────────┘
```

entry one); bibliographic level for nonmonographs ("[ANALYTIC]" in entry four); and form of an item ("[LARGE PRINT]" in entry two). You will notice that information sometimes appears to be duplicated, such as "Large print ed." and "[LARGE PRINT]" in entry two. This happens when similar information is recorded in several fields from which data is extracted for display. No attempt is made to eliminate such duplicate information from the display.

A brief display also includes a code for records cataloged by certain national libraries, but these codes use the full OCLC three-character institution symbol rather than the one-character codes used in a truncated display. In Figure 4–5, entry three shows the Library of Congress institution symbol ("DLC"). The final element displayed for every record is its OCLC control number preceded by the label "OCLC:." Some records also include a holdings symbol as an additional element. The holdings notation "In XXX" is displayed when the account used to conduct the search is registered to institution XXX and XXX has its holdings symbol attached to the record represented by that entry (see entry two). No information about any other institution's holdings is provided in a brief display.

A brief display provides more information about each record than the one-line truncated display and can frequently provide enough information to allow you to select a record that meets your needs directly from this display without needing to view a whole series of individual record displays. This is particularly true when an item has been issued in many similar formats for which no distinguishing information appears on a truncated or group display. For example, the brief display of three similar entries with the same author, title, and publishing information will allow you to distinguish easily among the audio CD, the cassette, and the vinyl disc because this display includes information from the physical description for those items.

Navigation and selection commands

All of the navigation and selection commands described above under truncated displays apply as well to brief displays. You can move forward and backward among multiple screens of brief entries by using PDN/PUP or FOR/BAC. You can select and view a single record from the brief display by entering its number or entering 'dis' and its number and pressing <SEND>. You can return to your brief display from an individual record with the GOB command or the 'gob br' command although there is no difference in the result between the two. You can request a display format other than the default with the 'dis' command.

You can also mark and display a subset of brief records that initially appeared over several screens. The system will display records from this set one at a time in the individual record format which is the next display level below a brief display. However, the FOR/BAC and PDN/PUP commands behave differently in single record displays than they did in brief and truncated displays (where they were virtually synonymous). In response to the 'dis' command following marking, the system will display the first record in your set. FOR will display the first screen of the next record in the set. PDN will display the next screen of the record currently on display. Similarly, you can subsequently use BAC (but not PUP) to return to the first screen of an earlier record in your set and PUP (but not BAC) to move to the previous screen of your current record.

Sometimes an initial truncated display is small enough that you may wish to view all of the records in a brief display to aid selection. You can enter 'dis br' and press <SEND> to have the system display all of the truncated entries in a brief display. For example, the sample derived name/title search for *Lana: the Lady, the Legend, the Truth* in Figure 4–3 resulted in only seven records.

You might decide to view them all in a brief display rather than sequentially examining many full record displays because information on the brief display can readily identify a record in which you are interested. Perhaps you are looking for a large-print edition and you are not concerned with a specific publisher or year. Examining one screen with four or five brief records at a time can be a very efficient strategy. However, be careful about selecting too many records at once for a brief display since the more spread out over many screens the display becomes, the more difficult the records are to work with. You may gain nothing in terms of work efficiency.

SINGLE RECORD DISPLAY

When only one record in the database matches a search, the system will respond with a single-record display immediately without any intermediate displays. Single-record responses are more likely to occur with numeric search keys than with other types of searches. You also get a single-record display when selecting an individual record from a group, truncated, or brief display.

Figure 4–6 illustrates a typical single-record display for a record that fits on one screen. Immediately below the header line in this display is an indication of whether your institution's symbol is in the accompanying locations record and how many other holdings symbols are listed there. The brief display included a statement about your institution's holdings only. This display includes a summary statement about all holdings. Figure 4–6 shows that the institution to which this account has been assigned ("XXX") does not own this title and that only two other institutions have indicated to OCLC that they do. The next two lines contain information related to system aspects of the record (rather than its cataloging properties). These lines contain such information as the record's OCLC system control number, when the record was added to the system, and when the record was last used.

Following the holdings statement and system information lines is a series of fields containing cataloging information relevant to this specific item. Each field begins with a start-of-message symbol (▶) and ends with an end-of-message symbol (¶). Fields are described in more detail in Chapter 6. They are mentioned briefly here only in terms of display and navigation.

The first field, called the "fixed field" in OCLC, generally runs four or more lines and contains certain coded information about the record (such as language and country of publication) spread out in columns across the width of the line. The fixed field is followed by a series of sequentially numbered variable fields,

---

Figure 4–6   One screen display of a single bibliographic record

```
                              ¶ CAT          SID: 00000        OL
Entire record displayed.
OLUC dp goul,ste,j                            Record 25 of 155
NO HOLDINGS IN XXX - 2 OTHER HOLDINGS
OCLC: 30749431        Rec stat:  n
Entered: 19940712     Replaced: 19940712    Used:  19940930
Type: a    ELvl: K    Srce: d    Audn:      Ctrl: eng   Lang: eng
BLvl: m    Form:      Conf: 0    Biog:      MRec: enk   Ctry: enk
           Cont:      Gpub:      Fict:      Indx: 0
Desc: a    Ills:      Fest:      DtSt: r    Dates: 1991, 1980 ¶
  ▶  1   040      EUN ǂc EUN ¶
  ▶  2   020      0140135340 (pbk.) ¶
  ▶  3   090      ǂb ¶
  ▶  4   049      XXXM ¶
  ▶  5   100 1    Gould, Stephen Jay. ¶
  ▶  6   245 10   Ever since Darwin : ǂb reflections in natural
history / ǂc Stephen Jay Gould. ¶
  ▶  7   260      Harmondsworth, England : ǂb Penguin Books, ǂc
1991. ¶
  ▶  8   300      285 p. : ǂb ill. ; ǂc 20 cm. ¶
  ▶  9   490 0    Penguin science ¶
  ▶ 10   650 0    Evolution (Biology) ¶
  ▶ 11   650 0    Natural selection ǂx History. ¶
```

containing such information as ISBN, author, title, publisher, physical description, series, and subject headings for the item represented by this record. As you can see in Figure 4–6, many fields fill only part of a line. Nonetheless, each new field is displayed beginning on a new line. This causes individual record displays to be very spread out down the screen and single records usually need multiple screens to display complete information. Figure 4–7 illustrates a multiple screen single record. Notice that the system message line now displays the message "Beginning of record displayed," rather than the "Entire record displayed" message in Figure 4–6. This message is the primary clue indicat-

---

Figure 4–7   Multiple screen display of a single bibliographic record

```
                              ¶ CAT              SID: 00000     OL
Beginning of record displayed.
OLUC  dp goul,ste,j                          Record 11 of 155
HELD BY XXX - 1601 OTHER HOLDINGS
OCLC:  23049373        Rec stat:  p
Entered:  19910111     Replaced:  19910615     Used:  19950507
 Type:  a    Elvl:      Srce:      Audn:      Ctrl:      Lang:  eng
 BLvl:  m    Form:      Conf:  0   Biog       Mrec:      Ctry:  nyu
             Cont:      Gpub:      Fict:  0   Indx:  0
 Desc:  a    Ills:  a   Fest:  0   DtSt:  r   Dates:  1991,  ¶

 ▶  1   010        91-6916 ¶
 ▶  2   040        DLC  ‡c DLC ¶
 ▶  3   020        0393029611 ¶
 ▶  4   050 00     QH45.5  ‡b .G68 1991 ¶
 ▶  5   082 00     508 ‡2 20 ¶
 ▶  6   090        ‡b ¶
 ▶  7   049        XXXM ¶
 ▶  8   100 1      Gould, Stephen Jay. ¶
 ▶  9   245 10     Bully for brontosaurus :  ‡b reflections in natural
history / ‡c  Stephen Jay Gould. ¶
 ▶ 10   250        1st ed. ¶
 ▶ 11   260        New York :    ‡b Norton,  ‡c c1991. ¶
```

```
                              ¶ CAT            SID: 00000          OL
  End of record displayed.
  OLUC     dp goul,ste,j                     Record 11 of 155
  HELD BY XXX - 1601 OTHER HOLDINGS
  ▶  12  300   540 p. :  ‡b ill. ;  ‡c 22 cm. ¶
  ▶  13  504   Includes bibliographical references (p. 513-524) and
  index. ¶
  ▶  14  650 0    Natural history ‡x Popular works. ¶
  ▶  15  650 0    Evolution  ‡x Popular works. ¶
```

ing that the display couldn't fit all on one screen and additional cataloging data is displayed on at least one more screen.

Many multiple screen records display very little descriptive information on the first screen, ending at the author field or perhaps the title field. The header and system information and the coded fixed field take up approximately half of the first screen and the rest of the screen can easily be filled with various numbers and codes that appear before the author, such as an LC control number, ISBNs, and classification numbers. With these records, the full display requires a second screen just to verify title, edition, publisher, or pagination. This situation occurs more frequently with records produced by a national agency such as the Library of Congress that include many number and code fields than with original records input by OCLC member institutions that typically have fewer such fields. Figure 4–8 shows the first screen for such a record.

Figure 4–8   First screen of a multiple screen display of a single bibliographic record

```
                         ¶ CAT                 SID: 00000      OL
Entire record displayed.

OLUC  dp goul,ste,j                          Record 35 of 155
 HELD BY XXX - 1701 OTHER HOLDINGS
 OCLC:  11814391         Rec stat:     c
 Entered: 19850226       Replaced:   19920615    Used:   19950519
 Type: a   Elvl: K    Srce: d    Audn:    Ctrl: eng   Lang: eng
 BLvl: m   Form:      Conf: 0    Biog:    Mrec:       Ctry: nyu
           Cont: b               Gpub:    Fict: 0     Indx: 1
 Desc: a   Ills: a    Fest:      DtSt: s Dates: 1985, ¶

 ▶ 1   010       85-4916//r90 ¶
 ▶ 2   040       DLC ≠c DLC ≠d UKM ¶
 ▶ 3   015       GB87-53072 ¶
 ▶ 4   019       17265421 ¶
 ▶ 5   020       0393022285 :  ≠c $17.95 ¶
 ▶ 6   050 00    QH81 ≠b .G673 1985
 ▶ 7   080       59:576.12 ¶
 ▶ 8   082 00    508 ≠2 19 ¶
 ▶ 9   090       ≠ b ¶
 ▶ 10  049       XXXM ¶
 ▶ 11  100 1     Gould, Stephen Jay. ¶
 ▶ 12  245 14    The  flamingo's  smile : ≠b reflections  in  natural
history  / ≠c Stephen Jay Gould
```

Navigation and selection commands

Many of the navigation and selection commands described above are not applicable to a single record. There is nothing to select (you have a single record) and very little navigation is possible. The basic navigation commands are PDN to view the next screen of data and PUP to view the previous screen of data. As mentioned above under brief displays, you can not use 'FOR/BAC' to navigate within a single record. Those commands will attempt to move you to the next or previous record, not to the next or previous screens within this record, and their use will produce error messages. The navigational messages "Beginning of record displayed" and "End of record displayed" will appear on the first and last screens respectively of a multiple screen display. No message appears on any middle screens. The lack of a message lets you know that you are at neither the beginning nor the end of the record but somewhere in the middle.

Another method (other than PDN) for displaying later information from a single record is to request a display beginning at a specific tag number or tag group. Tags and tag groups are explained in Chapter 6. For example, you may want to know what subjects have been assigned to a record and ask to begin the display with the subject tag group (the 6xx tag group). You would enter 'tag 6xx' and press <SEND>. The system will respond by beginning the display with the first tag in the subject tag group. This method is also quite useful when the information in which you are interested spans several screens and you wish to view it all on one screen to avoid repeated PDN/PUP commands. For example, the information displayed in Figure 4–8 ends with the title. The edition, publisher, and pagination are on the next screen. It might be easier for you to have everything from the author through the pagination displayed on one screen to make decisions about this record. You could accomplish this by entering 'tag 100' and pressing <SEND>. The system would redisplay this record beginning with the author (tag 100).

PHRASE INDEX DISPLAY

As mentioned in Chapter 3, the system responds to a phrase search by positioning you in an area of the corresponding index such that the closest match to your search key displays in the middle of the screen (at entry 9). This entry may or may not be a match or even a near match. The response does not depend on how many records in the system (if any) match your search request. Figure 4–9 is an example of a display following a title phrase search.

Figure 4–9   Phrase index display

```
                            ¶ CAT                  SID: 00000        OL

OLUC ti sound and the fury
        Phrase Index                                                Hits
▶    1¶   SOUND AND TELEVISION BROADCASTING STATIONS                  1
▶    2¶   SOUND AND TELEVISION BROADCASTING STATIONS FIELD STRENGTH CO 4
▶    3¶   SOUND AND TELEVISION BROADCASTING STATIONS 30 JUNE 1982      1
▶    4¶   SOUND AND THE CINEMA THE COMING OF SOUND TO AMERICAN FILM    1
▶    5¶   SOUND AND THE CLARINET                                       1
▶    6¶   SOUND AND THE DOCUMENTARY FILM                               2
▶    7¶   SOUND AND THE EAR                                            1
▶    8¶   SOUND AND THE FURRY                                          1
▶    9¶   SOUND AND THE FURY                                         50+
▶   10¶   SOUND AND THE FURY (FAULKNER)                                1
▶   11¶   SOUND AND THE FURY (MOTION PICTURE)                          2
▶   12¶   SOUND AND THE FURY (WILLIAM FAULKNER)                        2
▶   13¶   SOUND AND THE FURY & AS I LAY DYING                          6
▶   14¶   SOUND AND THE FURY A CONCORDANCE TO THE NOVEL                2
▶   15¶   SOUND AND THE FURY A CRITICAL COMMENTARY                     1
▶   16¶   SOUND AND THE FURY A STUDY IN PERSPECTIVE                    1
▶   17¶   SOUND AND THE FURY A STUDY OF JASON COMPSON AND HIS RELATION 1
▶   18¶   SOUND AND THE FURY A THEATRICAL COMEDY IN ONE ACT            1
▶   19¶   SOUND AND THE FURY AN ANECDOTAL HISTORY OF CANADIAN BROADCAS 1
```

A phrase index display is an alphabetical list of different index entries, not a list of records as were the earlier displays. Each entry occupies one line and consists of only two elements, a normalized index phrase and an indication of the number of records that contain that entry (shown under "Hits"). The normalization process performs such functions as capitalizing the entire phrase and removing properly coded initial articles, most of the punctuation (like commas, colons, and semicolons), and diacritical marks. The normalized version more closely represents how a phrase is stored in the index rather than how it appears in a record. For example, the record represented by entry 15 in Figure 4–10 has the title "The sound and the fury : a critical commentary" while its corresponding phrase index entry is all capitalized with both the initial article and colon eliminated.

A phrase index always fills all 19 entries on a page. There are no partial pages as with the other displays. For example, the group display in Figure 4–2 only had 11 entries and the truncated display in Figure 4–3 only had seven entries. Since the phrase index is not a list of records, the system message line never displays a list status message (e.g., "Beginning of list displayed" or "Entire list displayed") and the header line never includes a result set record count (e.g., "Records: 278"). Those features don't exist in this display. Additionally, an entry number is not associated with one particular record throughout a result set since there is no "result set" and no records in this display for a number to be associated with. Entry numbers go from one to 19 and merely indicate the relative position of an index entry on that display screen. For example, you will never see an entry 114 listed. Numbers start again at one every time you move to a different display screen.

The "Hits" column gives some indication of the number of records matching the corresponding phrase. With 50 or fewer matching records the number is accurate. If more than 50 records match that phrase, the system only shows "50+" rather than the actual number. For example, entry nine in Figure 4–9 shows "50+" records. You do not know from this display whether the number of matching records is actually 51 or 782 or 6,493.

Navigation and selection commands

You select an entry by entering its line number and pressing <SEND>, just as with the earlier displays. However, you can only select one entry at a time from a phrase index display, unlike the earlier displays which allowed you to select multiple entries at one time. Trying to select multiple entries or a range of entries (e.g., '9,11' or '8–12') returns an error message.

The system responds to an entry selection by displaying the records shown under "Hits" on that line in a default format appropriate to the number of records listed. For example, entry two in Figure 4–9 has four records which would be displayed in a brief display. Entry 16 has one record which would be displayed in a single record display. From the phrase index display you do not know exactly how many records matched entry nine, only that there were more than 50. If entry nine were selected, the system would respond with either a truncated display (for 51–99 matching records), a group display (for 100–1,500 matching records), or a message that the number of records exceeded the system limit (for over 1,500 matching records). Note that it is possible for an entry to appear in a phrase index even when the number of matching records at that entry exceeds the current system display limit and cannot be displayed.

Use the PDN command to move forward to the next screen of

entries and the PUP command to move back a screen of entries. The FOR and BAC commands do not work as equivalents to the PDN/PUP commands in the phrase display (as they did in several earlier display formats). Their use will generate an error message. As you move among screens, remember that the line numbering begins again with one on each new screen.

The 'GOB' command will return you to the phrase index display after viewing records under one of its entries. You can also enter 'gob bi' and press <SEND> to return directly to the phrase display if you are several display layers into an entry and wish to return without any intermediate steps. For example, suppose you are viewing a single record that was selected from a truncated display that resulted from selecting an entry from a phrase index display. The 'GOB' command will return you to the truncated display. 'Gob bi' will bypass the truncated display and return you directly to the phrase index display.

LOCATIONS RECORD DISPLAY

Accompanying most (but not all) bibliographic records is a locations record, an example of which is shown in Figure 4–10. The system message line and header line provide similar information as in bibliographic records. However, the summary holdings line has additional information. It begins with an indication of holdings display type (Figure 4–10 shows "Regional locations") before listing information about the institution assigned the account used to conduct the search (XXX in Figure 4–10), as well as how many total holdings symbols are attached to the locations record. The area beginning on the next line displays the same selected bibliographic information as the corresponding brief display for this record except that the holdings statement found on brief displays has been eliminated. Holdings are already covered in the line above this area.

The main body of a locations record lists the symbols for institutions that have indicated to OCLC that they own a copy of the item represented by that bibliographic record. Each unique three-character symbol has been assigned to a participating institution by OCLC. The complete list of symbols and their identity can be found in a set of OCLC publications, *OCLC Participating Institutions*, which are updated regularly. The identity of the symbols and the institutions they represent can also be found by looking in the online *Name-Address Directory*. To access the directory simply enter a colon followed by the three character symbol and press <SEND>. You will retrieve a record or records identifying the institution and providing a variety of

---

Figure 4–10   Regional Institution symbol display

```
                                ¶ CAT              SID: 00000      OL
Entire holdings displayed.
OLUC                      dp goul,ste,j       Record 44 of 155
Regional locations - NO HOLDINGS IN XXX - 303 OTHER HOLDINGS
Purcell, Rosamond Wolff.  Illuminations : a bestiary / [photographs
by] Rosamond Wolff Purcell ; [text by] Stephen Jay Gould.  1st ed.
New York : Norton, c1986.  DLC    OCLC: 13455962

STATE    LOCATIONS
NJ       CMO EOL MMT NPL NWM RID WAN
DE       DLM
NY       BNY NYP RRR RVE VGN VVP VVS VXJ VZU vzz XBM XSC yam YBM YDM
         YFM YGM ykc ypl YQR YXF ZQP ZRS ZWU
PA       ALL LFM mcn PAI PAU PGM PIS PLF PWC SQP SRU TEU UPM
```

---

information about it. To return to your previous screen enter <RET>.

The list of holdings symbols on a record is arranged in a standardized grouping in three levels which makes it easier to locate a specific symbol, should that symbol be in a particular display. At the first level there are three main groups: U.S. states, Canadian provinces, and all other countries. This level is used to group symbols at the other levels and has no display codes itself. The order in which first level groups display depends on where the authorization number that is being used to search the system has been registered. For example, if the number is registered to an institution in California, then the U.S. states group will display first. If the number is registered to an institution in France, then the other countries group will display first.

At the second level, each main group is divided into subgroups. Each subgroup is represented in displays by a unique two-character code. The United States states group is divided into states. The Canadian provinces group into provinces. The other countries group into countries. The display order among these subgroup codes depends on where the authorization number used to search the database is registered. The system will display your state, province, or country first with all other codes from the same main group listed alphabetically thereafter. Codes within any other main groups are all arranged alphabetically. For example, in Figure 4–10 the authorization is registered to a New Jersey institution. Therefore, NJ displays first followed alphabetically by the other three states in the region (DE, NY, PA).

At the third level, symbols for the individual owning institutions themselves are arranged alphabetically within the second level group. Figure 4–10 shows an alphabetical list of institutional symbols within each of the four states. In order to find a particular institutional symbol efficiently, you must know to which second level group it belongs. Of course, you can always look through all holdings symbols in a short list for that symbol but this can be very time consuming and inefficient with longer lists. When OCLC first started and had few members, three-character symbols were readily available and there was some relationship between an institution's location and name and the symbol assigned to it (e.g., "OSU" for Ohio State University and "PAU" for the University of Pennsylvania). As OCLC participation grew over time, and symbols became used up, such identifiable relationships ceased to be possible. There is frequently little apparent relationship today between many institutions and their symbols.

Although listing its symbol in the location record should indicate that a particular institution owns an item, there is nothing in the record to show you how many copies are owned, which branch may have the item, whether the copy is missing, or what the local call number might be. None of that information is readily available online. However, institutional symbols do tell you something about interlibrary loan policies. Uppercase symbols are used for institutions that participate in the PRISM Interlibrary Loan system. Lowercase symbols are used for institutions that do not. In Figure 4–10, notice that several of the institutions listed under New York are in lowercase ("vzz," "yam," "ykc," and "ypl"). Being listed in lowercase does not mean that an institution does not offer interlibrary loan of their items (although it indeed may not). This merely means that it does not offer interlibrary loan through PRISM.

Navigation and selection commands

To view a locations record when one is attached to a bibliographic record, enter 'dh' while displaying the bibliographic record and press <SEND>. The system will respond with an initial default display which depends on how many institutional symbols are in the record and where the institutions are located in relation to your institution. For example, the three display possibilities for an institution in the United States are:

state   (just institutions in your state)
region   (institutions in your state and all contiguous states)
all   (all institution symbols)

Similar display groupings exist for institutions in Canadian provinces and other countries. Basically, if there are enough holdings symbols in your state, the display will include just your state. If there are not enough in your state, but there *are* enough in your region, the display will include just your region. If there are not enough in your region, the display will include all institutions. Figure 4–10 is an example of a regional locations display.

You can directly request a specific locations display from a bibliographic record regardless of which default display the system might choose in response to a 'dh' request. To see your state display, enter 'dhs' and press <SEND>. To see your regional display, enter 'dhr' and press <SEND>. To see all the institutional holdings symbols, enter 'dha' and press <SEND>. You can also use those same commands to request a different holdings display once you are already on a locations record. For example, suppose that the system returned a state locations display in response to a 'dh' request. After examining the symbols you decide that you would like to see the regional display instead. You can now enter 'dhr' and press <SEND> to see the regional display.

Locations record displays that include all holdings symbols can be quite long and take many pages to display, especially when an item is held by institutions in many states, provinces, and countries. Each state begins on a line of its own. If an item is owned by institutions in 40 states, then the display takes at least 40 lines—even if only one institution in each state owns the item. Just as with bibliographic records, you can use PDN/PUP to move through screens within a record spanning multiple screens. You can not use FOR/BAC which will move you to the next or previous record (when there is one) rather than up and down within this record. And just as with bibliographic records, the systems message line will tell you when you are at the beginning or end of a locations record and tell you nothing when you are on some middle screen.

When you are viewing a long locations record with many screens, you can use the 'tag' command to request that the display begin with a specific state, province, or country. Enter a two-character state, province, or country code following 'tag' (e.g., 'tag oh' for Ohio) and press <SEND>. The system does not reorganize the list. It merely shifts the existing display so that holdings for the code you requested fall at the top of the current screen.

To return to a bibliographic record once you have finished viewing one of its locations displays, enter 'bib' and press <SEND>. Most navigation commands can be executed directly from a locations record, however, without returning to its bibliographic record. The system responds correctly to any navigation command that is a current valid option for the attached bibliographic record. It will respond as if you were on that bibliographic record. For example, suppose you are viewing the locations record for the third entry in a result set of four records. When you enter FOR from that locations record, the system will move forward to the bibliographic record for the fourth entry even though you were on a locations record. You can move directly from one locations record to another by chaining commands so that the display does not stop at the intermediate bibliographic record (e.g., 'for; dh').

AUTHORITY FILE DISPLAYS

The Authority File currently offers four basic display formats which parallel, but differ from, the four basic display formats in the Online Union Catalog. Unless otherwise instructed, the system will select one of these formats for a default record display as determined by the number of records in the search result set:

Quickview display   for a set of 101–600 records
Truncated display   for a set of 26–100 records
Brief display   for a set of 2–25 records
Single record display   for a set of 1 record

Several of these display formats share a common name with their Online Union Catalog counterparts, but the displays are different in the Authority File. This display hierarchy operates in the same way as the Online Union Catalog hierarchy. An initial record set consists of all the records that matched the search request, from one up to a maximum of 600 records. Notice that the Authority File maximum is substantially less than the 1,500 record maximum in the Online Union Catalog. The default initial display format and the default formats for any record subsets subsequently selected from this initial display are again determined by the number of records in the set or subset. For example, a subset of five records selected from a truncated display of 42 records will be returned in a brief display. A subset of one record selected from that same truncated display will be returned in a single record display. You can also request a specific display format if you prefer something other than the default. For example, you may prefer to view a set of 35 records in the brief display even though the default for that set would be the truncated display. The quickview display is the only one with restrictions in set size. While the quickview display is the default display for a result set over 100 records, you can request a quickview display for as few as 51 records. You will get the message "Illegal display format" if you request a quickview display of fewer than 51 records. Each of these display formats is discussed below.

COMMON INFORMATION IN ALL DISPLAYS

The common information in Authority File displays follows the same pattern as with the Online Union Catalog displays described earlier. The information on the first few lines of all displays is consistent. The system message line is again used to provide information about which screen in a particular display you are currently viewing. For example, the quickview display in Figure 4–11 shows the message:

```
Beginning of list displayed.
```

This message indicates that the display continues on to at least one additional screen. When a particular display takes up more than one screen, the system message line again displays a beginning indication on the first screen, an ending indication on the last screen, and no indication on any middle screens. Other example messages include:

```
Entire list displayed.
Entire record displayed.
Beginning of record displayed.
End of list displayed.
End of record displayed.
```

A header line again follows the system message line and a blank line. It contains context information for the particular search result display that you are viewing. The first element in this line indicates the database in which the search was conducted which is always "AUTH" in the Authority File. A restatement of your original index label and search strategy appears next. The system will always display an index label on this line, even when you entered your search in the old style without using a command and index label. For most searches, the end of the line shows either the total record count or the position of this record in relation to all records retrieved in the set. The specific information on this line will vary depending on your original search strategy, the size of the initial result set, and any intervening steps you may have taken since getting the initial display. The example in Figure 4–11 shows:

```
AUTH dn new,zea,c    Records: 182
```

This message indicates that this search was conducted in the Authority File, that a derived name search was done using the search key 'new,zea,c'. The result set includes a total of 182 records. Other example context lines from later Figures in this chapter are:

```
AUTH dn [hugo,vic,   Records: 42
AUTH dt sta,tr,,     Record 1 of 4
AUTH dn chri,aga,    Records: 18
```

Information on the rest of the screen will vary with each display format.

QUICKVIEW DISPLAY

Quickview is the default display format for a search result matching between 101 and 600 records. Figure 4–11 shows an example of a quickview display. The quickview display provides the same information as the truncated display. It is merely a compressed version of the truncated display. Each entry begins with a sequential number indicating that entry's position within the result set. The rest of the entry line consists of one indexed field from the corresponding authority record that matched the search key. The entry will display data from the field up to the length of one line (approximately 69 characters). It will not continue onto an additional line. Notice that entries 81 and 83 in Figure 4–11 both completely fill one line and even stop in the middle of a word. Compare entries 81 and 83 to entry 42, which is relatively short and complete.

Entries are arranged strictly alphabetically in the quickview display without regard for most internal punctuation. Notice in Figure 4–11 that the entries that begin with "New Zealand" without a following period (e.g., 42, 43, or 122) are filed in the same alphabetical sequence with the entries in which "New Zealand" is followed with a period.

The quickview display divides truncated entries into intervals and displays only the first three truncated entries in each interval with a line containing several ellipses (" . . . ") between intervals. The number of records contained in one interval is determined by the total number of records in the result set and

---

Figure 4–11 Quickview display

```
                              ¶ CAT              SID: 00000            AF
Beginning of list displayed.

AUTH  dn new,zea,c                               Records: 182
  Rec#    Field accessed
▶   1¶    Conference on the New Zealand Cretaceous (1973 : University
          of Aucklan
    2     New Zealand. Cabinet Committee on Family Affairs.
    3     New Zealand. Canteen Fund Board
      ...      ...        ...        ...
▶  41¶    New Zealand. Civil Engineering Division.
   42     New Zealand Civilization
   43     New Zealand Civilization American influences
      ...      ...        ...        ...
▶  81¶    New Zealand. Committee Appointed to Investigate Problems
          Associated wi
   82     New Zealand. Committee Appointed to Review the Operations
          of the Maori
   83     New Zealand. Committee Appointed to Review the Social Sciences
          Researc
      ...      ...        ...        ...
▶ 121¶    New Zealand. Committee to Review the Unit Titles Act, 1972,
          Special
  122     New Zealand Communicable Disease Centre
  123     New Zealand. Communications Advisory Council
      ...      ...        ...        ...
```

---

will vary in increments of five from a low of 20 (for a result set between 51 and 100 entries) to a maximum of 50 (for a result set between 226 and 600 entries). Figure 4–11 shows an interval size of 40 entries which the system selected based on a result set of 182 records. You can see that entries 41 and 81 follow ellipsis lines and, therefore, are the first entries of the second and third intervals respectively.

Navigation and selection commands

The quickview display provides several selection options. You can select the first entry from any one interval by entering its number in the home position and pressing <SEND>. Notice in Figure 4–11 that the first entry number in each interval (and only the first) is preceded by a start-of-message symbol (▶) and followed by an end-of message symbol (¶). These are the only entry numbers you can select from the home position without using the 'dis' command. Just as in the Online Union Catalog, you can also move your cursor onto the line with the entry that you want to select, position the cursor somewhere between the two symbols on that line, and press <SEND>. The system will respond to either of the above requests with a full screen of 19 entries in truncated display format. For most selections the entries will be arranged such that your selected entry number is in the middle of the screen (at the tenth line position). When you select the first interval, however, your selection appears at the top of the screen. When you select the last interval, the display will include fewer than 19 entries if there are fewer than nine entries following your selected entry, which will still be positioned in the middle of the screen (at the tenth line position).

You can also select a specific record or multiple records from the quickview display by using the 'dis' command followed by any entry number or series of entry numbers and a display format. When using the 'dis' command on a quickview display, you must always specify a display format or you will get the error message "Display format is required." The system will not select a default display format for you. Available display formats include truncated ('tr'), brief ('br'), and single record ('fu'—for full). When you select multiple records in a single record display format, the system displays each record individually beginning with the lowest entry number selected.

You can select any entry number with the 'dis' command, whether or not it displays as one of the first three entries in the interval. For example, in Figure 4–11 you could enter 'dis 82–88 br' and press <SEND>. The system would respond with a brief display of those seven records. However, from the information available on the quickview display all you know is that entries 82 and 83 are of interest. You cannot see entries 84–88 and would be guessing as to their relevance to your needs. It would be better to select entry 81 first (e.g., '81' <SEND>) and view a truncated display of the unseen entries 84–88 before making any decisions about their relevance. Although this selection method will work, the quickview display rarely provides enough information about unseen entries to make this an effective strategy in practice.

When a quickview display list contains more intervals than fit on a single screen, you can display successive screens of entries in the same way described earlier in the Online Union Catalog section. You can use successive PDN ("page down") or FOR ("forward") commands until the end of the list is reached. Successive PUP ("page up") or BAC ("backward") commands browse backward in a similar manner. For example, notice that Figure 4–11 shows only the first four intervals which cover through entry 160 while the header line indicates that there are 181 records in this result set. To see the entries from the additional interval in this list, enter either the PDN command or the FOR command. The remaining interval will display along with an "End of list displayed" message. To return to this first screen, enter the PUP command or the BAC command. The top of the list will display along with the "Beginning of list displayed" message. You can use successive PDN/FOR commands and PUP/BAC commands to navigate through multiple screen quickview displays. Remember that no location message (e.g., "End of list displayed") displays on any middle screens when there are three or more screens to display.

You can use the GOB (go back) command to return to the quickview display from the truncated, brief, or single record display that resulted from selecting one or more of its entries. The GOB command moves up one level higher in the display hierarchy from your current display just as it did in the Online Union Catalog displays. For example, perhaps you initially selected entries 41–48 from the quickview display in Figure 4–11 and, after viewing those records, you decide that you would like to view records from a different area. You can enter GOB—the system will redisplay your original quickview display and you can now select another entry or entries.

TRUNCATED DISPLAY

A truncated display is the default format for a search result containing between 25 and 100 entries as well as the default format for entries expanded from a quickview display. Recall that a quickview display is merely a compressed truncated display. Figure 4–12 shows a truncated display of some of the records that could result from a derived name search for Victor Hugo (using the key '[hugo,vic,').

A truncated display contains a series of one-line entries, each with selected information from one heading in a record in the search result set. As in the quickview display entries are arranged strictly alphabetically without regard for most internal punctuation. Each entry is uniquely identified by a sequential number that indicates its order in the initial search result set. The same number will be associated with one record throughout a search result set no matter which display format is subsequently selected. A truncated display entry contains only one other component: a one-line display (of up to approximately 71 characters) of the indexed field from the corresponding authority record that

```
┌─────────────────────────────────────────────────────────────────────────┐
│  Figure 4–12   Truncated display                                          │
├─────────────────────────────────────────────────────────────────────────┤
│                                                                           │
│                                 ¶ CAT              SID: 00000      AF      │
│  Beginning of list displayed.                                             │
│                                                                           │
│  AUTH  dn [hiugo,vic,                             Records: 42             │
│    Rec#    Field accessed                                                  │
│  ▸   1¶   Hugo Aboites Aguilar, Vicente                                   │
│  ▸   2¶   Hugo de Le´on, V´ictor.                                         │
│  ▸   3¶   Hugo Forjaz, Victor                                             │
│  ▸   4¶   Hugo, Victor Marie, comte, 1802-1885. Quatrevingt-trieze        │
│  ▸   5¶   Hugo, Victor, 1802-1885                                         │
│  ▸   6¶   Hugo, Victor, 1802-1885. Amy Robsart                            │
│  ▸   7¶   Hugo, Victor, 1802-1885. Angelo, tyran de Padoue. English & Italian │
│  ▸   8¶   Hugo, Victor, 1802-1885 Characters                              │
│  ▸   9¶   Hugo, Victor, 1802-1885 Characters Hernani                      │
│  ▸  10¶   Hugo, Victor, 1802-1885 Characters Javert                       │
│  ▸  11¶   Hugo, Victor, 1802-1885. Correspondence.                        │
│  ▸  12¶   Hugo, Victor, 1802-1885. Dernier jour d'un condamn´e. English   │
│  ▸  13¶   Hugo, Victor, 1802-1885. Ecrits de Victor Hugo sur la peine de mort │
│  ▸  14¶   Hugo, Victor, 1802-1885. Formes que prend la souffrance pendant le som │
│  ▸  15¶   Hugo, Victor, 1802-1885. Gavroche. Azerbaijani                  │
│  ▸  16¶   Hugo, Victor, 1802-1885. Hernani                                │
│  ▸  17¶   Hugo, Victor, 1802-1885. Histoire d'un crime. English           │
│  ▸  18¶   Hugo, Victor, 1802-1885. Homme qui rit. Chinese                 │
│  ▸  19¶   Hugo, Victor, 1802-1885. Lucr`ece Borgia                        │
│                                                                           │
└─────────────────────────────────────────────────────────────────────────┘
```

matched the search request.

One function of an authority record is to direct users to the authorized form of a heading when perhaps only an unauthorized form is known beforehand. Therefore, not only authorized headings but also related headings (e.g., "see also" references) and unauthorized variant forms of authorized headings (e.g., cross references) are indexed in the authority file. The indexed field that gets displayed in the truncated entry may not be the authorized form of the heading. It may be a cross reference. You cannot tell which form it is from this display format itself. For example, in Figure 4–12 the indexed heading at entry three ("Hugo Forjaz, Victor") is a cross reference to the authorized form of that name ("Forjaz, Victor Hugo"). However, you do not discover this until you look at this entry in a brief or full record display. You cannot assume that the heading you are viewing in a truncated display is the authorized form. Entry one is also a cross reference as well. When both an authorized and an unauthorized heading in the same record match the same search key, only the authorized form displays. For example, in Figure 4–12 the record represented by the heading at entry seven ("Hugo, Victor, 1802–1885. Angelo, tyran de Padoue. English & Italian") also has a cross reference containing the same author but with the English form of the title ("Hugo, Victor, 1802–1885. Angelo, the tyrant of Padua"). Since the form of name in the authorized heading and the cross reference both match the search key (they are the same name), only the authorized heading displays.

Navigation and selection commands

Just as in the Online Union Catalog, a truncated display in the Authority File shows a maximum of 19 entries on one screen although you can have as many as 100 records returned in the default truncated display and you can specifically request a truncated display for any number of records up to the maximum of 600 returned in a search result set. You can again use PDN/FOR and PUP/BAC to navigate through successive screens of truncated entries.

To view the single authority record for one of the listed entries, enter its corresponding sequence number and press <SEND>. Alternately, you could enter the sequence number following the 'dis' command. For example, to view the record in Figure 4–12 for Victor Hugo Forjaz, enter '3' or 'dis 3' and press <SEND>. The system will display the full authority record containing that name. You can also move your cursor to the line with the entry that you desire, place the cursor anywhere between the start-of-message (▸) and end-of-message (¶) symbols on that line, and press <SEND>. Unlike the quickview display where this option was available only on selected entries, notice that every entry in Figure 4–12 has both of these symbols surrounding the entry number. This method still has the same drawbacks mentioned earlier, namely, that it usually requires more cursor movement to accomplish the same procedure and that you can only select one entry at a time rather than multiple entries.

You can simultaneously select multiple entries from a truncated display by listing discrete entry numbers separated with commas and consecutive entry numbers separated with a dash (e.g., '8–10,16' or 'dis 8–10,16') or list all numbers separated with commas (e.g., '8,9,10,16' or 'dis 8,9,10,16') and press <SEND>. You are not required to name a display format when using the 'dis' command as you were when selecting records from the quickview display. Selecting a single entry will result in a single record display. Selecting any number of multiple entries will result in a brief display. Selections must be listed in ascending numerical order. For example, to display the two records in Figure 4–12 related to Hugo's Hernani, enter '9,16' or 'dis 9,16' and press <SEND>. The system will display your selected multiple entries in a brief display format. The system will return an error message if you enter '16,9' or 'dis 16,9' instead of '9,16' or 'dis 9,16.'

Selecting entries from several screens before displaying them all together as a group (marking entries) works the same way in the Authority File as it does in the Online Union Catalog. To select and mark entries, begin exactly as above but without using the 'dis' command. (Using the 'dis' command while marking produces an error message.) Select one or more entries from your current screen (e.g., '8–10,16'), but follow your final selection with a comma (e.g., '8–10,16,') and press <SEND>. The system responds with the message "Please complete marking." Now you can go to your next screen (PDN/FOR) or previous screen (PUP/BAC), select additional entries from that screen (e.g., 23–24,35–37), and press <SEND>. The ending comma is only required on the first selection screen to initiate the marking process. It is not required on subsequent screens.

You can view multiple screens in any order when marking entries but you must always select items from your current screen in ascending numerical order. If you return to a screen with previously selected entries, those selected entries appear highlighted. Should you select additional entries from this screen, the system will incorporate them into the record subset you are building. Once you have finished selecting all relevant entries of interest from the multiple screens, enter 'dis' and press <SEND> to display the subset of records that you have selected. The system will display your entries in a default brief display format. However, you can also specifically request either a truncated ('dis tr') or single record ('dis fu') display of this record subset.

Just as in the Online Union Catalog, the GOB ("go back") command will return you to your original truncated display from a subsequent truncated, brief, or individual record display of a record subset. Remember that the GOB command is used throughout the system to return one level higher in the display hierarchy from a current position. You can also skip an intermediate display level when returning to a higher level. For example, suppose you are viewing a single record that was selected from a brief display that was created from a subset of records that were selected from a truncated display. Entering GOB from the single record returns you to the brief display. Entering GOB again returns you to the truncated display. To return directly to the truncated display from the single record, enter 'gob tr' and press <SEND>. This works throughout the system to skip intermediate steps. You can enter 'gob br,' 'gob tr,' or 'gob qu' as appropriate, depending on what your initial search result was and how you arrived at your current display.

BRIEF DISPLAY

A brief display is the default format for a search result set between two and 25 records. It is also the default display format for any number of records (greater than one) that were selected as a subset from a truncated display. Figure 4–13 shows a brief display of some of the records that could result from a derived name search for Agatha Christie (using the key 'chri,aga,'). Figure 4–14 shows a brief display of a subset of seven records that might have been selected from a truncated display resulting from a derived name search for New Zealand commissions and committees (using the key 'new,zea,c').

The brief display is similar to the truncated display. Again each entry is represented by a sequential number that it retains throughout various displays of this result set. For example, Figure 4–14 contains records with the sequence numbers 75–78, 89, and 105–106. Entries are again arranged alphabetically without regard for internal punctuation. Notice that five, six, and seven in Figure 4–13 lack closing periods following the death date but nonetheless interfile properly according to the next word in the heading. A brief display, however, has a blank line between entries which causes this display to be more spread out than either the quickview or truncated display. In Figure 4–13 only nine entries now fit on one screen rather than the 19 entries that could fit on one screen of a truncated display.

There are two significant differences between truncated and brief displays. The first significant difference is that each entry can now contain two elements of information following the sequence number (rather than one): the accessed or indexed field and the established heading when that heading differs from the indexed field. Whereas the truncated display only contained the indexed field with no indication of whether or not that form was the established heading, the brief display always shows an established heading directly in the display. The indexed field always displays first. The established heading (when it differs from the indexed field) displays second following two right angle brackets (i.e., following ">>"). For example, in Figure 4–13 notice that entries two and three both contain indexed fields followed by right angle brackets and established headings. Were you to

---

Figure 4-13   Brief display

```
                            ¶ CAT               SID: 00000        AF
Beginning of list displayed.

AUTH    dn chri,aga,                             Records: 17
  Rec#  Field accessed >> Established heading
▶  1¶   Christie, Agatha, 1890-1976.

▶  2¶   Christie, Agatha, 1890-1976 >> Mallowan, Agatha Christie, 1890-1976

▶  3¶   Christie, Agatha, 1890-1976 >> Westmacott, Mary, 1890-1976

▶  4¶   Christie, Agatha, 1890-1976. And then there were none

▶  5¶   Christie, Agatha, 1890-1976 Characters

▶  6¶   Christie, Agatha, 1890-1976 Characters Hercule Poirot

▶  7¶   Christie, Agatha, 1890-1976 Characters Jane Marple

▶  8¶   Christie, Agatha, 1890-1976. Crooked house. German

▶  9¶   Christie, Agatha, 1890-1976. Easy to kill
```

---

view the full records for these entries, you would see "Christie, Agatha, 1890–1976" listed as a "see also" reference to these other established names under which she is also known. In Figure 4–14 notice that entries 78 and 106 also both contain indexed fields followed by right angle brackets and established headings. However, both of these indexed headings are "see" references to the established heading form. There is no indication on the brief display of the relationship between the accessed and established headings. You need to view the individual record to see what that relationship is. When there is no second heading, the indexed heading is the established heading.

The other significant difference between truncated and brief displays is that more of the indexed field (as well as more of the established heading when present) displays over several lines as required instead of having longer headings truncated at the end of one line. The two elements in a brief display together can be as long as several hundred characters over many lines. Notice that entries 75 and 106 in Figure 4–14 both extend on to a third line. This extra display length can be particularly advantageous with certain classes of headings, such as long corporate bodies or government agencies, where the main body might fill one line itself before any distinguishing sub-body can display. For example,

---

Figure 4–14   Brief display with multiple line entries

```
                              ¶ CAT              SID: 00000        AF
Entire list displayed.

AUTH   dn new,zea,c                              Records: 182
  Rec#    Field accessed >> Established heading
▶  75¶   New Zealand. Commission of Inquiry into the Explosion and Fire
         Which Occurred at the Factory of the Chemical Manufacturing Co.,
         Ltd. on 26 September 1974.

▶  76¶   New Zealand. Commission of Inquiry into the Heavy Engineering
         Industry

▶  77¶   New Zealand. Commission on Education.

▶  78¶   New Zealand. Commission on the Courts, Royal >> New Zealand.
         Royal Commission on the Courts.

▶  89¶   New Zealand. Committee of Inquiry into Solicitors Nominee Companies.

▶ 105¶   New Zealand. Committee on Health and Social Education.

▶ 106¶   New Zealand. Committee on Health Services Organisation, Special
         Advisory >> New Zealand. Special Advisory Committee on Health
         Services Organisation.
```

---

the several headings beginning with "United States. Interstate Commerce Commission. Bureau of Motor Carriers" already fill one line in a truncated display before revealing any distinguishing section information. A brief display of these headings would allow the section information to display on an additional line permitting you to select the appropriate heading from the brief display.

Navigation and selection commands

All of the navigation and selection commands described above under truncated entries apply here as well. You can move to the next screen of a multiple-screen display using either the 'PDN' or 'FOR' command. You can move to the previous screen using either the 'PUP' or 'BAC' command. You can select one record or a range of records from a single screen either with or without the 'dis' command (e.g., '3' or 'dis 3' or '4–6,8' or 'dis 4–6,8').

The default display format for one or more records selected from a brief display is a single record (or full) display. If you selected multiple records, the system responds by displaying the full single record for the first entry in your subset. Entering 'FOR' moves you to the full record of the second entry and so on through the list of selected records. Entering BAC reverses this process. For example, in response to selecting the subset of entries '4–6,8' in Figure 4–13, the system displays the full record for entry four. Entering FOR returns the full record for entry five. Entering FOR again returns the full record for entry six. Entering FOR again returns the full record for entry seven. If you enter FOR while on the last record of your subset, the system returns an error message indicating that "You are already at the end of the list." It does the same when you try to move beyond the end of any other list.

You can select entries from several screens of a multiple-screen display before displaying them by following the same record "marking" guidelines described above under the truncated display. The process works the same here. The GOB command also works the same in a brief display. Both of these operations are described more fully in the truncated display section.

SINGLE RECORD DISPLAYS

When only one record matches a search request or when you have selected a single record from a truncated display or one or more records from a brief display, the system responds with a single record display (of the first record when you have selected several). Figure 4–15 illustrates a typical single record display in the Authority File.

Just as in bibliographic records, the single authority record contains a series of fields containing information relevant to the heading being described—each field beginning with a start-of-message symbol ( ) and closing with an end-of-message symbol (¶). The first field is called the "fixed field" in OCLC. It displays coded data in a series of columns over several rows (or lines) that occupy approximately the first third of the available record display area. The fixed field in Figure 4–15 begins with "TYPE" and goes through "RULES." and contains much white space in addition to this coded data. The fixed field is followed by a series of sequentially numbered variable fields that contain such information as the established heading, any cross references or "see also" references (when appropriate), the item where this heading was found, a series publisher (when appropriate), etc. Even though each new field is displayed beginning on a new line, just like bibliographic records, most authority records are relatively short when compared to bibliographic records and generally fit on one screen. A much smaller percentage of authority records than bibliographic records continue on to additional screens.

Figure 4–15   Tagged display of a single authority record

```
                           ¶ CAT            SID: 00000          AF
Entire list displayed.
AUTH   dt sta,tr,,                      Record 1 of 4
                                        LC/NACO - NAME
ARN:       1069950
Rec stat:  c   Entered:       19840216
►Type:      z   Upd status:    a     Enc lvl:    n      Source:
 Roman:     ▮   Ref status:    a     Mod rec:           Name use:  a
 Govt agn:  ▮   Auth status:   a     Subj:       a      Subj use:  a
 Series:    a   Auth/ref:      a     Geo subd:   n      Ser use:   a
 Ser num:   b   Name:          n     Subdiv tp:  ▮      Rules:     c ¶
►  1  010      n 83700217  ‡z n 84744685 ¶
►  2  040      DLC ‡c DLC ‡d DLC ¶
►  3  005      19851213133103.6 ¶
►  4  130   0  Star trek. ¶
►  5  430   0  Star trek novel ¶
►  6  643      Boston ‡b Gregg Press ¶
►  7  644      f  ‡5 DLC ¶
►  8  645      t  ‡5 DLC ¶
►  9  646      s  ‡5 DLC ¶
► 10  670      McIntyre, V.N. The entropy effect, 1984, c1981; ‡b
CIP t.p. ¶
► 11  670      McIntyre, V.N. Star trek III, c1984: ‡b t.p. (A Star
trek novel)¶
```

There are actually two options for a full display of a single authority record: a tagged display and a mnemonic display. The primary difference between these two formats is the way in which the fixed fields (and some other coded data) are displayed. The tagged display is the default display for a single bibliographic record and the one you will most commonly see. In a tagged display, the fixed field elements show the codes themselves rather than any English language equivalents. Figure 4–15 illustrates a typical tagged display in the Authority File. A mnemonic display, on the other hand, shows the fixed field elements in English language words that represent the code values rather than showing the code values themselves. Also, some fixed field elements may not display at all. Figure 4–16 illustrates the same record as Figure 4–15 but in a mnemonic display,

As a demonstration of how the fixed fields are handled differently, notice that Figure 4–16 shows the word "UNNUMBERED" as the second column in the middle of the last fixed field row, immediately above the first variable field (the 010 field). Figure 4–15 shows this same information in its coded form, "Ser num: b," as the first column in the last fixed field row. All of the other word values in Figure 4–16 have coded values in Figure 4–15 as well (e.g., "MONO SERIES" = "Series: a," "EVALUATED" = "Ref status: a," etc.), although you will notice that the values do not appear in the same column and row within the fixed fields in the different display formats.

Additionally, some fixed field information in the tagged display may not appear in the mnemonic display. For example, the entry "Geo subd: n" in the tagged display fixed field of Figure 4–15 indicates that geographic subdivision practice is not applicable to this heading. Nothing appears for this element in the fixed field of the mnemonic display in Figure 4–16. Some information from the fixed field of a tagged display may also appear elsewhere than the fixed field area in a mnemonic display. For example, the fixed field value "Rules: c" in Figure 4–15 indicates that this heading was established under AACR2 rules. This information appears in Figure 4–16 as the "[AACR2]" notation following the main heading in line four of the variable fields. You do not see that notation on line four in the tagged display of Figure 4–15.

Navigation and selection commands

Few of the navigation and selection commands described above apply to a single record. The basic commands are PDN to view the next screen of the current record on display and PUP to view

```
┌──────────────────────────────────────────────────────────────────────────┐
│ Figure 4–16    Mnemonic display of a single authority record               │
├──────────────────────────────────────────────────────────────────────────┤
│                            ¶ CAT              SID: 00000        AF          │
│ Entire record displayed.                                                   │
│ AUTH     dt sta,tr,,                          Record 1 of 4                 │
│                                               LC/NACO - NAME               │
│ ▶ AUTHORITY RECORD                                                         │
│   ARN: 1069950            REC STAT: REVISED   ENTERED: 19840216             │
│                                                                            │
│   NAME/SUBJECT/SERIES      ESTABLISHED HEADING    EVALUATED                 │
│   LC                                                                       │
│   MONO  SERIES    UNNUMBERED       ¶                                        │
│ ▶  1    010       n 83700217  ‡z n 84744685 ¶                              │
│ ▶  2    040       DLC  ‡c DLC  ‡d DLC ¶                                     │
│ ▶  3    005       19851213133103.6 ¶                                       │
│ ▶  4    130   0   Star trek. [AACR2] ¶                                     │
│ ▶  5    430   0   Star trek novel ¶                                        │
│ ▶  6    643       Boston  ‡b Gregg Press ¶                                 │
│ ▶  7    644       f  ‡5 DLC ¶                                              │
│ ▶  8    645       t  ‡5 DLC ¶                                              │
│ ▶  9    646       s  ‡5 DLC ¶                                              │
│ ▶ 10    670       McIntyre, V.N. The  entropy  effect,  1984,  c1981;  ‡b  │
│   CIP t.p. ¶                                                               │
│ ▶ 11    670       McIntyre, V.N. Star trek III, c1984: ‡b t.p. (A Star     │
│   trek novel) ¶                                                            │
└──────────────────────────────────────────────────────────────────────────┘
```

the previous screen of the current record on display. Just as in bibliographic records in the Online Union Catalog, FOR and BAC do not behave the same as PDN and PUP within a single authority record even though they behaved the same when navigating around the authority record lists discussed previously. FOR will attempt to move you to a full display of the next record and BAC will attempt to move you to a full display of the previous record and both commands will produce an error message if there is only one record in your current set.

However, you may want to toggle between the mnemonic and tagged displays. To do this enter 'alt' in the home position and press <SEND>. The system will respond by displaying your record in the format that is not currently on display. Entering 'alt' while on a mnemonic display will change that record to a tagged display. Entering 'alt' again will return that record to the original mnemonic display.

PHRASE INDEX DISPLAYS

The system responds to a phrase search in the Authority File by positioning you in the area of the corresponding root index such that the closest match to your search key displays in the middle of the screen. You get this same response regardless of whether or not any index entries in the system actually match your search key. Figure 4–17 is an example of a possible root index display following a title browse using 'sca ti report unit' and Figure 4–18 is an example of a possible root index display following a personal author browse using 'sca pn hugo.'

A root index display contains an alphabetically arranged series of entries, each entry corresponding to one heading (either an established heading or a cross reference) in an authority record. Each entry is represented by a sequential number beginning with "R." However, the numbering sequence starts again with R1 on each new screen since these numbers are merely a convenient way to identify and select an item from a screen and do not rep-

---

Figure 4–17   Root index display

```
                              ¶ CAT                 SID: 00000            AF
        AUTH    ti report unit
                Root Index                                                 Hits
   ►   R1¶      REPORT TO THE STOCKHOLDERS & OTHER POEMS                      1
   ►   R2¶      REPORT TO THE STORTING                                        2
   ►   R3¶      REPORT TO THE THIRTEENTH CONGRESS OF THE ROMANIAN COMMUNIST PARTY   1
   ►   R4¶      REPORT TO THE TRILATERAL COMMISSION                           1
   ►   R5¶      REPORT TO UTAH STATE LEGISLATURE                              2
   ►   R6¶      REPORT TRITA LIB                                              2
   ►   R7¶      REPORT UAG                                                    4
   ►   R8¶      REPORT UNITED COMMUNITY PLANNING CORPORATION                  1
   ►   R9¶      REPORT UNITED STATES BUREAU OF INDIAN AFFAIRS PLANNING SUPPORT   1
                   GROUP
   ►   R10¶     REPORTE DE INVESTIGACION                                      4
   ►   R11¶     REPORTE DE INVESTIGACION (UNIVERSIDAD AUTONOMA CHAPINGO CIESTAAM)   1
   ►   R12¶     REPORTE DE INVESTIGACION (UNIVERSIDAD AUTONOMA METROPOLITANA   1
                   DIVISION DE CIENCIAS Y ARTES PARA EL DISENO)
   ►   R13¶     REPORTE DE INVESTIGACION (UNIVERSIDAD AUTONOMA METROPOLITANA   1
                   UNIDAD AZCAPOTZALCO DIVISION DE CIENCIAS SOCIALES Y
                   HUMANIDADES)
   ►   R14¶     REPORTE DE INVESTIGACION (UNIVERSIDAD AUTONOMA METROPOLITANA   1
                   UNIDAD XOCHIMILCO DIVISION DE CIENCIAS SOCIALES Y HUMANIDADES)
```

Figure 4–18   Root index display

```
                              ¶ CAT            SID: 00000        AF
AUTH        pn hugo
            Root Index                                          Hits
 ▶   R1¶    HUGO, SPINELLI                                         1
 ▶   R2¶    HUGO, T W (TREVANION W) 1848 1923                      1
 ▶   R3¶    HUGO, THOMAS 1820 1876                                 1
 ▶   R4¶    HUGO, TREVANION W 1848 1923                            1
 ▶   R5¶    HUGO, VALENTINE 1887 1968                              1
 ▶   R6¶    HUGO, VICTOR MARIE COMTE 1802 1885                     6
 ▶   R7¶    HUGO, VICTOR 1802 1885                               50+
 ▶   R8¶    HUGO, VIKTOR 1802 1885                                 1
 ▶   R9¶    HUGO, W B (WILLIAM BARRY)                              1
 ▶  R10¶    HUGO, WILLIAM BARRY                                    1
 ▶  R11¶    HUGODOT, FLORENCE                                      1
 ▶  R12¶    HUGODOT, PHILIPPE                                      1
 ▶  R13¶    HUGOKE                                                 1
 ▶  R14¶    HUGOLIN FATHER 1877 1938                               1
 ▶  R15¶    HUGOLIN P O F M 1877 1938                              1
 ▶  R16¶    HUGOLIN PERE 1877 1938                                 1
 ▶  R17¶    HUGOLIN R P O F M 1877 1938                            1
 ▶  R18¶    HUGOLIN VON ORVIETO D 1373                             1
 ▶  R19¶    HUGOLIN, L LUCIANO                                     1
```

---

resent an entry's relative position in a search result set (as do the sequence numbers in the other displays discussed above).

Following the sequence number is an entry representing a normalized authority heading. Normalization includes capitalizing all letters and replacing most punctuation (except for parentheses and some commas) with a space. For example, the dash and one comma were removed from the heading "Hugo, Victor, 1802–1885" in its representation as "HUGO, VICTOR 1802 1885" by entry R7 in Figure 4–18. An entry is not limited to a single line. It can be as long as 128 characters extending over several lines. For example, entry R13 in Figure 4–17 extends to three lines and entries R9, R12, and R14 extend to a second line. As a consequence, the number of entries that fill a screen will vary instead of being constant at 19 as in displays where entries are limited to one line each. Multiple line entries are much more likely to occur with title or corporate name headings which can both be quite long at times than with personal name headings which tend to be shorter. Notice that Figure 4–17, a title browse, only has 14 entries because several of them extend to additional lines whereas Figure 4–18, a personal name browse, has a maximum 19 entries because each entry is less than one line.

The final column in the root index display indicates the number of times that the corresponding entry appears as a heading. If a given heading appears more than 50 times in the system, this number merely indicates "50+" rather than giving an exact number as it does for fewer than 50 occurrences of a heading. However, there is not a one-to-one relationship between the number of heading occurrences as shown here and the number of records in which that heading appears. Some headings appear multiple times in a single record and each of those occurrences are counted in this number. For example, entry R7 in Figure 4–18 indicates that the heading ""HUGO, VICTOR 1802 1885" occurs more than 50 times ("50+"). However, those 50+ occurrences may appear in only 37 records because some records contain two or more Victor Hugo headings—usually one in an established heading (e.g., "Hugo, Victor, 1802–1885. Angelo, tyran de Padoue. English & Italian") and one or more in cross references (e.g., "Hugo, Victor, 1802–1885. Angelo, the tyrant of Padua").

The Authority File has a second phrase index display—the expanded index display. This display is an expanded view of the same headings found in the root index display. In this display, multiple occurrences of a heading are broken out into separate subheading entries. Figure 4–19 is an example of a possible expanded index display beginning from entry R6 in Figure 4–18. An expanded index display is requested from the root index display.

The first column of an expanded index display again contains a sequence number, this time beginning with "E" however. Again the number sequence begins with "1" on each new screen rather than remaining associated with a particular heading throughout a display. These sequence numbers serve the same function as the sequence numbers in a root index display.

The second column of the expanded index display begins by repeating the root heading found on the root index display. These repeated headings do not have a preceding sequence number in the first column. Only subheadings have preceding sequence numbers. Below a heading and preceded by a dash are individual entries for all subheadings that begin with that root heading. For example, Figure 4–18 indicates that entry R6 has six matches. Figure 4–19 shows those six matches as subheadings alphabetically arranged underneath that root heading. A root heading without a subheading is represented in the first subheading entry by

Figure 4–19   Expanded index display

```
                           ¶ CAT                    SID: 00000          AF

AUTH    pn   HUGO, VICTOR MARIE COMTE 1802 1885
                 Expanded Index                                       Hits
             HUGO, VICTOR MARIE COMTE 1802 1885 -
▶   E1¶    - [400]                                                     1
▶   E2¶    - CORRESPONDENCE ENTRE VICTOR HUGO ET PIERRE JULES HETZEL  [400]   1
▶   E3¶    - CORRESPONDENCE [400]                                      1
▶   E4¶    - HERNANI THE KINGS DIVERSION RUY BLAS [400]                1
▶   E5¶    - PLAYS ENGLISH  [400]                                      1
▶   E6¶    - QUATREVINGT TREIZE [500]                                  1


             HUGO, VICTOR 1802 1885 -
▶   E7¶    - [100]                                                     1
▶   E8¶    - AMY ROBSART  [100]                                        1
▶   E9¶    - ANGELO THE TYRANT OF PADUA [400]                          1
▶   E10¶   - ANGELO TYRAN DE PADDOUE ENGLISH & ITALIAN [100]           1
▶   E11¶   - CHANSONS DE VICTOR HUGO  [400]                            1
▶   E12¶   - CHANTS DU CREPUSCULE LES VOIX INTERIEURES LES RAYONS ET LE [400]  1
▶   E13¶   - CHRISTMAS STORY  [400]                                    1
▶   E14¶   - CORRESPONDENCE [100]                                      1
▶   E15¶   - DERNIER JOUR DUN CONDAMNE ENGLISH  [100]                  1
▶   E16¶   - DEVIANOSTO TRETII GOD  [400]                              1
```

a blank entry following the dash. Most root headings have at least one such entry without a subheading. E1 and E7 in Figure 4–19 are examples of entries for root headings without subheadings. The expanded index display inserts a blank line between separate root headings. Figure 4–19 shows two root headings (R6 and R7 from Figure 4–18) with a blank line between them.

Following each subheading is an indication in brackets of which field in the authority record that subheading came from—1XX (main heading), 4XX (see reference), or 5XX (see also reference). When a heading lacks a subheading (see E1 and E7 of Figure 4–19), then the field number is the only piece of data at that entry. One entry will not list two different field numbers. If a heading appears in different fields in different records (e.g., a personal name heading is a 100 in one record and a 500 in another record), then that heading is listed once for each different field even though the headings are otherwise identical.

The final column of the expanded index display shows how

many records contain that heading/subheading. For most headings this value will be "1" since a particular heading generally appears on only one record as a main heading (1XX) and is generally only a cross reference (4XX) on one record as well. The major exception is for a heading that appears as a "see also" (5XX) heading on several records. For example, one "broader term" heading may appear as a "5XX" in seven relevant "narrower term" records.

Navigation and selection commands

You must use the PDN command to move to the next screen and the PUP command to move to the previous screen of either the root or expanded index display. The FOR and BAC commands are not PDN/PUP equivalents on these displays and will not work.

You can select only one entry number at a time from either the root or expanded index display. Trying to select multiple entries or a range of entries returns an error message. Select an entry by entering its sequence number in the home position and pressing <SEND>. Alternately, you can move your cursor over the entry number between the start-of-message and end-of-message symbols on that line and press <SEND>. You can either include or exclude the letter prefix with the sequence number and the system will respond the same. For example, both '5' and 'r5' will retrieve the record for entry R5 in Figure 4–18. Also, both '8' and 'e8' will retrieve the record for entry E8 in Figure 4–19.

Selecting an entry from a root display has two possible results depending on how many "hits" that entry has. For an entry showing only one hit, the system returns the single record display directly. For example, selecting entry R5 from Figure 4–18 will return the single authority record for Valentine Hugo. For an entry showing multiple hits, the system returns an expanded index display beginning with the selected entry. For example, selecting entry R6 (which has 6 hits) from Figure 4–18 results in the expanded index display in Figure 4–19. You can bypass the expanded index display and go directly to a display of authority records by preceding your selected entry number in the root index with the 'fin' command. For example, if you use the 'fin' command to select entry R6 from Figure 4–18 (i.e., 'fin 6' or 'fin r6'), the system will display the retrieved records in an appropriate display format for the set size. Perhaps the six hits at entry R6 occur in only four records. Those four records would be displayed in a brief format. Selecting an entry from the expanded index display returns records directly (in an appropriate display format for the size of the record set).

The GOB command again returns you to your previous display. However, the system rearranges both the root and expanded index displays when you return to them. When returning to the root display, the system moves the entry you originally selected into the middle position in the new display with a corresponding change in sequence numbers for all other entries. For example, if you select entry R3 (Thomas Hugo) from Figure 4–18 and then return to the root index display, the former R3 entry will now appear as entry R9 with all the other sequence numbers adjusted accordingly. When returning to the expanded index display, the system moves the entry you originally selected into the first position (E1) and makes a corresponding change in the sequence numbers for all other entries. For example, if you select entry E8 (Amy Robsart) from Figure 4–19 and then return to the expanded index display, the former E8 entry now appears as entry E1 with the other entry numbers adjusted accordingly.

Just as with the other displays, you can skip any intermediate displays and return directly to your original root index display (enter 'gob rt' and press <SEND>) or expanded index display (enter 'gob ex' and press <SEND>). For example, perhaps you are viewing an individual record that was selected from a brief display that was selected from an expanded index display that was selected from a root display. GOB would return you to the brief display. GOB again would return you to the expanded index display. GOB again would return you to the root index display. However, 'gob ex' would return you directly to the expanded index display, skipping the brief display. 'Gob rt' would return you directly to the root display, skipping both the brief and expanded index displays.

TOO MANY MATCHES

When there are more matches to your search key than the limit that the system will process, the result is a "dead end search" using that approach. The current system limits are 1,500 matching records in the Online Union Catalog and 600 matching records in the Authority File. Your only search option when you have too many matches, other than stopping the search, is to try a search strategy which is likely to have fewer matches. This could be either a different search key or your original search key with some added qualifiers (qualifiers are discussed in Chapter 5). If you are unable to construct a better search strategy from the information that you have available, you must accept the fact that

Figure 4–20   Help/Revise/Return screen

```
                                                    SID: 00000
163459 records retrieved. Select one of the following:
►hlp ►revise ►return                                          ¶


Search Terms                                                Hits

au smith                                                1634591
```

you will not be able to discover an existing record for your item in the system. This occasionally happens, but luckily not often.

Each search category handles reaching the system limit slightly differently. A search key search is the least helpful. It will merely display the message "Number of records retrieved exceeds system limit" on the system message line and return your cursor to the home position. The system does not erase your search key so you are able to modify it if you choose. However, you have no idea of the total number of records retrieved with this search and no guidance as to whether it might be fruitful to modify the search in some way.

A keyword search, on the other hand, returns a system message line that tells you exactly how many records were retrieved and presents you with a second line containing three options: "hlp" to read the online help; "revise" to revise the search and submit it again; and "return" to abandon this search strategy, clear the screen, and return your cursor to the home position ready to enter a new command. Figure 4–20 is an example of a Help/Revise/Return screen. You must choose one of these options at this point to continue working. To choose an option, place your cursor somewhere over the word for that option and press <SEND>. In a response to a "help" request, the system displays an appropriate help screen from the online help facility. (Online help will be described more in Chapter 5.) In response to a "revise" request, the system displays the same revise search screen described in Chapter 3 and shown in Figure 3–5. In response to a "return" request, the system will clear the screen and you will get a "Find canceled" message on the system message line.

You never get too many matches with an index phrase search. You are always placed somewhere in an index and never see these messages.

5 QUALIFYING SEARCHES

Some of the example Online Union Catalog search keys shown in Chapter 3 match many hundreds of records in the database and others exceed the current system retrieval limits described in Chapter 4. Derived search keys (title, name, and name/title) can sometimes result in lengthy extended searches because they are not as unique as number search keys which generally retrieve only one or a few records. A large record result set is more time consuming and inefficient for you to examine than a search result of only a few records and should be avoided if possible.

One way to avoid extended searches is to use as specific a search key as you can construct from the information available to you. Depending on your particular author and title, one derived search key may retrieve fewer records than another, even several hundred fewer records. For example, suppose you are searching for a record for the book *The Greenwood House*, by Larry Hackenberg. The derived title key 'gre,ho,,' might produce a group display of 283 records, whereas the derived name/title search key 'hack,gree' might produce a truncated display of only 19 records.

Two other methods for narrowing a search result set are discussed in this chapter: *the use of the circumflex within a derived search key and the use of qualifiers with derived and keyword search keys.* Four types of qualifiers are covered: *format (type of material), date of publication, microform, and cataloging source.* These methods are not available with all search types and in all databases. For example, phrase searches use neither the circumflex nor qualifiers and no Authority File searches use qualifiers. The circumflex is the only technique used in both the Online Union Catalog and the Authority File but it can be used only with derived search keys (including the combined search key). Figure 5–1 lists which method can be used with which search type and in which database.

USE OF THE CIRCUMFLEX

The circumflex (^) was introduced in Chapter 3 as a method to limit the search result set with several numeric search keys (LCCN, government document number, and music publisher number). This chapter describes its use with derived search keys to limit result sets in both the Online Union Catalog and the Authority File.

Figure 5–1   Search types and qualifiers

TYPE OF SEARCH	CIRCUMFLEX	QUALIFIER			
		Format	Dates	Microform	Source
Online Union Catalog					
OCLC control number	no	no	no	no	no
Search keys	yes	yes	yes	yes	yes
Keyword	no	yes	yes	no	no
Phrase	no	no	no	no	no
Authority File					
OCLC control number	no	no	no	no	no
Search keys	yes	no	no	no	no
Keyword	no	no	no	no	no
Phrase	no	no	no	no	no

Some segments of a derived search key permit an optional number of characters in that segment between some minimum and maximum number. This ability to enter optional information in some search key segments provides greater flexibility in searching and increases your likelihood of retrieving any matching records that may be in the database when you start out with incomplete or suspect information.

For example, perhaps the citation from which you got an author's name came from a source that only listed an author's first initial and last name (e.g., J. Craig) while the heading on the corresponding bibliographic record in OCLC has a full first name and a middle initial (e.g., James E. Craig). If you enter a name search in OCLC and only include the first initial in the second search key segment (which is all you know from your citation), the system will still retrieve records matching the full name of the author in which you are interested along with potentially many other records. The second and third segments of a personal name search key both allow an optional number of characters. The second segment can have one, two, or three characters and the third segment can have zero or one character. The system will match anything at least as long as what you enter in this segment. Here are some possible search results from search keys of varying allowable lengths for the James E. Craig name example above.

SEARCH KEY	INDEX LABEL	RESULTING DISPLAY	NUMBER OF MATCHES
crai,j,	fin dp crai,j,	group	1415
crai,ja,	fin dp crai,ja,	group	375
crai,jam,	fin dp crai,jam,	group	304
crai,jam,e	fin dp crai,jam,e	truncated	9
[crai,j,	fin dn crai,j,	quickview	125
[crai,ja,	fin dn crai,ja,	truncated	40
[crai,jam,	fin dn crai,jam,	truncated	31
[crai,jam,e	fin dn crai,jam,e		0

This flexibility in a segment does not always work to your advantage. For example, suppose that you are searching for bibliographic records containing the actual personal name heading J. Craig— a name heading that only has a first initial. Since the system will normally retrieve headings containing a fuller name as well as headings with just the initial as in the example above, this flexibility will increase your search result by retrieving names in which you are clearly uninterested. However, you can use the circumflex to turn off this flexibility and limit the search result.

The circumflex is an optional element that can be used in some segments of derived search keys to make an otherwise general search key more specific when:

1. a segment of the search key allows a choice in the number of characters, and
2. the indexed word has fewer than the maximum allowable number of characters, but at least the minimum number of characters required.

The circumflex tells the system only to match characters that have been entered before the circumflex, not anything longer. It helps you to limit your search results to likely candidates. Since both of the above conditions apply in our "J. Craig" name example, we can reformulate our search using the circumflex with the following possible results.

SEARCH KEY	INDEX LABEL	RESULTING DISPLAY	NUMBER OF MATCHES
crai,j^,	fin dp crai,j^,	group	145
crai,j^,^	fin dp crai,j^,^	truncated	22
[crai,j^,	fin dn crai,j^,	brief	13
[crai,j^,^	fin dn crai,j^,^	brief	2

Notice the significant difference in the size of the above result sets using the circumflex compared with the earlier result sets with a similar construction where the circumflex was not used.

You can use a circumflex in several segments of a search key at the same time when each of those segments allow it. Using a circumflex in multiple segments usually further narrows a search result set. For instance, in the first and third examples above only one segment uses a circumflex and the result sets include names with the first initial "J." but also names with a middle initial or name. In the second and fourth examples two segments use circumflexes and the result sets are considerably smaller and include names with only a first initial and nothing else.

You only use one circumflex in a given search key segment no matter how many characters you leave out. For example, the above personal name search key for J. Craig only needs one circumflex for the two character positions not used in the second segment (e.g., 'crai,j^,^' rather than 'crai,j^^,^'). Some segments give you no option for the number of characters therein, in which case you cannot enter fewer characters unless the term that goes in that position actually has fewer than the maximum characters. In such segments, you do not need to use a circumflex. The system only matches what you enter, nothing longer. For example, the first segment of a derived title search key must contain three characters when the first significant word has at least three characters. Therefore, the first segment of the derived title search key for *The D. H. Lawrence Review* does not need a circumflex even though it only has the single character "d" (e.g., 'd,h^,la,r' rather than 'd^,h^,la,r'). The second segment can include a circumflex since the number of characters in the second segment has options. The following examples illustrate the use of the circumflex in several different derived search keys.

NAME/TITLE (4,4)	SEARCH KEY
Ken Kesey. One Flew over the Cuckoo's Nest	`kese,one^`
Sein Lin. Land Policies in Developing Countries	`fin da lin^,land`

TITLE (3,2,2,1)	
The D. H. Lawrence Review	`d,h^,la,r`
How Can I Say Goodbye?	`fin dt how,ca,i^,s`

PERSONAL NAME (4,3,1)	
W. Eugene Smith	`smit,w^,e`
Bo Johnson	`fin dp john,bo^,^`

Using the circumflex can often eliminate lengthy, multiple screen search result sets. For example, the derived name/title search key 'ker,cata' for *A catalogue of manuscripts containing Anglo-Saxon*, by N. R. Ker, might return a multiple screen truncated display of 58 matching records whereas the search key 'ker^,cata' might return a single screen truncated display of just eight matching records. A more specific or unique search key will usually generate a smaller, more manageable search result set that displays over fewer screens. The circumflex can be used alone or combined with any of the other qualifiers described next to increase search specificity and narrow result sets.

FORMAT QUALIFIER

Each record in the Online Union Catalog was cataloged in one of eight primary bibliographic record formats based generally on the type of material the record represents. Beginning in 1996, with *Format Integration Phase 2*, records can also include secondary format information representing secondary aspects of the material. For example, a weekly audio magazine issued on cassette may have a "sound recordings" primary format and a "serials" secondary format. Using the format qualifier as part of your search strategy narrows a result set only to items that were cataloged using that format either as a primary or secondary format. This limiting ability can add to the efficiency of your search strategy by potentially eliminating many records from your search result set. You can focus on the specific format in which you are interested. The format qualifier is currently available for use only with search key and keyword searching in the Online Union Catalog. Each of the eight formats could be a primary or secondary format and each is identified by a unique three character code. The current qualifier codes are:

FORMAT	CODE
Books	bks
Computer files	com
Maps	map
Mixed materials	mix
Music scores	sco
Serials	ser
Sound recordings	rec
Visual materials	vis

To limit your search result to only records cataloged in one specific format, add the appropriate three-letter qualifier code to your search request. There are two methods for doing this which parallel the two methods for entering a search key. The "old" method is to follow your derived search key or keyword search with a forward slash and the qualifier. This method was developed when all searches were constructed without commands. However, you can also use this "old" method with search keys that use commands.

FORMAT	QUALIFIED SEARCH KEY
Serials	`jou,of,po,s/ser`
	`fin dt jou,of,po,s/ser`
	`fin ti potassium/ser`
Books	`mob,di,,/bks`
	`fin dt mob,di,,/bks`
	`fin au christie/bks`
Sound recordings	`sym,al,mo,/rec`
	`fin dt sym,al,mo,/rec`
	`fin ti pastoral/rec`

Alternately, you can use the "new" method and append a qualifier label (similar to an index label) and format code to your search using 'and.' Figure 5–2 lists the current qualifier labels. Unlike the "old" method described above, you can only use this method with searches that were constructed using commands.

FORMAT	QUALIFIED SEARCH KEY
Serials	`fin dt jou,of,po,s and ft ser`
	`fin ti potassium and ft ser`
Books	`fin dt mob,di,, and ft bks`
	`fin au christie and ft bks`
Sound recordings	`fin dt sym,al,mo, and ft rec`
	`fin ti pastoral and ft rec`

Most of the time it will be clear which qualifier is appropriate for a given search. If you are looking for a recording of a Mozart concerto, it would never have been cataloged as a map. However, sometimes it is not always obvious which format qualifier would be appropriate for a given search. Was the serial map that you are looking for cataloged as a map or as a serial? If it is necessary to use a format qualifier, you may need to search both formats to discover a potential bibliographic record. Items cataloged after the introduction of secondary formats could be retrieved using

Figure 5–2	Qualifiers and their labels
QUALIFIER	LABEL
Format	ft
Date of publication	yr
Microform	mi
Cataloging source	so

either qualifier (when the record shows both primary and secondary formats), but older items will only be retrieved with one of them (since the record only has a primary format). The best solution is using a search strategy that does not require a format qualifier to be effective but that may not be possible depending on the information available to you when conducting the search.

DATE OF PUBLICATION QUALIFIER

Often the same work is published in more than one edition and/or with different publication dates. Sometimes the same search key or keyword retrieves many similar works or authors that share that search key or keyword. When you know a particular publication date, or a range of dates, for the work whose record you wish to retrieve, you can use a date of publication qualifier to limit your search results to only matches published within that date range. The date qualifier is currently available only in the search key and keyword indexes in the Online Union Catalog. There are a variety of ways in which the value in the date qualifier may be entered because dates have many possibilities. The following chart lists those possibilities.

DATES		EXAMPLE DATE QUALIFIER
Single year		1981
Decade		197?
	or	1970–9
Century		18??
	or	1800–99

Single year and all following years (e.g., 1950 to the present)			`1950-`
Single year and all earlier years (e.g., up to and including 1950)			`-1950`
Inclusive span of years:			
1962–1982			`1962-82`
1921–1923			`1921-23`
		or	`1921-3`
1878–1927			`1878-927`
		or	`1878-1927`

Those qualifiers with question marks (197?, 18??) will retrieve bibliographic records from all years in the corresponding decade or century. Optionally, you can enter the full decade or century range as shown above. This is equivalent to the form for a span of years when the span just happens to be a decade or century. For a serial or other item published over a span of years, use the date of the first year of publication. For all other works, use the date of publication.

The date of publication qualifier is based on the date that was entered by the cataloger in the date fixed field of the bibliographic record. If the date in the record is incorrect, the qualifier will not work properly. Some records have only an incomplete date of publication entered in the date field, with one or more **us** filling in for unknown digits, or have no date of publication at all with only **us** as fill characters in the date field (e.g., 197u if a cataloger knows a book was published sometime in the 1970s, but not the exact year). With search keys only, not with keywords, you can use four question marks (????) as a date qualifier to limit your search result just to records in these categories.

You enter the date qualifier in the same two ways described above under the format qualifier, either appending the date to your search term after a forward slash or adding a label and date value providing your search used a command and index label. The following examples show search keys and keywords qualified by date(s).

```
leak,ric,e/1979-82
fin dp leak,ric,e/1979-82
fin dp leak,ric,e and yr 1979-82

twai,mar,/-1900
fin dp twai,mar,/-1900
fin dp twai,mar, and yr -1900
```

```
moza,wol,a/192?
fin dp moza,wol,a/192?
fin dp moza,wol,a and yr 192?

fin ti pastoral/1990-
fin ti pastoral and yr 1990-
```

You need to be careful when using a date qualifier that your date is not so specific that you miss important related works which can help your cataloging. For example, if you restrict a search to 1994 only (looking for a record for the American paperback), you will miss the record for a 1992 edition (the British hardback) which could have provided valuable information about classification and subject headings that you could have used in cataloging the 1994 edition. Date qualifiers are valuable in reducing result sets that otherwise exceed the system limit but overly restrictive date qualifiers can hinder your search and be counterproductive. With experience, you learn to strike a balance between these two needs.

MICROFORM QUALIFIER

The microform qualifier acts like a toggle and lets you limit your search to only records that are in a microformat (such as microfilm or microfiche) or only records that are not in a microformat. This simple either/or qualifier can be useful when you are looking for a microform version of a title and wish to eliminate the non-microform records from your search result or you are looking for the reverse. The microform qualifier can only be used currently with search key searches in the Online Union Catalog. The two microform qualifiers are:

	QUALIFIER
Microform reproduction	mf
Not a microform reproduction	nm

The system determines whether a record is in a microformat or not by examining a fixed field in the record that carries a code with this particular piece of information. Again we must rely on the accurate coding of that field by the cataloger in order to effectively use this qualifier.

You enter the microform qualifier in the same two ways described above under the format qualifier, either using a forward slash with any search or using a label and value with a command search. The following examples show search keys and keywords qualified by microform.

```
leak,ric,e/nm
fin dp leak,ric,e and mi nm
fin dp moza,wol,a/mf
fin dp moza,wol,a and mi mf
twai,mar,/mf
fin dp twai,mar,/mf
```

CATALOGING SOURCE QUALIFIER

Many libraries prefer Library of Congress (LC) records or records produced through certain recognized national cataloging programs (like CONSER) that conform to LC standards. The source qualifier can be used with search keys in the Online Union Catalog to limit a result set to only such records. The result set will also include member-input records that are coded as based on LC cataloging even though LC did not add those records to the database itself (e.g., retrospective conversion of old manual LC cards). This qualifier only has one value ('dlc') and again has the same two entry options as the earlier qualifiers.

```
leak,ric,e/dlc
fin dp moza,wol,a and so dlc
fin dp twai,mar,/dlc
```

USING MULTIPLE QUALIFIERS

You can use any combination of different qualifiers in the same search statement, provided they are all valid for that type of search, but you can only use one qualifier of each type. For example, you can qualify a search by date '1981' and format 'bks' but you can not qualify one search by both format 'bks' and format 'ser.' If you choose to use several qualifiers, you can enter them in any order you wish using any combination of the permitted methods for that qualifier as described previously. For example, you could enter:

```
search-key/date/format/microform
search-key/format/date/microform
fin index-label search-key/date/format/microform
fin index-label search-key/format/date/microform
search-key/microform and ft format
search-key/format and mi microform
fin index-label search-key/microform and ft format
fin index-label search-key/format and mi microform
search-key and ft format and yr date
search-key and yr date and ft format
fin index-label scarch-kcy and ft format and yr date
fin index-label search-key and yr date and ft format
```

A common search strategy for prolific names and popular titles is to use *several qualifiers* as shown above. Such an approach further specifies the search and definitely will limit the system's response to your search request. For example, using the search strategy 'mur,on,th,o/1990-/med' or 'mur,on,th,o/med/1990-' will retrieve fewer records for a current video of *Murder on the Orient Express* than would the same search without any qualifiers or with just one of the qualifiers.

The following examples show several methods for entering the same two qualifiers in a derived title search and title keyword search for the same item. All of these searches will have the same result set.

```
aph,of,si,p/bks/1807
aph,of,si,p/1807/bks
fin dt aph,of,si,p/1807 and ft bks
fin dt aph,of,si,p/bks and yr 1807
fin dt aph,of,si,p/1807/bks
fin dt aph,of,si,p/bks/1807
fin dt aph,of,si,p and ft bks and yr 1807
fin dt aph,of,si,p and yr 1807 and ft bks
fin ti aphorisms/bks/1807 and ti sidney
fin ti aphorisms/bks and ti sidney/1807
fin ti aphorisms and ft bks and ti sidney and yr 1807
```

Even when you use several qualifiers, there is no guarantee that you will retrieve only one record matching your search key. For example, many popular works are issued by multiple publishers in the same year (e.g., American and British editions) or a popular recording may come out in several versions in the same year (e.g., cassette and compact disc). The best qualified derived search key will still most likely retrieve several matches in either of those cases. Your goal in devising a search strategy is not necessarily to devise a complex strategy that only retrieves one record but to devise a reasonable strategy that is easy to enter and retrieves a manageable number of records for you to review. Properly used, qualifiers can add greatly to this goal.

SET QUALIFIERS

Sometimes you may wish to use the same qualifier for an entire series of searches because all of the searching in a given part of your search session shares some common characteristic for which you are able to qualify searches. Perhaps you are searching a video collection and wish to qualify every search with the visual materials format. Perhaps you are searching newly received books that have all been published no earlier than 1994 and wish to qualify every search with a date of 1994 or newer. Perhaps you are searching a big band record collection containing items that were all published before 1950 and wish to qualify every search with the sound recordings format and date before 1950. In all of these examples, there is a common qualifier that is shared by many consecutive searches. OCLC offers the ability to set session qualifiers that apply to all subsequent search key searches until the qualifiers are inactivated or the search session is ended. Using this feature, you do not need to append a qualifier to every search key to have it apply. Searches are automatically qualified until the feature is inactivated. However, you will still need to use specific qualifiers for any keyword searches that you may use in that search session since setting qualifiers only applies to search key searches. And remember that qualifiers do not apply to phrase searches.

There are two ways to set qualifiers for a search session (or part of a search session). You can either type the 'set qual' or 'sho qual' command in the home position and press <SEND> to bring up a template listing the various qualifier options that can be selected. Figure 5–3 shows this set qualifiers template. You can enter one option for each qualifier by typing a selection in place of the default value "any" following the corresponding qualifier name. If you do not wish to use a particular qualifier type, then "any" is the appropriate value so you can just leave it there. In addition to selecting options, you must activate the qualifiers by changing the default status from "inactive" to "active." The selected qualifiers will remain in effect for all search key searches until you make them "inactive" again or select different qualifiers.

Figure 5–3   Set qualifiers screen

```
                                        SID: 00000
▸hlp                 ▸ret                                    ¶

   Select Qualifiers

   ▸ Qualifiers are: inactive
     Format: any   Microform: any Source: any    Dates: any    ¶

   Qualifiers:          (inactive, active)
   Format:              (any, bks, com, map, mix, rec, sco, ser, vis)
   Microform:           (any, mf, nm)
   Source:              (any, dlc)
   Dates:               (yyyy, -yyyy, yyyy-, yyyy-y, yyyy-yy,
                         yyyy-yyy, yyyy-yyyy, yy??, yyy?, ????)
```

The other method to set qualifiers is to enter the 'set' command in the home position followed by an appropriate string of qualifier label/value pairs and include 'act' somewhere in the string to make the qualifiers active. For example, the qualifiers suggested in the opening paragraph could be entered as:

```
set ft vis and act
set act and yr 1994-
set yr -1950 and ft rec and act
```

Any qualifiers can be subsequently changed at any point in the search session by merely entering a new choice using one of the methods described above. For example, perhaps you just finished searching a shipment of new CDs with searches limited to 'ft rec' and next you want to search a shipment of videos and searches now limited to 'ft vis' instead. You can either call up the template again and change the format qualifier or enter the command string 'set ft vis' and press <SEND> to make this change. The new value will supersede the old value since only one format value can be active at a time. You did not need to append "and act" to the new qualifier because your qualifiers are already active. You are just changing them.

This same strategy can be used to remove one qualifier while maintaining other qualifiers. You enter the default "any" value for a specific qualifier to remove previous limits and allow searches to retrieve records with any value for that qualifier. For example, again suppose you just finished searching a shipment of new CDs (using the qualifiers 'ft rec and yr 1993-') and now want to search some records that are not all new. You still want to limit your searches to 'ft rec' but now you want to remove the year limits. You can either call up the template and change the year value to "any" or enter the command 'set yr any' and press <SEND> to remove the year limits.

You may also wish to inactivate all of your qualifiers at some point in the session. For example, perhaps you just finished searching a shipment of new videos and now you are moving on to search a mixed group of materials from several formats published over a range of years. You no longer want a format or year qualifier to apply to every search. You can inactivate the current qualifiers either by calling up the template again and replacing "active" with "inactive" or by entering the command 'set inact' and pressing <SEND>. The session qualifier values remain unchanged but they no longer apply to searches unless activated again (e.g., by entering 'set act' the same way you just entered 'set inact').

You can override a session qualifier for a specific search by explicitly qualifying that one search with some other value using the techniques for qualifying an individual search described earlier in this chapter. For example, suppose you are searching a group of newly published books and have set the session year qualifier to "1994-" and among these new books you discover one book published in 1980. You can simply qualify this one search with a different year (e.g., "title/1980" or "fin dt title and yr 1980"). This will override your session qualifiers for this one search without inactivating them for subsequent searches.

SEARCH HISTORY

The system retains a search history containing up to the ten most recent searches that you conducted in each database that you used during your current search session. That is, the system will retain a list of the ten most recent searches in the Online Union Catalog as well as a separate list of the ten most recent searches in the Authority File. To review the search history list in your current database, enter 'rev' in the home position and press <SEND>. Figure 5–4a is an example of a search history display of ten searches in the Online Union Catalog.

The database in which the searches were conducted is shown in the upper right corner of the screen ("OL" in Figure 5–4). Each entry has three elements: a sequential set number, the search query

Figure 5–4   Search history screen

```
                          ¶ CAT            SID: 00000        OL


                       Search History

    Set   Search Query                                 Records
  ▸ S1 ¶ dt bul,,,/1985-                                  1159
  ▸ S2 ¶ an *27976571                                        1
  ▸ S3 ¶ da turn,lana                                        7
  ▸ S4 ¶ dp hugo,vic,                                   > 1500
  ▸ S5 ¶ dp mgui,and, and yr 1994-                           0
  ▸ S6 ¶ mn mn:ge17^                                         1
  ▸ S7 ¶ ti "SOUND AND THE FURY"                            97
  ▸ S8 ¶ ti "SOUND AND THE FURY & AS I LAY DYING"            6
  ▸ S9 ¶ dt gre,ho,,                                       278
  ▸ S10¶ dt us,so,re,i                                       1
```

a) A full list of ten searches

```
                          ¶ CAT            SID: 00000        OL


                       Search History

    Set   Search Query                                 Records
  ▸ S1 ¶ an *27976571                                        1
  ▸ S2 ¶ da turn,lana                                        7
  ▸ S3 ¶ dp hugo,vic,                                   > 1500
  ▸ S4 ¶ dp dp mgui,and, and yr 1994-                        0
  ▸ S5 ¶ mn mn:ge17^                                         1
  ▸ S6 ¶ ti "SOUND AND THE FURY"                            97
  ▸ S7 ¶ ti "SOUND AND THE FURY & AS I LAY DYING"            6
  ▸ S8 ¶ dt gre,ho,,                                       278
  ▸ S9 ¶ dt us,so,re,i                                       1
  ▸ S10¶ bn 0719543320                                       1
```

b) The same list after a new search

represented by that set number, and the number of records in the corresponding result set. For example, the third search set ("S3") in Figure 5–4a represents a derived author/title search in the Online Union Catalog for *Lana: the Lady, the Legend, the Truth*, by Lana Turner ("da turn,lana") which retrieved seven records. This is the same search with the same result set used earlier to demonstrate the truncated display shown in Figure 4–3. Searches are listed in the order in which they were done with S1 being the oldest and S10 the most recent search.

Once you have executed an eleventh search, the first search in the history list is dropped and all remaining searches are renumbered with the new eleventh search listed in the tenth position. This is demonstrated in Figure 5–4b. After an ISBN search for 0719543320 is executed in this example, it becomes set S10 and all earlier searches move up one number. The search formerly at S1 ("dt bul,,,/1985-") is dropped entirely from the search history list and can no longer be retrieved.

All correctly constructed search key and keyword searches (i.e., "find" command searches) are listed in the search history regardless of how many records match the search request, including zero matches and more matches than the current system limit will display. In Figure 5–4a notice that the search shown at entry S4 ("dp hugo,vic,") retrieved more than the current system limit of 1,500 matching records and that the search shown at entry S5 ("dp mgui,and, and yr 1994-") had no matching records. Only incorrect or incomplete search keys that returned an error message of some kind are not listed.

No phrase searches (i.e., "scan" command searches) are listed in the search history as such. However, if you select any entries from a phrase index display, each of the corresponding search sets (equivalent to a "find" search) is listed. For example, entries S7 and S8 in Figure 5–4a were each selected from the index display following the title phrase search "sca ti sound and the f" and each is listed in the search history even though the original title phrase "scan" search is not listed.

You can redisplay any one of the ten search result sets listed by entering its corresponding set number in the home position and pressing <SEND>. You must include the "S" with the set number and you can only select one set at a time. The system will respond with a display appropriate for the number of records in that result set and the database in which you are working. For example, to select the search set for "dt gre,ho,," in Figure 5–4a, enter 's9' in the home position and press <SEND>. The system will respond with a group display of those 278 records.

PRISM HELP FACILITY

PRISM includes a well developed online help facility which covers searching, cataloging, the Online Union Catalog, and the Authority File among its topics. Entries provide enough detail to answer most questions quickly.

A good way to explore the help facility is to enter 'help help' (or 'hlp hlp') and press <SEND>. This retrieves the main menu of available topics in the help system. One of the entries on this main menu is a "List of Help Topics" which are available in the system. The list contains many (but not all) terms indexed in the help system and is an excellent place from which to begin exploring the help facility. Once you find the name of a relevant topic from the list, you can enter 'help [the topic]' and press <SEND> to get fuller information on that selected topic. For example, you can enter 'help forward' and press <SEND> to go directly to the help screen that describes the "forward" command. You can also start at the main menu and select appropriate menu and submenu entries until you arrive at the help screen for the topic (in this case "forward"). However, asking for a topic directly is frequently faster and more efficient. Entering 'help topics' retrieves the list of available help topics.

Figure 5–5 shows the structure of a topic help screen. The home position line contains a message showing that you are in the "PRISM Help" facility and reminds you how to exit help and return to your previous display. Following a blank system message line, the system displays a menu line containing several commands primarily used to navigate within the help facility itself. Your cursor appears on the first of these commands. The commands include:

- "ret" to return from the help facility to the screen from which you requested help;
- "for" and "bac" to go to the next and previous help display screens;
- "gob" to return to a menu one level higher in the help facility than your current topic; and
- "hlp" to return directly to the help main menu from any help screen.

To use one of these commands from the menu line, place your cursor anywhere over the desired command and press <SEND>. Using <TAB> and <BACKTAB> can help you move easily between adjacent commands on this line. Alternately, you can enter RET,

---

Figure 5–5   Help screen layout

```
PRISM Help - <F10> on RET to exit Help            SID: 00000

 ▶ret   ▶for   ▶bac   ▶gob   ▶hlp                               ¶
[Title of this help topic]                       Display 1 of 3



          [ Up to 19 lines of Help Text ]
```

FOR, BAC, and GOB in the home position and press <SEND> or use the same function key equivalents for these commands that you use in other PRISM activities to perform these actions. They work the same in the help facility.

Immediately below the menu line is the title of the particular help topic covered in the text on that screen, for example "OLUC Index Labels" or "Qualifying Searches." To the right of the topic title is an indication of how many help screens are available on this topic and which of those screens you are currently viewing, for example "Display 1 of 1" or "Display 2 of 3." The system provides from one to approximately eight help screens on each available topic. Some multiple screen topics have the same title on all screens (e.g., "View Search Results Display 2 of 4" and "View Search Results Display 3 of 4") and some have different titles on each screen (e.g., "Corporate/Conference Stoplist Display 1 of 2" and "Keyword Stoplist Display 2 of 2"). Some later screens of multiple screen topics append "(cont.)" to the title (e.g., "OLUC Index Labels (cont.)") but this is not always the case. The main body of the display contains up to 19 lines devoted to the text of that particular help message. Because topics can be rather brief, the system performs better as a short reference source than as a source of in-depth answers to complex questions.

The help system also provides some level of context sensitive help. If you merely enter 'hlp' (or 'help') without a topic, the system will display the help screen that corresponds to your current place in the system. For example, if you request help while viewing a group display, the system will return the "Group Display" help screen. When there is no corresponding help screen to display, or there are several possibilities, the system will display the main help menu for you to select a topic.

SEARCH EXERCISES

Now that you have finished the searching section of this manual, here are three online exercises that will help you develop your OCLC searching skills. These exercises also show how different search strategies for the same item can frequently produce very different search results. You must have access to the OCLC Online Union Catalog to complete the exercises. These exercises concentrate on both derived search keys and qualifiers. Exercise 1 compares both the old and new forms for entering derived search keys and qualifiers. Exercise 2 demonstrates a variety of search strategies that can be used to search for a single item and the range of result sets that those strategies generate. Exercise 3 demonstrates the different results that you get from using the same search key both with and without qualifiers.

Since OCLC is a dynamic and constantly changing system with new records added to the Online Union Catalog daily, your search results may differ slightly from those given in the answers to the exercises. While these exercise examples were chosen to minimize the probability of differing results, nothing can eliminate the possibility entirely. Even with different search results these exercises can still demonstrate a range of searching and allow you to compare different strategies.

EXERCISE 1 (Answers at Back of Book.)

Directions:

Search each example below in the Online Union Catalog using the old style qualified derived search keys. Record the initial display you get in response to your search request: group, truncated, brief, or single record. If your search results in a multiple record display, request entry 1 at each step until you have a single bibliographic record on display. Record the contents of the 100 field (author) if present, the 245 field (title), and the OCLC control number for each final single record you retrieve. Next perform the same search using commands and index labels. You should get exactly the same result.

Example:

```
hugo,vic,/1985                 Group display
                               (100) Hugo de Leon, Victor
                               (245) La informacion en radio
                               #15317891
   fin dp hugo,vic, and yr 1985
```

EXERCISE 1

syke,chr,/1975	fin dp syke,chr, and yr 1975
boo,an,pr,/1963	fin dt boo,an,pr, and yr 1963
jou,of,ar,e/ser/1932-9	fin dt jou,of,ar,e and ft ser and yr 1932-9
stei,legw/rec/-1972	fin da stei,legw and ft rec and yr -1972
kese,one^/rec	fin da kese,one^ and ft rec
stei,joh,/mf/191?	fin dp stei,joh, and mi mf and yr 191?
smit,w^,e/1934-51	fin dp smit,w^,e and yr 1934-51
goul,ste,j/-1969	fin dp goul,ste,j and yr -1969
chri,agat/-1944	fin da chri,agat and yr -1944
twai,inno/????	fin da twai,inno and yr ????

EXERCISE 2

Directions:

Construct a set of five search keys for each of the following items before going to the terminal, including: derived personal name, derived title, derived name/title, combined derived personal name and derived title, and title phrase. Do not use qualifiers for this exercise. Go to the terminal and enter each of the five search keys you constructed. Record the number of records in each result set except for the title phrase. For the title phrase, record the entry you select from the index display and the number of records in that entry's result set. Locate the specific item within each result set (for result sets that are less than the system maximum) and record its OCLC control number. Notice the differences in the result sets and displays as you search.

Example:

James Fenimore Cooper. The last of the Mohicans. Penguin Books, 1986.

	SEARCH KEY	RECORDS IN SET
personal name:	coop,jam,f	exceeded system limit
title:	las,of,th,m	703
name/title:	coop,last	607
combined:	fin dp coop,jam,f and dt las,of,th,m	584
title phrase:	sca ti last of the mohicans	9–308

OCLC control number: #13270825

EXERCISE 2

A. Daniel Defoe. A journal of the plague year.
　　Norton, 1992.

B. Victor Hugo. Les miserables.
　　Modern Library, 1992.

C. Virginia Woolf. To the lighthouse.
　　Harcourt Brace Jovanovich, 1990.

D. Nadine Gordimer. July's people.
　　Penguin Books, 1982.

E. Henry James. The portrait of a lady.
　　Vintage Books, 1992.

EXERCISE 3

Directions:

Construct unqualified and qualified derived search keys for each example below before going to the terminal. Once at the terminal, enter the suggested unqualified derived search key in the Online Union Catalog for one of the items and follow the result until the desired single bibliographic record is displayed. Record the initial display, any intermediate displays, and the OCLC control number of the final record. Next, enter the qualified search key for the same item, recording the same information as you did for the unqualified search key. Note the differences in the result sets as you search. Continue through all the items.

Example:

Personal name/title search for the book:

    Agatha Christie. Agatha Christie, five classic
    murder mysteries. Avenel Books, 1985.

UNQUALIFIED SEARCH	QUALIFIED SEARCH
Search key:	Search key:
chri,agat	chri,agat/bks/1985
Outcome:	Outcome:
1. truncated display	1. brief display
2. #11468463	2. #11468463

EXERCISE 3

A. Personal name search for the book:

    Ian Fleming. Chitty Chitty Bang Bang.
    Random House, 1964.

B. Personal name/title search for the book:

    Mark Twain. The innocents abroad, or, The new
    pilgrim's progress. Harper, 1924.

C. Title search for the video (visual format):

    The Count of Monte Cristo.
    Video Images, 1986.

D.   Title search for the book:

```
Stephen Crane. The red badge of courage.
Dent, 1992.
```

E.   Personal name/title search for the book:

```
Michael Crichton. Jurassic park : a novel.
G.K. Hall, 1991.
```

6 THE BIBLIOGRAPHIC RECORD

This chapter provides a basic and brief introduction to the structure of machine-readable cataloging (MARC) records as implemented by OCLC in the Online Union Catalog. MARC records conform to an agreed upon standard within the library automation community that allows for the easy transfer of records between various systems and institutions. For example, the Library of Congress transmits its records to OCLC in a MARC format. The MARC standards provide some flexibility in areas of the record that allow individual organizations to accommodate local needs. For example, OCLC has defined the 049 field (containing a holding library code) to meet its own local needs. The OCLC implementation of the MARC standard with its local extensions is generally referred to as OCLC-MARC. For complete information about the OCLC-MARC bibliographic record, refer to the latest edition of OCLC's *Bibliographic Formats and Standards*.

MARC records organize information into discrete units of data, some of which contain codes specifically for computer manipulation (such as language codes) and some of which are easily readable by people (such as titles). Each data unit is labeled in such a way that users of a record understand the function of that piece of data in the record. Some of those labels are described later in this chapter. Because data is clearly labeled, MARC records can be used by computers to produce a variety of products such as catalog cards, online catalog displays, or printed bibliographies.

The OCLC-MARC record consists of a series of fields organized into two parts: one fixed-length field and multiple variable-length fields. Figure 6–1 shows this division within the basic structure of a books format record in the Online Union Catalog and includes a brief description of some variable fields. Figure 6–2 uses the Library of Congress record for the book *The Greenwood House,* by Larry Michael Hackenberg, as a specific example of the books format record outlined in Figure 6–1.

FIXED FIELD

The fixed field is the first field in each record. This field contains a "fixed" set of elements appropriate for each format. A fixed

---

Figure 6–1   Selected OCLC-MARC fields (books format)

```
OCLC:                        Rec stat:
Entered:                     Replaced:                Used:
```

FIXED FIELD

```
Type: a      Elvl:      Srce:      Audn:      Ctrl:      Lang:
BLvl: m      Form:      Conf:      Biog:      Mrec:      Ctry:
             Cont:      Gpub:      Fict:      Indx:
Desc:        Ills:      Fest:      DtSt:      Dates:
```

VARIABLE FIELDS

TAG	IND		DATA
	1	2**	
010			LCCN (Library of Congress control number)
040			Symbols for cataloging, inputting, and modifying institutions
020			ISBN (International Standard Book Number)
041	–		Language codes
050	–	–	LC class number ‡b item number
082	–	–	DDC class number ‡b item number
090			Locally assigned LC-type class number ‡b item number
092	–		Locally assigned DDC class number ‡b item number
049			Symbol for institutional account currently logged in on this terminal (system supplied)
1XX	–		Main entry (personal, corporate, or meeting name, or uniform title)
245	–	–	Title : ‡b other title information / ‡c statement of responsibility ; subsidiary responsibility
250			Edition statement
260			Place of publication : ‡b Publisher, ‡c Date of publication
300			Extent of item : ‡b other physical data ; ‡c size
4XX	–	–	Series statement from item
5XX	–		Notes
6XX	–	–	Subject added entries
7XX	–	–	Other added entries and linking entries
8XX	–	–	Series added entries (when traced differently than in the 4XX)

** Indicators: 1 = 1st indicator position; 2 = 2nd indicator position
XX The second and third positions can take several different numbers depending on the exact contents of the tag. See the Appendix for some examples.

Figure 6–2   Example of a bibliographic record (books format)

```
    OCLC: 1735469        Rec stat:  P
    Entered:  19751002   Replaced:  19780410  Used:  19950930
►   Type: a    Elvl:      Srce: d    Audn:      Ctrl:      Lang: eng
    Blvl: m    Form:      Conf: 0    Biog:      Mrec:      Ctry: vau
               Cont: b    Gpub:      Fict: 0    Indx: 1
    Desc: i    Ills: a    Fest: 0    DtSt: s    Dates: 1976,        ¶
►    1   010       75-33166 ¶
►    2   040       DLC ‡c DLC ¶
►    3   020       0813906466 ¶
►    4   050  0    TH4818.W6  ‡b H3 ¶
►    5   082       728 ¶
►    6   090       ‡b ¶
►    7   049       XXXM ¶
►    8   100  1    Hackenberg, Larry Michael,  ‡d 1942- ¶
►    9   245 14    The greenwood house :  ‡b how to design, build, and own
an inexpensive beautiful house / ‡c Larry Michael Hackenberg. ¶
►   10   260       Charlottesville : ‡b University Press of Virginia,  ‡c
1976. ¶
►   11   300       139 p. :  ‡b ill. ;  ‡c 23 cm. ¶
►   12   504       Bibliography: p. 135. ¶
►   13   500       Includes index. ¶
►   14   650  0    Wooden-frame houses. ¶
►   15   650  0    Building, Wooden. ¶
►   16   650  0    Lumber. ¶
```

---

field element set is consistent for all records within one format but varies from one format to another. The length of the data which can be input into each element is also "fixed" by the system and is limited to a specific set of prescribed codes or values for that element. Each element is identified by a unique mnemonic label and always appears in the same position within the field.

The fixed field is used primarily for data manipulation and record retrieval by computer systems and should be fully and correctly coded for those systems to function properly. For example, information from the fixed field is used by OCLC for the various qualifiers discussed in the last chapter. Notice that the fixed field element "Dates:" in Figure 6–2 has the value "1976." OCLC uses the value in "Dates:" for the year of publication qualifier. When you fail to code the fixed fields properly, you hinder everyone's chances of finding the record. OCLC also uses fixed field elements in some of its printing and display programs. For example, the fixed field element "Desc:" is used to tell the system what kind of punctuation to supply on printed catalog cards. As the OCLC system develops and gets more sophisticated, it is taking greater advantage of the information stored in the fixed field to help users navigate through the increasing numbers of records in the database.

The Appendix contains an abridged list of fixed field elements containing the values encountered most frequently in the examples and exercises used in this manual.

VARIABLE FIELDS

Following the fixed field is a series of variable fields containing all of the "variable" length free text data appropriate for a given bibliographic record. The amount of information stored in each field is restricted only by the definition or nature of that particular field and by the general system limits on the size of a record (currently 4,096 characters) and the size of one variable field (currently 1,230 characters). Each variable field with a different kind of information is identified by a different three-digit code, called a tag, that describes the nature of the data contained in that field. A "tag" often becomes a shorthand way of referring to a specific field. For example, we usually refer to a personal name main entry field as a 100 and a bibliography note field as a 504. Notice that Figure 6–2 contains the personal name "Hackenberg, Larry Michael" in a 100 field and a bibliography note in a 504 field.

The assignment of these three-digit codes to pieces of information is not random. Certain tags that store similar kinds of information and share a similar function within a record also share the same first digit. These similar tags constitute a "tag group." Figure 6–3 shows the general tag groups for bibliographic records. Note that the meaning of a specific tag group varies with different kinds of MARC records, although they all have tag groups. For example, the 5XX tag group in MARC authority records contains "see also" references, not the "notes" found in the 5XX tag group in MARC bibliographic records.

Within a tag group, the second and third digits of a tag further define the specific contents of that tag. For example, within the bibliographic record 1XX tag group (main entry headings), a 100 tag is a personal name main entry while a 110 tag is a corporate name main entry. You must be very careful to tag all information that you enter into a record correctly or you may cause problems

TAG GROUP	DESCRIPTION
Figure 6–3	**Bibliographic record tag groups**
0XX	Control numbers and codes (such as call numbers, ISBNs, government document numbers)
1XX	Main entry headings
2XX	Title statement paragraph (such as title, edition, publisher)
3XX	Physical description (such as pagination, size)
4XX	Series statements from item
5XX	Notes (such as contents, summary, bibliography)
6XX	Subject added entries
7XX	Other added entries and linking entries (such as added author, editor, former title)
8XX	Series added entries that are traced differently than in the 4XX
9XX	These tags are reserved for local use

with the system handling of the erroneously tagged record. For example, the system extracts information from certain tags to build each index, such as extracting information from the 100 tag and adding it to the personal name index. If you have incorrectly tagged a personal name as a corporate body (110 instead of 100), the system will add the name to the wrong index and retrieving that record becomes much more difficult.

Each field contains two positions for characters between the tag number and the text of the field. These characters are called *indicators*. Different fields have different combinations of indicators defined for them: either none, just the first, just the second, or both. When a field has both indicator positions defined, each indicator operates independently of the other. There is no "joint" meaning with two indicators. The underscores following several of the tags in Figure 6–1 indicate some places where indicators may occur as part of the field data.

Indicators have different meanings in different tags. Some indicators signal the system to make certain responses or perform certain actions. For example, the second indicator ("4") in the 245 tag in Figure 6–2 tells the system to skip the first four characters (i.e., T, h, e, and space) before beginning to index the title. An incorrect second indicator in a 245 will cause the title to index incorrectly. Other indicators help to define the contents of a tag.

For example, the second indicator ("0") in each 650 tag in Figure 6–2 tells you that the source for each of those subject headings is the Library of Congress. An incorrect second indicator in a 650 could cause the subject heading to be indexed in the wrong file or to link to the wrong authority record (e.g., the system processes the subject as a medical heading rather than an LC heading). The proper entry of indicators is important to the creation of a complete and accurate catalog record that can be handled correctly by our automated systems.

Within some fields in Figure 6–1, and many fields in Figure 6–2, you find a delimiter pair created by the symbol " ǂ " (called a delimiter), followed by a lowercase alphabetic character. (Numeric characters may also follow a delimiter although there are none in these examples.) These delimiter pairs segment field data into separate "subfields" containing smaller discrete pieces of information. For example, subfield b (ǂb) of tag 260 in Figure 6–2 contains the name of the publisher and is separated from the place of publication by that delimiter pair (ǂb). Another delimiter pair (ǂc) separates the publisher from the date of publication. When the first segment of data in a field is in subfield a (ǂa), the delimiter pair is implicit and does not display on the screen in front of that segment. Generally, only internal subfields show the delimiter pair in OCLC.

The system uses subfield information for many things, including indexing and record display. For example, only the main title in ǂa of the 245 title field is indexed in the derived title index. The subtitle from ǂb is not indexed. However, both the ǂa and ǂb of the 245 title field display in a brief display. Inappropriately entering a ǂb in a 245 title could cause that title to index incorrectly and could adversely affect record retrieval. The cataloger's correct division of a field into its constituent subfields and proper assignment of a delimiter pair for each subfield are essential for the system to function properly.

The Appendix also contains a selected listing of those variable fields, indicators, and subfields that are used in most of the bibliographic records found in examples or exercises in this manual.

SYSTEM INFORMATION

The first two lines of an OCLC bibliographic record display contain some system-generated information about that record, including its OCLC control number, the status of the record, when it first entered the system, the last time it was replaced, and when it was last used for a Produce or Update transaction. You are not able to change this information. Only the system can do that.

In Figure 6–2, notice that the fixed field and each variable field begins with a start-of-message symbol (▸) and ends with an end-of-message symbol (¶). These are the same symbols that have been used consistently throughout the system to mark the beginning and end data. We will sometimes need to input these symbols as part of the data entry process.

For your convenience when communicating with the OCLC system, each variable field tag is assigned a sequential line number starting with 1. The line number appears in front of the three-digit tag. These line numbers are merely for easy reference and have no particular association with a specific tag number. When you add or delete variable fields during the record editing process, the remaining fields will be renumbered to accommodate your changes. For example, if you were to add an edition statement (tag 250) to the record in Figure 6–2, it would logically go between line 9 (tag 245—title) and line 10 (tag 260—publisher). After redisplaying the edited record, the edition statement would now be line sequence number 10, the publisher would now be line sequence number 11, and all subsequent lines would get new sequence numbers accordingly.

7 BASIC INPUTTING CONSIDERATIONS

Up until now, this manual has been concerned entirely with how to search for information within the OCLC Online Union Catalog and how to interpret it once you find it. You have been taught how to find bibliographic records and authority records, and also how to determine which libraries are in possession of each item. This is only the first part of the cataloging process. The bibliographic information that you find in OCLC must then be used to create catalog records for your own local institution.

The great popularity of databases containing machine-readable bibliographic records, such as the OCLC Online Union Catalog, lies in their ability to greatly increase the productivity and efficiency of catalog departments by making catalog records for items readily available worldwide. It is no longer necessary for every institution to do all the cataloging work for every item they acquire. With records for over 35,000,000 items available in the Online Union Catalog and thousands more being added every day, the likelihood of being able to find a catalog record created by someone else is correspondingly high. When found, the record can be used as the basis for a catalog record for the local institution's own catalog. Either an online catalog record, catalog cards, or both can then be ordered from OCLC by entering the appropriate commands. In addition, at the same time that a local catalog record is created, the individual library's holdings are added to the bibliographic record's location record within the Online Union Catalog so that other library's will be able to determine if they own it for interlibrary loan purposes.

As valuable as this service is, however, the information in the Online Union Catalog may sometimes be inadequate for your cataloging purposes. Libraries frequently have their own local standards and practices for cataloging which they expect their catalog records to reflect. Your library's needs may not be met by the records as they exist in OCLC. On some occasions, a bibliographic record may be lacking there altogether. In cases such as this, it becomes necessary to modify the information present in OCLC to bring it into agreement with your local requirements, or even to create a new, entirely original record in OCLC before you can utilize it in your local system or use it to produce catalog cards. The rest of this manual will attempt to deal with the basic principals of using PRISM for inputting into OCLC for the purpose of modifying or creating bibliographic records.

Chapter 7 provides a brief discussion of some of the basic facts involving bibliographic records in the OCLC database as well as a listing of the inputting options available to you when preparing to either enter a new record into the Online Union Catalog or to modify an existing record.

THE MASTER RECORD

Whenever you access a bibliographic record in OCLC what you are actually retrieving is a working copy of the master record. The master record is maintained permanently within the OCLC system and, for the most part, can be altered by only a relatively small number of people who have been authorized by OCLC to be able to do so. The working copy, on the other hand, is maintained by the system only temporarily, until either some final action on it is taken or the system is logged off. Unless you save it, the technique of which will be discussed below, once the system has been logged off there is no way to retrieve the same working copy again. Multiple libraries can use working copies created from the same master record simultaneously. There is no danger that because one person has retrieved a record from OCLC someone else will not be able to do so.

The working copy can be altered in any way that one wishes without affecting the master record. The edited working copy can then be used to create a catalog record for the local institution. Once it has been either updated or produced (these terms will be discussed), OCLC creates a permanent archive record that preserves the way in which your library has modified the working copy and which serves as the basis for your own catalog record. The system maintains separate archive records permanently for each institution that has used a master record to create a catalog record for themselves. These archive records do not interact with the master record in any way. If the master record is modified subsequent to an institution using it to create a catalog record, their archive record remains unaffected.

INPUTTING OPTIONS

There are essentially three different options for inputting that involve bibliographic records within the OCLC system:

1. You can modify a preexistent record to bring it into accordance with your local cataloging practices.
2. You can utilize a pre-existing record and, by means of various OCLC commands, transform it into a record new to the Online Union Catalog.
3. You can call up any of a number of different kinds of blank workforms and create an entirely original new record.

MODIFYING A RECORD

If you find a bibliographic record in the Online Union Catalog that matches the item that you wish to catalog, you can edit the bibliographic record in OCLC to reflect any changes that you wish to make in the cataloging for your own local use. When you update or produce on the record, OCLC will create a catalog record for you that reflects the edits that you have made and store it as an archive record within the system. Under ordinary circumstances, none of the edits you make are preserved on the permanent master record in the Online Union Catalog.

There are, however, several circumstances, which may be briefly mentioned here, under which edits that are made are preserved on the master record. If OCLC has granted an institution "Enhance" status, it is possible for it to lock, edit, and replace most bibliographic records in the Online Union Catalog that are within the same bibliographic format. OCLC grants this capability according to format only to those institutions that have passed a qualifying examination for cataloging and inputting within that format. Enhance institutions render a valuable service to the library community by upgrading and correcting out-of-date or incorrectly cataloged records. The provisions of the OCLC Enhance program are, however, beyond the scope of this manual.

Another case in which it is permissible to edit the master record is if the record is a minimal level catalog record. Under MARC there are different "levels" of cataloging available to a cataloger. These levels are differentiated by the degree of completeness of the catalog record. A minimal level catalog record contains less bibliographic information than does one done according to higher levels of cataloging. You can tell which level a record has been cataloged at in OCLC-MARC by looking in the ELVL (Encoding level) element of the fixed field. A "K" in this element indicates a minimal level record. Whereas only those who possess enhance status may modify most master records, anyone with at least full authorization may upgrade a minimal level catalog record to a full level catalog record by locking, editing, and replacing the record. Once upgraded, a record possesses the same status as any other full level catalog record. More information on locking and replacing records and the situations in which it is permissible to do so will be discussed in Chapter 8.

If any changes have been made to the master record since its initial inputting into the system, that fact is reflected in the 040 field. The subfield d of the 040 field lists the OCLC symbol of any institution, including OCLC itself, that has revised the original cataloging of the record. Revising a catalog record is always open to anyone with the proper authorization. A record may be revised many times and many different institutions may revise the same bibliographic record. The 040 field gives no indication what any of the individual revisions may have consisted of. There is no way of telling whether any given institutution listed in subfield d of 040 has upgraded the record from minimal level, or if they have enhanced a record that was already at a higher level, or if they have performed yet some other form of revision.

CREATING A NEW RECORD

If there is no record in the Online Union Catalog that matches the item you need to catalog, you must enter a new bibliographic master record into the system. To assist catalogers in determining when they have found a record that sufficiently resembles the item they are searching to be considered a match, OCLC has created guidelines. These guidelines may be found in Chapter 4, "When to input a new record," in OCLC's *Bibliographic Formats and Standards*. This should always be consulted before any decision is made to enter a new master record. You should take every precaution to avoid adding duplicate records to the Online Union Catalog. Duplicate records for the same bibliographic item needlessly complicates searching and consumes space in the database. They can also cause problems in local systems that rely upon OCLC control numbers to avoid duplicates within the local system. OCLC is very concerned in maintaining the quality of its database and regularly runs duplicate detection and resolution software in an attempt to keep the database as free of duplicates as possible.

Once you have decided to enter a new master record into OCLC, you must decide upon the method you wish to use to input it.

There are two basic methods by which a new record may be created in the OCLC Online Union Catalog. You can either key in a new record entirely from scratch or you can utilize a labor saving option by utilizing much of the data from a preexistent record. Which method to choose and how to apply it will be discussed in detail in Chapter 9.

8 EDITING BIBLIOGRAPHIC RECORDS

Chapter 8 presents a basic overview of editing commands within PRISM. The emphasis in this chapter will be on the editing of records already present in the Online Union Catalog, but much of the material is valid for the creation of new records as well. Concerns specific to the creation of new master records will be dealt with in Chaper 9.

Since the basic editing commands for all three of the different modes of inputting introduced in Chapter 7 are the same, this manual will make no attempt to distinguish between those modes in discussing basic editing techniques. The descriptions in this section are valid for all situations, whether you are merely editing a bibliographic record already present in OCLC or editing a new record that you are in the process of creating.

NAVIGATION COMMANDS

Just as there are a large number of commands for navigating among the various records and screens that result from a search request, there are also a large number of commands for navigating within individual records in order to facilitate their editing. The following figure lists the principal navigation commands for editing. Most of these commands are either standard in word processing or have already been described above in connection with their function in navigating searches and therefore will receive no further explanation here beyond that which is given in Figure 8–1. A few extra words, however, do need to be added about the following commands.

TAG

With the tag command you can move directly to the particular field you want to edit. This command is particularly useful if you have a multi-screen record and you wish to go directly to one of the higher numbered fields in the record rather than repeatedly typing PDN until you find what you are looking for. To use this command type "tag [field number]" and press <SEND>. You can also make the command less specific by typing xx for the last two

Figure 8–1 Bibliographic record navigation commands	
NAVIGATION COMMAND	DESCRIPTION
Cursor	Move left, right, up, or down one key at a time, or by holding the key down, more rapidly
PUP	Move back one screen
PDN	Move forward one screen
<HOME>	Return cursor to the home position
<END>	Move cursor to bottom right corner of screen
<CTRL><_>	Move cursor to first letter of word to right
<CTRL><_>	Move cursor to first letter of previous word to left
<TAB>	Move cursor one tab to the right
<SHIFT><TAB>	Move cursor one tab to the left
<CTRL> <END>	Move cursor to end of same line
<CTRL> <HOME>	Move cursor to beginning of same line
<ENTER>	Move cursor to beginning of next line
TAG	See below
LINE	See below

digits in the field number. For example 'tag 6XX'<SEND>. The system will move to the screen containing the first subject heading field irrespective of which particular 6XX field it is. In both cases, if the record in question does not actually have the field that you request, the system will move to the next closest tag number.

LINE

With the line command you can move to a specific line number in the record. The command is 'line [line number]' and press <SEND>. As with the tag command if the requested line number is not present on the record the system will move to the line number closest to it.

BASIC EDITING

A large variety of word processing capabilities are available through PRISM for editing bibliographic records. All the standard sorts of commands, such as character insert or delete, that must of necessity be present in any word processing program are also available in PRISM as well as many other options, to be described below, designed to be of particular use in cataloging.

The most important general consideration to keep in mind while editing in OCLC is that any edit that you make to a record must be "sent" to the system before the system can recognize it and make it a part of your edited record. If you enter any other command in OCLC after making an edit, without having first sent your edit to the system, you will lose it. There are two different methods for sending edits to the system within PRISM. They can either be sent one line at a time or an entire screen at a time.

LINE-BY-LINE EDITING

Throughout the remainder of this manual the term "line" refers to an entire variable field that is labeled with a specific line number within OCLC (see Chapter 6). An individual OCLC "line" may consist of a number of actual lines visible on the screen. Indeed, in the case of a 505 (contents note) field, the "line" may be a great number of actual lines long.

To "send" the edits for any single line it is simply necessary to position the cursor at any point on the edited line and press <SEND>. The system responds:

```
1 line(s) modified
```

FULL-SCREEN EDITING

One of the great improvements in editing capabilities that was instituted when OCLC initiated PRISM was the option of doing full-screen editing. Under the predecessor to PRISM, the first system, line-by-line editing was the only available option. Within PRISM, it is possible to edit all the fields present on a single screen and send all the edits with one command. It is not possible to send all the edits on an entire record at once, but full-screen edit still represents a substantial reduction in the number of keystrokes necessary in editing.

The full-screen edit option can be turned on or off. The default setting is on. To turn full-screen editing off type <alt>< F9>. The system responds:

```
Full screen edit now off.
```

This message will continue to be displayed until another command is entered. To turn full-screen edit back on, also type <Alt> <F9>. The system responds:

```
Full screen edit now on.
```

Once you are in full-screen edit mode, edit as many different lines as you wish. As each line is edited, the system marks it by changing the start-of-message symbol to reverse video. If you edit a line, and the system does not change its start-of-message symbol to reverse video, full-screen edit is not on.

Once you have completed your edits you can send them all together by typing <Alt>< F10>. The system responds:

```
Screen edits sent.
```

You can then go on to the next screen and edit it. Remember, you must send your edits for one screen before going on to the next screen or you will lose them.

If, when you attempt to send your edits you receive the message "No marked fields," the full-screen edit is not on and your edited lines have not been marked. You can still salvage your work by marking your edited lines manually. Position the cursor at the beginning of the line you want to mark and type <Alt>< F8>. The start-of-message will change to reverse video. When you have marked in this way all the fields that you have edited, you can then type <Alt>< F10> to send them. Alternatively, you could first turn on full-screen edit by typing <Alt><F9>. Then by overwriting any single character on a line, you can mark it.

Similarly, if you have edited a line but then change your mind and do not wish to keep the edits as part of your record, move the cursor to that line and type <Alt>< F8>. The start-of-message sysmbol returns to normal video. When you send the screen edits, this line will not be sent and will not be modified.

REFORMATTING A RECORD

If at any time during the editing process, you wish to see what the record would currently look like with all your edits included, you can use the reformat command. When you enter the reformat command, the system redisplays the record taking into account all edits that have been made to the current working copy of the record. It adds, deletes, rearranges and renumbers lines as necessary. It also deletes any unused fields, though this is principally of relevence if you are inputting a new record into OCLC.

To reformat a record, type rf at the home position and press <SEND>.

UNEDITING A RECORD

If, after you have made and sent any edits to a record, you change your mind and decide that you do not want to edit that record after all, you can remove all your edits from the record with one command. To execute the unedit command, type 'ue' and press <SEND>. All the edits that have been made will be removed and the record will redisplay as it was before any edits were made. Remember that if you use the unedit command, *all* of your edits will be removed from the record. There is no way of designating a partial unediting.

SIMPLE EDITS

Simple edits within lines can be made as they are made in most word processing programs. You can overwrite, insert or delete characters as necessary by using the appropriate keys. Overwrite is the default mode.

For more complex editing PRISM has available a number of options designed to simplify and increase the efficiency of inputting.

EDITING FIELDS

FIXED FIELD EDITING

You can edit the entire fixed field from the home position. To do this type the fixed field element's mnemonic, a colon, the value you wish to add or modify and press <SEND>. For example, to add a 'b' (for bibliography) to the contents element, type 'cont:b' <SEND>.

You can edit multiple characters simultaneously by separating them with blank spaces. For example, to add the 'b' to contents and an 'a' to illustrations, type 'cont:b illus:a' <SEND>.

006 FIELD

One of the greatest difficulties with using MARC, until recently, has been its division into multiple independent formats according to the type of material involved. Monographs, serials, sound recordings, videos, computer files, and so on all had separate for-

---

Figure 8–2   Bibliographic record possessing characteristics of two formats

---

```
                                ¶ CAT      MOD      SID: 00000            OL

Beginning of record displayed.

OLUC su maps and su periodicals                    Record 427 of 434
NO HOLDINGS IN XXX - 8 OTHER HOLDINGS
OCLC: 25240411          Rec stat: c
Entered:      19920207     Replaced:    19960523 Used:    19960108
▶ Type:  e    ELvl: I    Srce: d    Relf:      Ctrl:       Lang: eng
  BLvl:  s    SpFm:      GPub: s    Prme:      MRec:       Ctry: ilu
  CrTp:  c    Indx: 1    Proj:      DtSt:  m   Dates:  1991,9999
  Desc:  a ¶
▶    1 040      SPI ‡c SPI ‡d OCL ¶
▶    2 007      a ‡b j ‡d a ‡e a ‡f n ‡g z ‡h n ¶
▶    3 034 0    a ‡d W0913000 ‡e W0873000 ‡f N0423000 ‡g N0370000 ¶
▶    4 052      4101 ¶
▶    5 090      G4101.P2 year/quarter ‡b .I46 ¶
▶    6 049      XXXM ¶
▶    7 110 1    Illinois. ‡b Dept. of Transportation. ¶
▶    8 245 10   Illinois interstate road work alert ‡h [map] ¶
▶    9 255      Scale not given ‡c (W 91°30'—W 87°30'/N 42°30'—N 37°00'). ¶
▶   10 260      [Springfield, Ill.] : ‡b Illinois Dept. of Transportation,
  ‡c 1991 - ¶
▶   11 300      maps ; ‡c on sheet 46 x 40 cm., fold. to 23 x 10 cm. ¶
▶   12 310      Quarterly. ¶
```

---

mats, with their own unique fields defined only for that format. In recent years, as more and more items were published that partook of elements of more than one format, it had become increasingly difficult to adequately reflect the nature of the item when one was restricted to describing it according to the precepts of only one format. A book published with a CD, a video with an accompanying book, a map issued serially all presented difficulties in description that could not really be met under MARC.

Format integration was designed to remedy this situation. In several stages, the last of which occurred in March of 1996, the tagging of bibliographic records has been made far more consistent across all the various formats. All MARC tags and subfields have now been validated for use in any bibliographic record regardless of format. The different formats themselves, however, have not been eliminated. The fixed field still determines which format a record belongs to with all its attendent implications for indexing in the Online Union Catalog. In order to establish a means by which aspects of the item that diverge from the format of the item as a whole could be represented in the bibliographic description of the record, and thereby be made indexable, a new field was instituted during Format Integration, part 2 in March, 1996: *the 006 field.*

The purpose of the 006 field, which is named "Fixed length data elements—additional material characteristics," is to provide a bibliographic record with a secondary collection of fixed field elements which can be utilized for describing those elements of an item that cannot be subsumed under the description of the bibliographic record as a whole. Thus if you have, for example, a book on computer technology with an accompanying CD of computer files, you can now provide coding that covers the presence of both formats within the same item. A format must still be chosen to be the principal format, but it is now possible to code elements of however many other formats are relevant to a given item by placing them in 006 fields. The 006 field is repeatable and can be used as many times as is required. In the above example, the actual fixed field would still be that of a monograph, but by means of an 006 field the record can also be coded to reflect that it possesses computer files as well. You can use 006 fields to code for secondary formats of accompanying materials as in the case of the book and CD example or to identify a secondary characteristic of the principal material itself, such as a map serial.

It is not within the scope of this manual to discuss in detail technical aspects of how to decide upon the use of or coding of an 006 field. For relevant guidelines see OCLC's *Bibliographic Formats and Standards.* Rather, the subject has been broached here because the inputting commands for this new field are unlike those of any other.

Adding an 006 field

To add an 006 field to a record you type the command 'n006' or 'new006' followed by the format qualifier you would use in searching in the Online Union Catalog for the format you wish to add to the record. Thus, if you find a map serial that has been entered into the Online Union Catalog on the maps format, you would type 'n006 ser'<SEND> in order to bring up a blank 006 field that will reflect those aspects of the work that are serial in nature. After you have entered the command, the system clears the screen of the bibliographic record and displays the 006 field.

The 006 field for serials consists of those fixed field elements specific to the serials format that are necessary for the descrip-

---

Figure 8–3   Blank 006 display

```
                                    ¶        new006     SID: 00000
 ▸ ret

                        Serials Format 006 Information

 ▸ T006:  s       Freq: ▌       Regl: ▌        ISSN:        SrTp: ▌
   Orig:          Form:         EntW:          Cont:        Gpub:
   Conf:  0       Alph:         S/L:  0           ¶
```

---

tion of the serial aspects of the item. The mnemonics utilized are the same as those used in the regular serial fixed field and they are used in the same way. Once you have modified those elements you wish, press <SEND>. The system returns the bibliographic record to the screen, now including the 006 field. Within the normal record display, the 006 field appears as a single line variable field. The system deletes the mnemonics and collapses the display down to a straight string of the characters, including blanks, contained in the 006 field.

Modifying an 006 field

The 006 field can be edited just like any other variable field. To edit an 006 field, type 'm006' or 'mod006' <SEND>. If there is more than one 006 field, you must specify the one you wish to modify by adding the line number to the command, for example, 'm006 2'<SEND>. The system removes the bibliographic record from the screen and displays the 2006 field in mnemonic mode. You can then edit the 006 just as you would any fixed field. Press <SEND> and the system returns the record to the screen with the modified 006 returned to its position within the variable fields.

The 006 field can also be edited without accessing the mnemonic prompts. Simply move your cursor to the 006 field and edit and send the line just like any other variable field. Obviously, great care needs to be exercised when editing without the mnemonic prompts, but if all you wish to do is replace one character with another, it is certainly a reasonable and time-saving option.

Because the presence or absence of 006 fields affects the indexing and thus the searchability of the record in the Online Union Catalog, OCLC has elected to allow anyone with at least full authorization to add 006 fields to the permanent master record of any record except CONSER-authenticated serials. To do this you must first lock the master record. See the section on locking and replacing records in Chapter 9 for the proper procedure. Once

```
┌─────────────────────────────────────────────────────────────────────┐
│  Figure 8–4   Bibliographic record containing 006 field              │
├─────────────────────────────────────────────────────────────────────┤
│                              ¶ CAT       MOD     SID: 00000     OL    │
│  Beginning of record displayed.                                       │
│  OLUC su maps and su periodicals                    Record 427 of     │
│  434                                                                   │
│  NO HOLDINGS IN IAY - 8 OTHER HOLDINGS                                 │
│   OCLC: 25240411          Rec stat:    c                              │
│   Entered:    19920207    Replaced:   19960523 Used:    19960108      │
│ ▸ Type:  e    ELvl: I   Srce:  d    Relf:       Ctrl:       Lang: eng │
│   BLvl:  s    SpFm:     GPub:  s    Prme:       MRec:       Ctry: ilu │
│   CrTp:  c    Indx: 1   Proj:       DtSt:  m    Dates: 1991,9999      │
│   Desc:  a ¶                                                           │
│ ▸  1   040     SPI ‡c SPI ‡d OCL ¶                                     │
│ ▸  2   006     [sqr  p  SD  0]                                         │
│ ▸  3   007     a ‡b j ‡d a ‡e a ‡f n ‡g z ‡h n ¶                       │
│ ▸  4   034 0   a ‡d W0913000 ‡e W0873000 ‡f N0423000 ‡g N0370000 ¶     │
│ ▸  5   052     4101 ¶                                                  │
│ ▸  6   090     G4101.P2 year/quarter ‡b .I46 ¶                         │
│ ▸  7   049     XXXM ¶                                                  │
│ ▸  8   110 1   Illinois. ‡b Dept. of Transportation. ¶                │
│ ▸  9   245 10  Illinois interstate road work alert ‡h [map] ¶         │
│ ▸ 10   255     Scale not given ‡c (W 91°30'—W 87°30'/N 42°30'—N       │
│                37°00'). ¶                                              │
│ ▸ 11   260     [Springfield, Ill.] : ‡b Illinois Dept. of             │
│                Transportation, ‡c 1991 - ¶                            │
│ ▸ 12   300     maps ; ‡c on sheet 46 x 40 cm., fold. to 23 x 10 cm. ¶ │
│ ▸ 13   310     Quarterly. ¶                                           │
└─────────────────────────────────────────────────────────────────────┘
```

the record is locked, add one or more 006 fields as described above. When you have completed your modifications, replace the record as described below.

Although anyone with at least full authorization is allowed to add 006 fields to the master record of most records in OCLC, to edit a preexistent 006 field on a full-level master record requires Enhance status just as modifying full-level records usually does.

FIELD ORDER

In addition to editing characters one at a time, by inserting, deleting, or overwriting, it is also possible to add, delete or move whole fields with a single command. The order in which fields display in OCLC is determined by a combination of line number and tag number. For the most part the system arrays the fields in a predetermined order based on tag number. The following lists the order of tags as automatically assigned by the system.

010
040
066
006–089
090–099*
049
1xx*
2xx
3xx
4xx*
5xx*
6xx*
7xx*
8xx*
9xx*

Those tag numbers that belong to groups of numbers that are not asterisked always display in an absolutely fixed order. An 066 always displays between 040 and 006 or the number nearest to it. All fields between 006 and 089 always display in strict numerical order. All 2XX fields display in numerical order and always between the last 1XX field and the first 3XX field. These orderings cannot be changed by the inputter. If you add an 043 field to the record, for example, it does not matter what line number you give it while inputting, when you reformat the record, the system will move it to its assigned place. Only in those cases where the field is repeatable, such as the 006 field, can the inputter exercise any control over the order of fields. All 006 fields will always display together, but their order can be designated by the inputter.

Those tag numbers that belong to groups that are asterisked above do not have their order totally preset. The tag groups themselves are still arranged by number. All 5XX fields will always precede all 6XX fields, but the inputter is allowed to determine the order of the fields within these tag groups.

REORDERING LINES

Because of the system controls over the ordering of tag numbers within records, the system will handle much of the need for reordering fields for you. If, in editing a field, you alter its tag number from 100 (main entry) to 700 (added entry), because of a change in cataloging rules since the time the record was originally created, when you reformat the system will automatically move the line down to the 7XX area of the record. You do not have to worry about moving it yourself.

Within those tag groups where the order of fields is not predetermined, field order is determined by line number. In the following example you want to change the 3rd 500 field to a 538 (system requirements) field and make it the first 5XX field in accordance with the current requirements of AACR2. To do this, simply type over the line numbers while in full-screen edit mode to reflect the desired order of fields. Type <Alt>< F10>, then reformat and the system will display the fields in their new order.

Remember, you can only change the order of lines within the parameters the system allows.

You can also renumber lines by using the cut, copy, and paste commands. These will be discussed separately as follows.

SEGMENTED FIELD EDITING

OCLC places a limit of approximately 600 characters on how many characters are allowed to be contained within a single line. Any field that is longer than that, such as a contents note, must be displayed in segments. When the system breaks a field into segments, the entire field continues to retain the same line num-

---

Figure 8–5 Bibliographic record with lines renumbered

```
▶  1 010    95-77530 ¶
▶  2 040    DPL ‡c DPL ‡d VHB ¶
▶  3 020    1568847033 ¶
▶  4 082 00 005.75 ‡2 20 ¶
▶  5 090    TK5105.888‡b .F68 1995 ¶
▶  6 090    ‡b ¶
▶  7 049    XXXM ¶
▶  8 245 00 Foundations of World Wide Web programming with HTML & CGI / ‡c
   [Ed Tittel, et al.] ¶
▶  9 260    Foster City, CA :‡b IDG Books Worldwide, Inc., ‡c c1995. ¶
▶ 10 300    xlii, 648 p. : ‡b ill. ; ‡c 23 cm. + ‡e 1 computer optical disc
   (digital : 4 3/4 in.) ¶
▶ 12 500    "For the working programmer"--Cover. ¶
▶ 13 500    Includes index. ¶
▶ 11 538    "Mastered following the ISO-9660 standard, so it should be
   mountable and readable from DOS/Windows, Macintosh, and UNIX machines (as
   well as any other platforms that adhere to this standard)."--Chapter 34. ¶
```

Figure 8–6   Renumbered lines after reformatting

▶ 1 010   95-77530 ¶
▶ 2 040   DPL ‡c DPL ‡d VHB ¶
▶ 3 020   1568847033 ¶
▶ 4 082 00 005.75 ‡2 20 ¶
▶ 5 090   TK5105.888 ‡b .F68 1995 ¶
▶ 6 090   ‡b ¶
▶ 7 049   XXXM ¶
▶ 8 245 00 Foundations of World Wide Web programming with HTML & CGI / ‡c
[Ed Tittel, et al.] ¶
▶ 9 260   Foster City, CA : ‡b IDG Books Worldwide, Inc., ‡c c1995. ¶
▶ 10 300   xlii, 648 p. : ‡b ill. ; ‡c 23 cm. + ‡e 1 computer optical disc
(digital : 4 3/4 in.) ¶
▶ 11 538   "Mastered following the ISO-9660 standard, so it should be
mountable and readable from DOS/Windows, Macintosh, and UNIX machines (as
well as any other platforms that adhere to this standard)."--Chapter 34. ¶
▶ 12 500   "For the working programmer"--Cover. ¶
▶ 13 500   Includes index. ¶

---

ber. The line, however, is broken into discrete segments that are numbered sequentially. The number of the individual segment displays in brackets to the right of the line number and to the left of the tag number. See the line 12 segments in Figure 8–7.

When editing segments, you can treat each segment just as if it were an individual line and edit it separately. This means that each segment must possess correct tags and indicators in its own right. If you edit a segment, you must make certain that it continues to contain correct tagging. If you wish to change either the tag or indicator of a segmented line it is only necessary to make the change to any one segment of the line. The system will automatically make the changes to all other segments.

If you add text to any but the last segment of a segmented field, when you send your edit, the system will automatically redisplay, creating a new subsegment below the segment to which you have added text. This is necessitated by the fact that the segment to which you have added text is already at maximum allowable length. The subsegment remains until you reformat the record at which time the system redistributes the text of the entire field.

If, in adding to the length of a line while editing, you surpass the 600 character limit, the system will automatically segment the line for you. No special action on your part is necessary. Figure 8–8 shows such a new segment between the existing line 12 segments shown in Figure 8–7.

| **Figure 8–7 Example of segmented field** |

▶ 8 245   02 A Festschrift for Albert Seay : ‡b essays by his friends and colleagues / ‡c edited by Michael D. Grace. ¶
▶ 9 260   Colorado Springs : ‡b Colorado College, ‡c 1982. ¶
▶ 10 300   xviii, 260 p. : ‡b ill. ; ‡c 24 cm. ¶
▶ 11 504   Includes bibliographical references. ¶
▶ 12 [1]   505 0   Suggestioni teoriche nel Lucidarium di Marchetto da Padova, dai "generi" alla "musica colorata" / Giuseppe Massera — The manuscript transmission of Hothby's theoretical works / Gilbert Reaney — De l'attribution áa Tinctoris des exemples musicaux du Liber de arte contrapuncti / Nanie Bridgman — La vie musicale áa la cour du pape Mâedicis Clâement VII (1523-1534) / Anne-Marie Bragard — Repertory and performance practice in Santa Maria Novella at the turn of the 17th century / Frank A. D'Accone — Self-destructive paradox in Antony and Cleopatra / Thomas W. Ross — Arthur Bedford, English ¶
▶ 12 [2]   505 0   polemicist of the Restoration / James W. Pruett — Mâehul's Ariodant and the early Leitmotif / Michael D. Grace — Bemerkungen zur Theorie der Vokalmusik in der Kompositionlehre von Adolf Bernhard Marx / Kurt von Fischer — Busnois, Brahms, and the syntax of temporal proportions / Carlton Gamer — Trinitarian symbolism in the "Engelkonzert" of Hindemith's Mathis der Maler / H. Wiley Hitchcock. ¶
▶ 13 650 0 Music. ¶
▶ 14 600 10 Seay, Albert. ¶
▶ 15 700 1 Grace, Michael D. ¶

ADDING A LINE

You can add a new line from the home position, from within the record, or from the end of the record. In each case you must assign the new field a line number. If the location the system will assign the new field to is already automatically determined by its tag number, it does not matter what line number you assign it as long as it has not already been used.

For example, if you wish to add an 043 field to a record that possesses 14 lines, you can type in a new line assigning it number 15. This is demonstrated in Figure 8–9. Once you reformat, the system will automatically place it in the correct location, as shown in Figure 8–10.

If, on the other hand, the field you wish to add belongs to one of those tag groups where the order of fields is not predetermined, you need to assign the correct line number for it to display where you wish. Use a decimal number to place it in between the two

---

Figure 8–8   Segmented field after making further additions

▸   8 245 02 A Festschrift for Albert Seay : ‡b essays by his friends and colleagues / ‡c edited by Michael D. Grace. ¶
▸   9 260   Colorado Springs : ‡b Colorado College, ‡c 1982. ¶
▸ 10 300   xviii, 260 p. : ‡b ill. ; ‡c 24 cm. ¶
▸ 11 504   Includes bibliographical references. ¶
▸ 12 [1]   505 0   Suggestioni teoriche nel Lucidarium di Marchetto da Padova, dai "generi" alla "musica colorata" / Giuseppe Massera — The manuscript transmission of Hothby's theoretical works / Gilbert Reaney — De l'attribution áa Tinctoris des exemples musicaux du Liber de arte contrapuncti / Nanie Bridgman — La vie musicale áa la cour du pape Mâedicis Clâement VII (1523-1534) / Anne-Marie Bragard — Repertory and performance practice in Santa Maria Novella at the turn of the 17th century / Frank A. D'Accone — Self-destructive paradox in Antony and Cleopatra / Thomas W. Ross — Bibliography of works of ¶
▸ 12 [1.1]   505 0 Albert Seay / William M. Mclellan — Arthur Bedford, English ¶
▸ 12 [2]   505 0   polemicist of the Restoration / James W. Pruett — Mâehul's Ariodant and the early Leitmotif / Michael D. Grace — Bemerkungen zur Theorie der Vokalmusik in der Kompositionlehre von Adolf Bernhard Marx / Kurt von Fischer — Busnois, Brahms, and the syntax of temporal proportions / Carlton Gamer — Trinitarian symbolism in the "Engelkonzert" of Hindemith's Mathis der Maler / H. Wiley Hitchcock. ¶
▸ 13 650 0 Music. ¶
▸ 14 600 10 Seay, Albert. ¶
▸ 15 700 1   Grace, Michael D. ¶

---

lines that are on either side of where you want the new line to go. In Figure 8–10, if you wanted to add the subject heading Reengineering (Management) and make it the first 650 (subject heading) field, you would designate it line 13.1.

To add a new line from the end of the record, move the cursor to the beginning of the line after the final field. Enter a start-of-message symbol, assign the new field a line number, and type the new field in with the proper MARC tagging and spacing. Press <¶SEND>. A new line must contain an end-of-message symbol. The system responds:

1 line added.

To add a new line from within the record, move the cursor to

Figure 8–9 Adding a line

```
                              ¶ CAT                    SID: 00000    OL
Beginning of record displayed.

OLUC dp loh,mic,                                   Record 11 of 155
 HELD BY XXX - 40 OTHER HOLDINGS
 OCLC: 32430525      Rec stat:  p
 Entered: 19950414   Replaced:  19960409    Used:  19960506
▶ Type: a    Elvl:     Srce:        Audn:       Ctrl:      Lang: eng
 Blvl: m    Form:     Conf: 0      Biog        Mrec:      Ctry: enk
            Cont: b   Gpub:        Fict: 0     Indx: 1
 Desc: a    Ills: a   Fest: 0      DtSt: s     Dates: 1995, ¶
▶  1  010        95-12674¶
▶  2  040        DLC ‡c DLC ¶
▶  3  020        056607642X (hardcover) ¶
▶  4  050 00     HD58.87 ‡b .L64 1995 ¶
▶  5  082 00     658.4/063 ‡2 20 ¶
▶  6  090        ‡b ¶
▶  7  049        XXXM ¶
▶  8  100 1      Loh, Michael, ‡d 1957- ¶
▶  9  245 10     Re-engineering at work / ‡c Michael Loh. ¶
▶ 10  260        Aldershot ; ‡a Brookfield, Vt. : ‡b Gower, ‡c c1995. ¶
▶ 11  300        xix, 167 p. ‡b ill. ; ‡c 23 cm. ¶
```

```
                           ¶ CAT               SID: 00000        OL
 End of record displayed.

 OLUC dp loh,mic                            Record 11 of 155
  HELD BY XXX - 40 OTHER HOLDINGS
 ▶ 12  504     Includes bibliographical references (p. 149-156) and index. ¶
 ▶ 13  650 0   Benchmarking (Management) ¶
 ▶ 14  650 0   Organizational change. ¶
 ▶ 15  043     n-us-- ¶
```

the end of the field above the point where you want to add the new line. Press <ENTER>. The system opens a new blank line. Type in the new line as above. For example, Figure 8–11 illustrates adding a subject heading to Figure 8–10 as mentioned above.

To add a new line from the beginning of the record, move the cursor to the home position. It is not necessary to begin with a start-of-message symbol when you are in the home position. Simply type in the new line as above and press <¶SEND>.

Another method of creating a new line that can be useful in

Figure 8–10   Reformatted record with added line

```
                              ¶ CAT              SID: 00000   OL
Beginning of record displayed.

OLUC dp loh,mic,                              Record 11 of 155
  HELD BY XXX - 40 OTHER HOLDINGS
  OCLC: 32430525        Rec stat:     p
  Entered: 19950414   Replaced: 19960409   Used:  19960506
▶ Type: a      Elvl:    Srce:      Audn:     Ctrl:     Lang: eng
  Blvl: m      Form:    Conf: 0    Biog      Mrec:     Ctry: enk
               Cont: b  Gpub:      Fict: 0   Indx: 1
  Desc: a      Ills: a  Fest: 0    DtSt: s   Dates: 1995, ¶
▶  1   010         95-12674¶
▶  2   040         DLC ‡c DLC ¶
▶  3   020         056607642X (hardcover) ¶
▶  4   043         n-us--- ¶
▶  5   050 00      HD58.87 ‡b .L64 1995 ¶
▶  6   082 00      658.4/063 ‡2 20 ¶
▶  7   090         ‡b ¶
▶  8   049         XXXM ¶
▶  9   100 1       Loh, Michael, ‡d 1957- ¶
▶ 10   245 10      Re-engineering at work / ‡c Michael Loh. ¶
▶ 11   260         Aldershot ; ‡a Brookfield, Vt. : ‡b Gower, ‡c c1995. ¶
```

```
                              ¶ CAT              SID: 00000     OL
  End of record displayed.

  OLUC dp loh, mic                           Record 11 of 155
   HELD BY XXX - 40 OTHER HOLDINGS
▶ 12   300    xix, 167 p. : ‡b ill. ; ‡c 23 cm. ¶
▶ 13   504    Includes bibliographical references (p. 149-156) and index. ¶
▶ 14   650 0  Benchmarking (Management) ¶
▶ 15   650 0  Organizational change. ¶
```

some circumstances is to use a pre-existent line as the basis of the new line. In the example cited above which adds the subject heading Reengineering (Management) to a record, you could save a few keystrokes by cursoring to line 14, altering the 14 to any decimal number lower than 14, and typing Reengineer directly over Benchmark (using insert to enter the final r). When you reformat, the new line will be inserted in the proper place. This method is probably only efficient when the line you wish to add is very similar to a line already present on the record.

Full-screen edit mode is operative when adding new lines as well. Type in as many new fields in the body or at the end of the record as you wish. Make sure they all have start-of-message and end-of-message symbols and a unique line number. Type <Alt> <F10> and all the new fields will be added at once.

DELETING A LINE

To delete a line simply move the cursor to the home position, type the line number, and press <SEND>. The system responds:

```
1 line(s) deleted.
```

To delete more than one line simultaneously, separate the line numbers by a hyphen. For example, typing '5–7' <SEND> will delete lines five through seven. You can also delete a line by moving the cursor to the line you want to delete, positioning it directly after the line number and pressing <¶SEND>.

CUT, COPY, AND PASTE

Like most word processing programs, PRISM gives you the ability to cut, copy, or paste lines of text. You can use cut, copy or paste either to rearrange fields within records, to transfer fields between bibliographic records, or to transfer fields from authority records to bibliographic records. Not only is this option capable of saving you considerable time by reducing the amount of keying in of data required, but, equally importantly, it also markedly decreases the possibility of typographic errors. Instead of needing to key in long complicated corporate names or personal names loaded with diacritics, for example, once you find the heading in the Authority File, you can simply copy it directly from the authority record to your bibliographic record thus eliminating any possibility of making an error.

Cut

With the cut command, you can cut one or more lines out of a bibliographic or authority record. You can use this command either to delete lines from a record or as part of a process in which you remove them from one place and move them to another. To cut lines, use the command 'cut [line number(s)]' <SEND>. The system responds:

```
1 line(s) moved.
```

The cut line, or lines, have now been removed from the record. When you reformat the record, they will no longer be present.

Figure 8-11   Adding a line from within the record

```
                                    ¶ CAT                 SID: 00000              OL
Beginning of record displayed.

OLUC dp loh,mic,                                    Record 11 of 155
 HELD BY XXX - 40 OTHER HOLDINGS
 OCLC: 32430525          Rec stat: p
 Entered: 19950414       Replaced: 19960409      Used: 19960506
▸ Type: a      Elvl:       Srce:        Audn:       Ctrl:       Lang: eng
  Blvl: m      Form:       Conf: 0      Biog        Mrec:       Ctry: enk
               Cont: b     Gpub:        Fict: 0     Indx: 1
  Desc: a      Ills: a     Fest: 0      DtSt: s     Dates: 1995, ¶
▸  1   010          95-12674¶
▸  2   040          DLC ‡c DLC ¶
▸  3   020          056607642X (hardcover) ¶
▸  4   050 00       HD58.87 ‡b .L64 1995 ¶
▸  5   082 00       658.4/063 ‡2 20 ¶
▸  6   090          ‡b ¶
▸  7   049          XXXM ¶
▸  8   100 1        Loh, Michael, ‡d 1957- ¶
▸  9   245 10       Re-engineering at work / ‡c Michael Loh. ¶
▸ 10   260          Aldershot ; ‡a Brookfield, Vt. : ‡b Gower, ‡c c1995. ¶4
▸ 11   300          xix, 167 p. ‡b ill.; ‡c 23 cm ¶
```

```
                                    ¶ CAT                 SID: 00000              OL
End of record displayed.

OLUC dp loh, mic                                    Record 11 of 155
 HELD BY XXX - 40 OTHER HOLDINGS
▸ 13  504     Includes bibliographical references (p. 149-156) and index. ¶
▸ 13.1 650 0 Reengineering (Management) ¶
▸ 14  650 0  Benchmarking (Management) ¶
▸ 15  650 0  Organizational change. ¶
```

Cut multiple lines by separating them with a hyphen such as 'cut 17–19'<SEND>. The lines which you wish to cut need not be present on the same screen. They may overlap more than one screen.

The system moves the cut lines to a storage area. The data remain stored there until such time as another cut or copy command is made. If you are using the cut command simply to remove lines from a record, nothing further need be done. The cut lines have been deleted. Although it is possible to paste the cut lines back into another or the same record, it is seldom advisable to use the cut command as part of a process to transfer lines from one record to another. Remember that cutting lines from a record means that you have edited it. You will have to take some final action upon the record you have cut the lines from as well as the record you are moving the lines to. Unless for some reason you really want to remove the lines from the first record, you should always use the copy command when transferring fields.

You can cut a segmented field as a whole or you can specify a selected segment or segments. Designate the segment or segments by line number as you would in any other cut command. For example 'cut 13 [2]' will delete the second segment of line 13. If you wish to cut the segmented field as a whole, simply specify the line number and all segments will be cut.

Copy

With the copy command, you can copy one or more lines out of a bibliographic or authority record without removing them from the original record. When you use the copy command, the system moves the designated lines into storage without modifying the original record in any way. By using the paste command described below, they can then be transferred into any record you wish. To copy lines use the command "ctx [line number(s)]" <SEND>. The system responds:

```
1 line(s) copied.
```

As with the cut command, the lines remain in storage until another cut or copy command is used. Also as with the cut command, you can copy multiple lines by separating them with hyphens.

Paste

Once you have moved text into storage, you can insert it at any point you wish. First call up the record you wish to add the text to. Then specify where you wish to paste the text. To do this use the command 'pst [line number]' <SEND> where the line number equals the line above the point where you wish the text to be added. The system automatically assigns the new lines line numbers that will display them where you have requested and automatically "sends" them. It is not necessary to do it manually. If you wish the system to add the lines after the last line of the record you need only type 'pst'. In this instance, specifying a line number is not necessary.

The copied text will remain in storage until replaced by text from another cut or copy command. As long as it remains in storage, it can be pasted as many times onto as many records as is necessary.

Passport cut, copy and paste

If you are using PRISM through PASSPORT software you have another option for using cut, copy, and paste available to you. You can use the PASSPORT block-editing capabilities just as you used the commands above.

You can execute PASSPORT block-editing commands either through function keys, through the keyboard, or if you are using PASSPORT for Windows, through the pull-down menus. To cut or copy text via the function keys, first position the cursor at the beginning of the block of text that you wish to mark. Press <F8>. The system responds:

```
Move to end of block.
```

With the cursor you can now mark the text you wish to cut or copy. Cursor across or down until you have marked all the text you wish. Marked text appears in reverse video. Press <F8> again. The system responds:

```
Press Cut/Copy Text key.
```

If you wish to cut the block of text press <F6>. If you wish to copy the block of text press <SHIFT> <F6>. If you choose the cut command, the block of text disappears. If you choose the copy command, it returns to normal video. The system has stored the text. To paste the block, position the cursor at the point where you wish to insert the text and press <F7>. The system inserts the text from the point indicated without overwriting any text that is already present. Unlike the PRISM paste command, the PASSPORT command adds the lines to the record but it does not send them. You must send them for them to be added to the record. Use <alt> <F10> to send the pasted lines and add them to the record.

You need to exercise caution in using the PASSPORT paste option. The system does not automatically renumber the lines to make them fit into the new record. It simply copies them exactly. Therefore, if you are copying a 100 field that is line four on an authority record onto a bibliographic record, you must renumber the line yourself after adding it to the record on the screen but before sending it or it will overwrite whichever field is already line four on your record.

As is the case with the PRISM cut, copy, and paste facility, the text remains stored until another block is either cut or copied. It can be used as many times as necessary.

To cut, copy, and paste in PASSPORT using the keyboard, first position the cursor where you wish to begin to mark the block. Press <Alt><B>. The system responds:

```
Move cursor to last character, press ENTER.
```

Follow the directions. When you press enter, a list of options appears. Cursor to either cut or copy in the list and press <ENTER>. The text is now stored. To paste the text, position the cursor where you wish to enter the text. Press <Alt><G>. As with the function key method of pasting text in PASSPORT, you must still add the pasted lines for them to be retained in the record being edited.

To cut, copy, and paste in PASSPORT for Windows, first position the mouse over the beginning of the text you wish to mark. Holding down the left mouse button, drag the mouse to the end of the text and release the mouse button. Marked text appears highlighted. Click on edit in the upper left of the screen. A drop-down menu appears. Click on cut or copy and the text is stored. Position the cursor at the point where you wish to add the text. Click on edit again and then on paste. The text is added.

When deciding which method of cut, copy and paste to use there are several factors to keep in mind. The PRISM method is probably the preferable method to use in most circumstances, however, the PASSPORT method does contain a couple of features that makes it more attractive in a few specific situations. Ordinarily, the fact that the PASSPORT paste function is capable of overwriting text is a hazard that makes it less desirable to use. In some cases, however, you may want to overwrite a line. Say that you discover that a form of entry on your record is incorrect because the authority record has been modified. Rather than typing over the change yourself, or cutting the line on the bibliographic record with the old form of heading, copying the line on the authority record with the new form of heading, and then pasting it into the bibliographic record with the PRISM paste command, you can use PASSPORT paste to paste over the incorrect heading directly, thereby combining two steps in one.

Another advantage that PASSPORT cut, copy, and paste has is a greater flexibility in your ability to designate what you want to move. With the PRISM cut, copy and paste commands you can only designate entire lines to be moved. With the PASSPORT commands, you can mark for yourself exactly how much text you wish to move. You can move parts of lines, single words, even as little as one character if you wish.

MOVING A RECORD

If you have edited a record in any way, you will not be able to access any other record, either bibliographic or authority, until you first take some action on the edited record. If you try to call up any other record, you will get the display shown in Figure 8–12.

You must execute one of the commands listed here before proceding further. To execute the command of your choice, move your cursor over until the cursor is resting on top of the desired command and press <SEND>. The listed commands have the following meanings:

- *Cancel "Find"*: If you choose this command, the system will cancel the command you have just attempted to execute and return you to the edited record on the screen.
- *Remove record*: If you choose "remove record," the system will unedit the record, remove it from the screen and execute the command you entered.
- *Save record*: If you choose "save record," the system will move the edited record to the save file, assign it a save number, and execute the command you entered. See more on saving records below.
- *Move record*: In addition to the Main Display, in which the record that you view on the screen at any given moment is stored, there is also a Copy Display area in which a bibliographic or authority record can be stored temporarily.

If you choose "move record," the system will move the edited record from the Main Display to the Copy Display and execute the command you entered. The edited record will remain stored in the Copy Display until it is recalled or you log off the session. You can do as many searches in the Authority File or the Online Union Catalog as you wish before returning to the Copy Display. You can even take final actions on another record while the first record remains in the Copy Display. You retrieve the first record from the Copy Display by entering TOG. You can move the edited record back to the Copy Display and redisplay the record in the Main Display also by entering TOG. You can toggle back

Figure 8–12 Move record display

```
[goul,ste,j¶                        ¶ CAT      MOD    SID: 00000          OL
You have a modified record in the Main Display. Select one of the following:
▶hlp ▶cancel "Find" ▶remove record ▶save record ▶move record              ¶
OLUC an #11814391                                    Record 1 of 1
HELD BY IAY - 1751 OTHER HOLDINGS
   OCLC: 11814391         Rec stat:  c
   Entered: 19850226      Replaced:  19920615      Used:  19960614
▶ Type: a    ELvl:       Srce:       Audn:       Ctrl:       Lang: eng
   BLvl: m    Form:       Conf: 0     Biog:       MRec:       Ctry: nyu
              Cont: b     GPub:       Fict: 0     Indx: 1
   Desc: a    Ills: a     Fest: 0     DtSt: s     Dates: 1985, ¶
▶  1    010         85-4916//r90 ¶
▶  2    040         DLC ‡c DLC ‡d UKM ¶
▶  3    015         GB87-53072 ¶
▶  4    019         17265421 ¶
▶  5    020         0393022285 : ‡c $17.95 ¶
▶  6    050 00      QH81 ‡b .G673 1985 ¶
▶  7    080         59:576.12 ¶
▶  8    082 00      508 |2 19 ¶
▶  9    090         ‡b ¶
▶ 10    049         XXXM ¶
▶ 11    100 1       Gould, Stephen Jay. ¶
▶ 12    245 14      The flamingo's smile : ‡b reflections in natural history / ‡c
Stephen Jay Gould. ¶
```

and forth between the Copy Display and the Main Display as many times as you wish.

When you move a record into the Copy Display, the system displays a lowercase "C" among the system messages at the top of the screen. It remains there while you proceed with other transactions to remind you that you still have a record stored in the Copy Display. When you toggle back to the Copy Display, the display changes the lowercase C to a capital C. As long as a record is stored in the Copy Display, one or the other C will display among the system messages: a capital C when you are in the Copy Display, a lowercase C when you are in the Main Display.

The edited record will remain in the Copy Display until such time as it is removed or the session is logged off. Only one record at a time can reside in the Copy Display. If you attempt to move a second record into the Copy Display when a record is already present there, you will receive the display visible in Figure 8–13.

At this point you can either cancel this command, toggle back to the Copy Display, take some final action on the edited record and enter your new search again, or you can select one of the listed actions. The system will take that action and then proceed with your new command.

A record can be removed from the Copy Display by deleting it or by replacing it with a different record. Once some final action, such as update or produce, has been taken on it, the Move Record command will automatically replace the record in the Copy Display with another.

You can move a record directly into the Copy Display, bypassing having to go through the prompt screen in Figure 8–12. To do this type 'MRD' <SEND>. A record does not have to have been edited to be moved into the Copy Display. You can store any bibliographic or authority record there that you wish.

If you have modified a record but then decide that you do not wish to proceed any further, you can remove the record directly, rather than from the "Remove record" prompt in Figure 8–12 by using the following command. Combine the return and remove commands by typing 'ret;rem' and pressing <SEND>. The system will unedit and remove the record and return to a blank screen.

LOCK AND REPLACE

Although you can edit a record as extensively as you like for your own local use, the edits that you make are not retained by the master record. OCLC realizes that in order to maintain the Online Union Catalog in as accurate, complete, and up-to-date a condition as possible, it is also necessary to allow for the modification of master records.

In addition to running many automated maintenance programs designed to correct errors and modernize headings in the database, OCLC has also established guidelines under which individual libraries may modify master records in the Online Union Catalog. The enhance program was mentioned briefly above, but it is an option that is not available to many. There are, however, a number of other situations in which libraries that merely possess full authorization, rather than enhance authorization, may revise master records. Some of these situations can be described briefly as follows:

Figure 8–13 Record already in Copy Display

```
[goul,ste,j¶                        ¶ CAT      MOD    SID: 00000         OL
You have a modified record in the Main Display. Select one of the following:
▸hlp ▸cancel "Find" ▸remove record ▸save record ¶
OLUC an #11814391                   Record 1 of 1
HELD BY IAY - 1751 OTHER HOLDINGS
   OCLC: 11814391          Rec stat:  c
   Entered: 19850226       Replaced:  19920615      Used:  19960614
 ▸ Type: a      ELvl:      Srce:        Audn:       Ctrl:        Lang: eng
   BLvl: m      Form:      Conf: 0      Biog:       MRec:        Ctry: nyu
                Cont: b    GPub:        Fict: 0     Indx: 1
   Desc: a      Ills: a    Fest: 0      DtSt: s     Dates: 1985, ¶
▸ 1   010         85-4916//r90 ¶
▸ 2   040         DLC ǂc DLC ǂd UKM ¶
▸ 3   015         GB87-53072 ¶
▸ 4   019         17265421 ¶
▸ 5   020         0393022285 : ǂc $17.95 ¶
▸ 6   050 00      QH81 ǂb .G673 1985 ¶
▸ 7   080         59:576.12 ¶
▸ 8   082 00      508 ǂ2 19 ¶
▸ 9   090         ǂb ¶
▸ 10  049         XXXM ¶
▸ 11  100 1       Gould, Stephen Jay. ¶
▸ 12  245 14      The flamingo's smile : ǂb reflections in natural history / ǂc
Stephen Jay Gould. ¶
```

1. Upgrading a minimal-level catalog record to a full-level catalog record.
2. Upgrading a CIP (Cataloging-in-Publication) record.
3. Enriching a record by adding subject headings, a call number, or a contents note.
4. Revising a catalog record that your own institution has input and that no other institution has yet placed their holdings on.

For more information you should see OCLC's *Cataloging User Guide*. However, as it is probable that most libraries will wish to avail themselves of one or more of the above opportunities at some time, it is important that anyone who inputs into OCLC understand the basic principals of editing master records.

To modify a master record one "locks" the record that one wishes to alter, makes the necessary edits, and then "replaces" the current master record with the version you have modified.

When you lock a record you are able to access the master record directly. Any edits that you then make, provided you have the proper authorization, modify the master record permanently. In order to avoid the confusion that might result if two different libraries were trying to edit the same master record at the same time, a given record can be locked by only one institution at a time. If you attempt to lock a record that has already been locked, the system responds:

```
Record locked by another user
```

To lock a record, first retrieve the record you wish to replace. Type 'loc' and press <SEND>. The system responds:

```
Record locked
```

If you know the OCLC control number of the record you wish to lock, you can retrieve and lock the record with one command. You need only type 'loc [OCLC control number]' and press <SEND>. The system will retrieve the record and lock it. Once a record has been locked, "LOC" displays in the upper right hand corner of the screen to the left of the session ID number. It continues to display there to remind you as long as the record is locked.

If you wish to edit a master record, you must lock the record before doing any editing. Until you lock the record, you are merely accessing a working copy of the master record, not the master record itself. For the same reason, you cannot lock a record that has been edited. Edits cannot be carried from a working copy to the master record. You must edit the master record directly. If you have begun to edit a record and then decide that you want to lock it, you will have to unedit it before you can lock it.

After you have made whatever edits to the locked record that you wish, in order for the edits to remain on the master record, it is necessary to use the replace command. When you use the replace command, the system replaces the old form of the master record with the edited form you have created and unlocks the record. The master record is once again available to others to edit. It also adds your library's OCLC symbol in a subfield d of the 040 field and changes the date in the "replaced" display at the top of the record. Anyone looking at the record will be able to tell the date that it was last revised.

To execute the replace command, type 'rep' in the home position and press <SEND>. Before executing the replace command, make absolutely certain that everything is as you want it. If you are upgrading a record from minimal level to full-level, unless you have enhance authorization, once you have replaced the master record you will not be able to go back and re-edit it. Similarly, any fields that you are adding to a record already at full level will not be available for revision once you have replaced the master record.

Using the replace command affects the master record only. OCLC does create an archive record for the transaction for your institution but it cannot be used to create a catalog record for your library. Once you have replaced the record you still need to take some final action—such as update or produce—in order to create a local catalog record.

Anyone with a higher authorization than Search can lock a record. Being able to lock a record, however, does not necessarily mean that one is able to replace it. That may require a higher authorization level. There is obviously no reason to lock a record if you cannot ultimately replace it. Since only one institution at a time can lock a record, locking a record prevents others from editing it and improving the OCLC database for as long as it remains locked. If you lock a record and then realize that you will not be able to modify the master record as you first thought, you can unlock or "release" the record so that others will once again be able to modify it.

To execute the release command, with the locked record on the screen, type 'rel' in the home position and press <SEND>. The system responds:

```
Record released
```

If you have already made any edits to the locked record, they will not be lost. They will remain on the working copy of the master record that remains on the screen after you have released the record. You can then proceed with the inputting process.

You can place a locked record in the save file just as you would any other bibliographic record. The record will stay locked as long as it remains in the save file. Once again, as long as you keep the record locked, no one else will be able to revise it. You should complete any work on locked records as quickly as possible so as not to prevent others from being able to revise them themselves.

9 ENTERING NEW RECORDS

This chapter presents a basic overview of some of the options available for inputting new master records into OCLC using PRISM.

CHOOSING AN ENCODING LEVEL

One of the first decisions that must be made after it has been determined that a new record needs to be entered into the Online Union Catalog is the encoding level that it will be assigned. There are a large number of different possible encoding levels that are validated within OCLC-MARC. The different levels indicate differing levels of complexity of bibliographic information and means by which that information was input into the OCLC system. A complete list of the possible encoding levels and their meanings is contained in OCLC's *Bibliographic Formats and Standards*.

Despite the large number of valid encoding levels, however, there are only two that are available for use to most inputters: K and I. K indicates a less-than-full or minimal level bibliographic record. I indicates a full-level catalog record as input by a non national level library.

The I "full level" record is the level most commonly applied at most libraries and the encoding level generally preferred when inputting, but there are nonetheless occasions when entering a K "minimal level" record is the appropriate thing to do.

No one can be conversant with all aspects of cataloging. Most large cataloging departments will try to divide their cataloging amongst people with different expertises. Smaller cataloging departments do not always have that luxury. In a position where one simply has to catalog an item with which one does not feel particularly comfortable—whether for reasons of language, format, subject matter, or whatever—there is nothing wrong with inputting it as a K level record. That way it will be much simpler for someone with a greater expertise in that area to review your work and upgrade and replace the record if necessary. If you input such an item as an I level record, only those relative few who have enhance status within the appropriate format will be able to modify and improve it.

You also need to be aware if your institution has any policies or guidelines governing the selection of encoding level in specific situations.

OCLC's *Concise Input Standards* lists guidelines for the completeness of cataloging required to be eligible for each encoding level when inputting new records into OCLC. For a record to be assigned a full-level encoding level it must meet the relevant guidelines. You need to be careful not to assign your record a higher encoding level than it is entitled.

MARK FOR TRANSFER

With PRISM, even if one needs to input an original record, there are still a number of labor saving devices that can be used to diminish the amount of typing, with its attendant potential for typographic errors, that is required.

One such option that is available is to "mark" data for transfer from a pre-existent record to a new one. With this command, you can "mark" as many fields as you want on a record in the Online Union Catalog and, by executing a command, carry them over into a new master record without having to do any keying in.

The clearest case of when to use the mark-for-transfer option is if you find a record for a different edition of the work you are inputting. Most of the cataloging information available on the record already in the Online Union Catalog will probably still be valid for the newer edition. By transferring fields into the new record, you may be able to avoid almost all keying in of new data. Another instance when Mark for transfer might be a valid option is if you find a record for another volume in the same series as the one you are inputting, provided your library does not already have a "constant data record" (see below) for inputting numbers of this series.

There are no exact guidelines as to when to apply the mark-for-transfer option. It is up to the individual inputter to decide when there is enough data in common between the existing record and the one you wish to create to make its application worthwhile.

To transfer data, first call up the record you want to mark for transfer and type 'mft' <SEND>. The display will not alter except that some of the fields will change to reverse video and the word "Marking" will display in the system messages to the left of the session ID number.

Those fields which are in reverse video are those that have been "marked" to be transferred to the new record. Those that are not will not be transferred without further effort. The system automatically marks for transfer all variable fields between 100 and 830. You can select additional fields for transfer or deselect fields you do not want to transfer by marking individual lines. To do this, from the home position, type the individual line number or numbers, separated by commas or a hyphen, and then press <SEND>. The system will respond:

```
"Text marked."
```

For example, you can mark lines three through five either by typing '3,4,5', or '3-5' from the home position.

To mark the fixed field type 'ff' and press <SEND>.

You can combine mark and unmark commands in one. Thus if line six represented a 090 (call number) field that you wanted to transfer and line 10 a 250 (edition) field that you did not want to transfer, you would type 'ff,6,10.' The system will mark for transfer the fixed field and the 090 field and unmark the 250 field.

After marking and unmarking whichever lines you wish, redisplay the record ('rds' <SEND>). The lines you have selected for marking should now be highlighted and those you deselected should no longer be. Once you have the record in the form you wish, type 'new' and press <SEND>. The system creates a new master record workform incorporating all the fields you have marked. Any further editing can then be completed in the ordinary manner.

One recent enhancement to PRISM is the ability to transfer data to records that are in a different format than the original. Say you have a new edition of an atlas and you find a record in the Online Union Catalog for a previous edition that is in books format. Since the initiation of Format Integration part 2 atlases are to be cataloged within the maps format. You can now use that books format record to transfer data to the new maps format record. To do this, first mark fields for transfer as usual. Type 'new' plus the command that you would use in requesting a blank workform within the new format. In this case type 'new wfme' and press <SEND>.

If you choose to use mark-for-transfer to create new records, you must be careful to edit all those fields that need it. The greatest danger in using the mark-for-transfer option lies in forgetting to edit some field that has been transferred. You must be extra careful and make certain that you have edited publication date, pagination, or any other field that has been transferred where the information in the new record differs from that of the source record.

CONSTANT DATA

One of the best labor saving devices available within PRISM is the ability to create and utilize Constant Data records. By means of Constant Data records, you can save commonly used bibliographic data and use it whenever needed. With Constant Data, not merely can you save yourself considerable inputting time, you can also assure that the data is input the same way every time, thereby cutting down on typographic errors and subsequent maintenance work. As much or as little information as is needed can be stored in the Constant Data record and it can be applied both to pre-existent records and to original workforms.

Prior to PRISM, it was possible on some OCLC terminals to program a limited number of function keys of finite length with data—generally single commonly used fields. Constant Data records are superior in that they are unlimited in both number and, within reason, length. They also do not have to be entered on each terminal individually. OCLC stores the Constant Data records for each institution within the system. They are available on any terminal to anyone who possesses the proper authorization number for your library. A complete list of Constant Data records for use at your institution is available in the Constant Data Information List. It is accessible by entering 'cdi' and pressing <SEND> while in the Online Union Catalog. Figure 9–1 is a sample list.

To view the contents of an individual Constant Data record, type the line number and press <SEND> or simply move the cursor down to the appropriate line and press <SEND>.

In the example in Figure 9–2, the library has created a Constant Data record to assist in the inputting of catalog records for theses granted by their institution. Those fields or portions of fields that are the same on every thesis catalog record have been included here.

A Constant Data record is stored under a name assigned by its creator. In order to make use of it, it is necessary to know that name. If you do not know, or cannot remember the name of the record you wish to use, you can use the 'Cdi' command to find it. Once you know the name, call up the record to which you wish to apply the Constant Data. This can be either a pre-existent bib-

Figure 9–1   Constant Data List

```
                              ¶ CAT          SID: 00000          OL

   Entire list displayed.

   Constant Data List                              Records: 19
            Name           FMT           Date Modified

 ▶    1¶    01SCI          bks           19911210
 ▶    2¶    02MATH         bks           19911210
 ▶    3¶    03REF          bks           19911210
 ▶    4¶    04ART          bks           19911210
 ▶    5¶    05QAMAIN       bks           19911210
 ▶    6¶    11PER          ser           19920130
 ▶    7¶    AUD            rec           19931110
 ▶    8¶    AUDCD          rec           19960403
 ▶    9¶    JOE            vis           19931013
 ▶   10¶    MICR           bks           19960612
 ▶   11¶    PELICANA       bks           19940119
 ▶   12¶    PELICANO       bks           19960103
 ▶   13¶    SOUND          rec           19950923
 ▶   14¶    SPANSKYC       vis           19940404
 ▶   15¶    T92            bks           19930729
 ▶   16¶    T93            bks           19960515
 ▶   17¶    THESIS         bks           19960104
 ▶   18¶    VIDEO          vis           19960329
```

liographic record or a blank workform. It is necessary to specify what kind of fields you wish the Constant Data record to add. If the Constant Data record contains only modifications to the fixed field, enter 'acd [CD Name] fix' <SEND>. If the Constant Data record contains only modifications to the variable fields enter 'acd [CD Name] var' <SEND>. Finally if the Constant Data record contains data in both kinds of fields enter 'acd [CD Name] both' <SEND>. In the above example, you would type 'acd thesis both' and press <SEND>.

The Constant Data record will overlay the information for every non-repeatable field it contains, add a new line for every repeatable field it contains, and automatically send the new information. It is not necessary to "send" any lines on your record after applying Constant Data. The usual system rules for overlaying lines based on line number, which was a potential problem in using cut, copy, and paste with PASSPORT, is also not a prob-

---

Figure 9–2   Constant Data Record

```
                                    ¶ CAT      C       MOD  SID: 00000    OL
Entire record displayed.

CD

▸  Constant data name: THESIS
   Entered:  19960104    Replaced:  19960104
   Type: a      ELvl: L     Srce: d    Audn:      Ctrl:    Lang: eng
   BLvl: m      Form:       Conf: 0    Biog: 0    MRec:    Ctry: xxu
                Cont: b     GPub:      Fict: 1    Indx: 0
   Desc: a      Ills: a     Fest: 0    DtSt: s    Dates: 1990,       ¶
▸  1  099      THESIS ‡a 1990 ‡b nnn ¶
▸  2  090      ‡b ¶
▸  3  049      XXXM ¶
▸  4  260 1    ‡c 1990. ¶
▸  5  300      leaves : ‡b ill ; ‡c 29 cm. ¶
▸  6  533      Typescript (photocopy). ¶
▸  7  502      Thesis (Ph. D.)—Central Plains University, 1990. ¶
▸  8  500      Vita. ¶
▸  9  504      Bibliography: leaves nnn-nnn. ¶
▸ 10  590      Library has: 3 copies. ¶
```

lem here. Line four, for example, in the above example, would not overlay line four of a bibliographic record it was applied to. It would be added in accord with OCLC system controls over the ordering of tag numbers and all lines would be renumbered as necessary. In those cases where there is a field present on the record being added to, that is within the same tag group as a field being added from Constant Data, the new field will be added after those fields already present. In those cases where the Constant Data record contains a non-repeatable field, it will automatically overwrite that field regardless of line number.

To create a Constant Data record you must first be in the Online Union Catalog. Enter 'cho ol' <SEND> if necessary. To request a blank workform, you must include both a format and a name in your command. The commands take the form of cd [format] [name]. For format, supply the same term as if you were requesting a blank bibliographic workform within that format. For name, supply a name that relates to the content of the record and that is easy to remember. Since it is necessary to know the Constant Data name in order to use the record, it is best to choose as simple and relevant a name as possible. Thus, if you wanted to create a Constant Data record to assist in the inputting of theses, such as the one in Figure 9–2, you would call up a blank workform by typing 'cd wfm thesis' and pressing <SEND>.

Input your Constant Data information exactly as if you were inputting a new bibliographic record. When you have input as much information as you wish, save the record by typing 's' and pressing <SEND>. If you assign it a name that has already been used, you will receive the error message "Constant Data record name already exists." Type a new name over the name you attempted to use and try to save it again. You should receive the message "Constant Data record saved." Unlike the bibliographic save file, there is no time limit on the Constant Data record save file. Records will remain there until they have been deleted.

To edit a Constant Data record, use the command 'ecd [CD Name]' to call up the record. Thus, to edit the record in Figure 9–2, you would type 'ecd thesis' and press <SEND>. Once the record has been accessed, you can edit it just as you would any bibliographic record.

ORIGINAL INPUTTING

If you cannot find a bibliographic record in the Online Union Catalog that matches the item which you are cataloging and you also cannot find a record with enough information in common to make using mark-for-transfer worthwhile, you must request a blank workform for inputting a new record. Blank workforms are available for each MARC format. To request a workform, type the command 'wf[format code of workform desired]' and press <SEND>. Thus, to request a blank workform for a monograph, you type 'wfm' and press <SEND>. Figure 9–3 contains a list of all workforms available listed by format, with commands for retrieving each one.

Figure 9–4 illustrates how a blank monographic workform appears.

The blank workform serves as a template to assist you in inputting. The fixed field and a representative collection of empty variable fields, complete with subfields, from all the major tag groups are displayed. This spares you the time-consuming effort of having to create all the lines on a workform yourself. Blank spaces or "fill characters" guide you to the proper place for locating elements in the fixed field and indicators in the variable

Figure 9–3	Workform commands	
	WORKFORM	COMMAND
	Books	wfm
	Print serials	wfs
	Visual materials	wfmg
	Mixed materials	wfmp
	Maps	wfme
	Scores	wfmc
	Sound recordings	wfmj
	Computer files	wfmm

fields. Those fixed field elements that display as fill characters in the workform must be assigned valid values before the system will accept the record. Other fixed field elements, in order to simplify editing, are filled in with their most commonly used values as default characters. They may be accepted as is or altered to other values as required.

You may edit the blank workform just as you would any other bibliographic record. You may use Constant Data, cut, copy, and paste, and full-screen editing to save on keystrokes while inputting. You can either ignore those blank lines that contain fields that are not needed or you can type over them any fields that are needed, but for which no empty lines are provided. The latter method will save you the trouble of creating new lines.

Any empty line that has not been used will be automatically deleted when you reformat the record. The same is also true when you save the record. In order to get the most value from the labor saving aspects of the many empty fields provided for you by blank workforms, you should avoid reformatting or saving new records until at least most, if not all, of your inputting has been completed.

Figure 9–4 Blank monographic workform

```
                                    ¶ CAT       SID: 00000            OL
   Beginning of record displayed.

   OLUC
     OCLC: NEW            Rec stat:    n
     Entered:   19960619  Replaced:  19960619   Used:    19960619
  ▸  Type: a   Elvl: █     Srce: █    Audn:       Ctrl:       Lang: █ █ █
     Blvl: m   Form:      Conf: 0    Biog        Mrec:       Ctry: █ █ █
               Cont:      Gpub:      Fict: 0     Indx: 0
     Desc: █   Ills:      Fest: 0    DtSt: █     Dates: █ █ █ █,  ¶
  ▸  1   010        ¶
  ▸  2   040        ‡c XXX ¶
  ▸  3   020        ¶
  ▸  4   041 █      ‡h ‡b ¶
  ▸  5   050 █      ‡b ¶
  ▸  6   090        ‡b ¶
  ▸  7   049        XXXM ¶
  ▸  8   1█ █ █     ¶
  ▸  9   245 █ █    ‡b ‡c ¶
  ▸ 10   246 █ █    ¶
  ▸ 11   250        ¶
  ▸ 12   260        ‡b ‡c ¶
  ▸ 13   300        ‡b ‡c ¶
```

```
                                    ¶ CAT       SID: 00000            OL
   End of record displayed.

   OLUC

  ▸ 14    4█ █  █ █ ¶
  ▸ 15    5█ █  █   ¶
  ▸ 16    6█ █  █ █ ¶
  ▸ 17    6█ █  █ █ ¶
  ▸ 18    7█ █  █   ¶
  ▸ 19    8█ █  █ █ ¶
```

10 FINAL ACTIONS

Once you have finished either editing a bibliographic record or inputting a new record, you must still take some final action upon what you have done for your work to be preserved. By either updating or producing the record, you can create a catalog record for your library. Alternatively, you may choose to store your work and wait to complete it at some future date. To do this you must place your edited record in the save file.

SAVING A RECORD

It is not necessary to complete all your work on a bibliographic record or workform in one session. You can suspend work temporarily by placing the record into the OCLC save file and resume work at a later time. Make certain that all your changes have been sent to the system before you save the record. Changes to any field not sent will not be recorded and will not be present on the record when you call it up later.

To place your record into the save file, type 'save' and press <SEND> or simply 's' <SEND> from the home position. The system responds:

```
Bibliographic record saved under [number]
```

The number, which will be between 1 and 9,999, indicates the record's place within the OCLC save file. Be sure to record this number in some place where you will be able to find it again later. You will need it to retrieve the record at a later time.

When you are ready to resume work, you can call up the record by typing '/[save number]' <SEND>. Thus if the record was saved under no. 7,445, enter '/7445' and press <SEND>, and you will access your record again. Unlike OCLC bibliographic records, the saved record can be accessed by only one terminal at a time, so if you are using it, it is inaccessible to any other user. Any user attempting to access a record already in use will receive the message:

```
Record in use by another user
```

When you recall a saved record it is lodged in the Main Display. The characters "mod" in small letters appear to the left of the session ID number to remind you that you are looking at an edited record. Until recently it was necessary to either resave the record or move it to the Copy Display before proceeding with any other transaction. A recent enhancement to PRISM has changed this. Retrieving a saved record is now no different than retrieving any other bibliographic record. You may move the record to the Copy Display or proceed with another transaction as desired. If you do not move the saved record to the Copy Display before you enter another command, you will have to call it up again by its save number if you wish to return to it.

If you make any new edits to the saved record after retrieving it, the "mod" at the top of the display changes to capital letters indicating that the record has been modified since it was last saved. It then does become necessary to move the record to the Copy Display or resave it before proceeding. Once you resave the record, "mod" will be displayed once again in small letters when you reretrieve it.

The record can be resaved as many times as necessary and still retain the same save number. If, however, any final action is taken on the record, such as updating or producing on it, it is automatically deleted from the save file. If the record is then resaved it will be assigned a new save number.

THE SAVE FILE

If you forget to write down the save number you can still retrieve the saved record by looking at the Save File Information List. The Save File Infomation List is a listing of all the records currently placed in your institution's save file. To access the Save File Information List type 'si' and press <SEND>. You will see a display that looks like Figure 10–1.

The phrase "RECORDS: [no.]" that displays in the upper right-hand corner refers to the number of records currently stored in the individual institution's save file. In this instance there are 117 records in the save file.

You can navigate through the list a page at a time by using either PDN, PUP or FOR, BAC or you can move to a specific spot in the list by specifying the number of lines to move forward or back. If, for instance, in searching for a saved record, you use the 'si' command and determine that there are 143 records in the

---

Figure 10–1   Save File Information List

```
                              ¶ CAT                SID: 00000        OL

Save File Information                              Records: 117
           OCLC #    Title                FMT   First      Last      Age  P
 ▶ 9113¶   34243747  An introduction to the history   bks   19960604   19960612   8   y
 ▶ 9165¶        NEW  World cement. Bulk materials h    ser   19960605   19960614   6   y
 ▶ 9169¶        NEW  Konzert-Rondo in form von Vari    sco   19960605   19960614   6   y
 ▶ 9178¶   16708016  Champaign-Urbana street map /     map   19960606   19960619   1   y
 ▶ 9184¶   30519378  Peoria and vicinity /             map   19960606   19960619   1   y
 ▶ 9189¶        NEW  Bloomington - Normal street ma    map   19960606   19960619   1   y
 ▶ 9190¶   32349489  Making gender work : managing     bks   19960606   19960607  13   y
 ▶ 9192¶   30941865  Springfield, Illinois : includ    map   19960606   19960619   1   y
 ▶ 9204¶        NEW  DeKalb, Sycamore, Rochelle, Il    map   19960606   19960619   1   y
 ▶ 9211¶   27657108  Fox River Valley /                map   19960606   19960619   1   y
 ▶ 9215¶   28214143  La batalla de las vâirgenes /     bks   19960606   19960606  14   n
 ▶ 9217¶   19658751  The religion of the Veda = Die    bks   19960607   19960607  13   y
 ▶ 9221¶   29909016  Virginia Peninsula : including    map   19960607   19960619   1   y
 ▶ 9232¶        NEW  West Houston /                    map   19960607   19960619   1   y
 ▶ 9238¶        NEW  F.I.E.P. bulletin : journal of    ser   19960607   19960614   6   y
 ▶ 9261¶   25832164  Calamity of the realm /           bks   19960610   19960610  10   y
 ▶ 9279¶   33280704  Inside Visual C++ : the standa    bks   19960610   19960610  10   n
 ▶ 9294¶        NEW  Research Service bibliographie    ser   19960611   19960617   3   y
 ▶ 9301¶   34774520  Middle East wastewater managem    bks   19960612   19960612   8   y
```

save file, and if you just recently placed the record in the save file and are therefore certain it must be near the end of the list, you can move immediately to the final screen by typing in the total number of records in the save file. In this instance one would type in 'for 143' and press <SEND>.

In addition to being useful in finding individual save records, the Save File Information List also contains much useful information about the status of the save file and the records contained in it.

The display at the top of the screen consists of the following columns.

Save file number: The left most column contains the save file number. As each record enters the save file it is assigned a number. Records are numbered consecutively from 1 to 9,999 and then begin over again at 1. When you access the Save File Information List, remember that the save records are displayed in strict numerical rather than chronological order. If the save file numbering has recently turned over and started again at 1, the latest records to be saved will not be at the end of the list.

OCLC number: The next column displays the OCLC control number of the saved record. If the record represents original input that has not yet been added to the Online Union Catalog, "NEW" is displayed in this column.

Title: Title gives the beginning of the title field of the saved record to assist in identifying each record while viewing the list.

Format: FMT refers to the MARC format of the saved record.

First and Last: The next two columns refer to dates. First indicates the date the record was initially placed in the save file. Last indicates the last date the record was resaved. If the record has not been resaved the dates will be the same. Records will remain in the save file for 14 days, not counting the date of input. If by that point the record has not been resaved, it is automatically deleted from the save file. If at any point the record is resaved, another 14 days is granted from that date. A record may be resaved as many times as desired.

Age: The next column indicates how many days it has been since the record was last resaved. The Save File Information List should be checked regularly and any saved records approaching the 14-day limit should be resaved.

P: P refers to whether the record was initially saved in prime-time or not. System charges for producing or updating a record are determined from the time when the record was initially saved rather than the time final action on it was taken. The Save File Information List indicates yes or no whether the record was initially saved in prime time.

Once you find the save record you wish to access, you can retrieve it either in the ordinary way or by moving the cursor down to the beginning of the desired line and pressing <SEND>.

A recent enhancement to PRISM makes it possible to move forward and back through the records in the save file without having to return to the Save File Information List between each one. The procedure works just like moving forward and back between records within a truncated display in the bibliographic file. After you use the 'si' command and have retrieved a record you can use the FOR and BAC commands just as you would there.

If you decide at any time to remove a record that you have placed in the save file, you can delete it by calling up the record, typing 'del' and pressing <SEND> from the home position.

VALIDATING RECORDS

The validation of records should always be part of the cataloging process. The validation command checks bibliographic records for a wide variety of possible errors in inputting. The errors it seeks, however, are format rather than content related. The system looks to make sure that the assigning of tags, indicators and subfields in the various fields has been done correctly. It cannot, however, evaluate the content of these fields. There is no spellcheck or any other function designed to judge the quality of the data being submitted. The only fields where the system will check content are those where the possible correct entries represent a finite set of values such as the components of the fixed field or the 043 field.

The most opportune time to validate a record is just before taking final action on it. In this way the system can validate your entire work before you submit it to the system. To validate a record, type 'val' and press <SEND>. If the system detects no errors it will respond with the message:

```
Record Validated.
```

If the system detects any errors it displays a message similar to the one shown in Figure 10–2.

The message indicates the total number of errors detected and displays information about the first of them. In Figure 10–2, the message indicates that the fixed field contains an invalid value for country of publication. To see a description of the next error, type FOR. In Figure 10–3, the message now indicates that line 11 contains an invalid indicator. Continue to type 'FOR' as many times as necessary to see all the listed errors.

When you exercise the validate command, the system validates the entire record—not just the part that you have edited. It is quite possible for the system to discover and report an error that was already present on the record even if you have not edited that field.

Correct the errors by editing the record as usual. When you believe you have fixed all the errors, validate the record again to make certain. When you receive the "Record Validated" message you are ready to take final action on your record.

Even if you do not validate your cataloging record, if you have edited any part of it other than the 049 (local holdings) field, when you try to produce or update it, the system will automatically validate it anyway. It will display error messages in precisely the

---

Figure 10–2   Error screen no. 1

```
                               ¶ CAT          MOD    SID: 07953      OL
Error 1 of 2: Fixed fields: Invalid code in Ctry

OLUC  an #11814391                    Record 1 of 1
HELD BY XXX - 1751 OTHER HOLDINGS
  OCLC:  11814391        Rec stat:  c
  Entered:  19850226     Replaced:  19920615  Used:  19960614
▶ Type: a      ELvl:      Srce:      Audn:    Ctrl:      Lang: eng
  BLvl: m      Form:      Conf: 0    Biog:    MRec:      Ctry: nzu
               Cont: b    GPub:      Fict: 0  Indx: 1
  Desc: a      Ills: a    Fest: 0    DtSt: s  Dates: 1985,   ¶
▶  1  010          85-4916//r90 ¶
▶  2  040          DLC ‡c DLC ‡d UKM ¶
▶  3  015          GB87-53072 ¶
▶  4  019          17265421 ¶
▶  5  020          0393022285 : ‡c $17.95 ¶
▶  6  050  00      QH81 ‡b .G673 1985 ¶
▶  7  080          59:576.12 ¶
▶  8  082  00      508 ‡2 19 ¶
▶  9  090          ‡b  ¶
▶ 10  049          XXXM ¶
▶ 11  100  10      Gould, Stephen Jay. ¶
▶ 12  245  14      The flamingo's smile : ‡b reflections in natural
history / ‡c  Stephen Jay Gould. ¶
```

---

same way it does when the validate command is intentionally exercised and the errors can be dealt with in exactly the same way. If all you have edited is the 049 field in order to add your holdings to OCLC, the system will not automatically validate the record.

UPDATE AND PRODUCE

There are two different commands with which a transaction may be completed and a local catalog record created. Which one to choose is dependent on the nature of the contract your institution has with OCLC. Put succinctly, if your institution is still producing catalog cards, you will probably want to conclude your trans-

---

Figure 10–3   Error screen no. 2

```
                                      ¶ CAT          MOD    SID: 07953      OL
Error 2 of 2: Line 11: Invalid code in 100, Ind 2

OLUC  an #11814391                                        Record 1 of 1

HELD BY XXX - 1751 OTHER HOLDINGS
   OCLC:  11814391          Rec stat:  c
   Entered:  19850226       Replaced:  19920615 Used:       19960614
▸ Type: a      ELvl:        Srce:       Audn:       Ctrl:       Lang: eng
   BLvl: m      Form:        Conf: 0     Biog:       MRec:       Ctry: nzu
                Cont: b      GPub:       Fict: 0     Indx: 1
   Desc: a      Ills: a      Fest: 0     DtSt: s     Dates:1985,      ¶
▸  1  010          85-4916//r90 ¶
▸  2  040          DLC ‡c DLC ‡d UKM ¶
▸  3  015          GB87-53072 ¶
▸  4  019          17265421 ¶
▸  5  020          0393022285 : ‡c $17.95 ¶
▸  6  050  00      QH81 ‡b .G673 1985 ¶
▸  7  080          59:576.12 ¶
▸  8  082  00      508 ‡2 19 ¶
▸  9  090          ‡b  ¶
▸ 10  049          XXXM ¶
▸ 11  100  10      Gould, Stephen Jay. ¶
▸ 12  245  14      The flamingo's smile : ‡b reflections in natural
history / ‡c  Stephen Jay Gould. ¶
```

action by using the produce command. If your institution is no longer creating catalog cards, you will probably want to use the update command.

When you use the update command, the system first automatically validates the record. If the record is original, it then adds it to the Online Union Catalog. If you have only edited a record already present in the Online Union Catalog, it adds your symbol to the list of OCLC holdings associated with that record. It also creates an OCLC-MARC subscription record in accordance with your contract with OCLC. The update command will *not* create catalog cards. If you wish catalog cards to be created, you must use the produce command. To update a record, type 'u' and press <SEND>. The system responds with:

```
Record updated.
```

When you use the produce command, the system procedes as it does when you use the update command, plus it produces cards in accordance with your institution's card profile with OCLC. If your institution has no card profile with OCLC, then cards will not be created by the produce command. If your library has no card profile, there is essentially no difference between using the update and produce commands. To produce a record, type 'p' and press <SEND>. The system responds:

```
Record produced.
```

EXERCISE 4

Record Content Exercise

While the following examples give you an opportunity to practice your searching skills, they are designed primarily to help you become more familiar with the format of bibliographic records in OCLC's Online Union Catalog. The questions emphasize record content. Answer them carefully and completely and include the tags, indicators, and subfields in your answers where appropriate. You can refer to the abridged list of variable field tags in the Appendix or to OCLC's *Bibliographic Formats and Standards* for assistance with the tagging.

Remember that the Online Union Catalog is a dynamic database with new and changed records added daily. While this exercise was designed to minimize the likelihood of your finding a different record than the one to which the questions apply, nothing can eliminate that possibility entirely.

A. ISBN 0-688-03076-9

1. Search key _____ OCLC # _____

2. Main entry? _____

3. What is the meaning of 240 tag? _____

4. What is the original title of the book? _____

5. Geographic subject heading? _____

_____

B. ISBN 0-679-50697-7

1. Search key _____ OCLC # _____

2. What institution input the record? _____

3. Library of Congress (LC) assigned Dewey Classification number? _____

4. Main entry? _____

5. Original cost of book? _____

6. Personal name added entry? _____

C.   ISBN 0-440-09343-0

1. Search key _____ OCLC # _____

2. LC Classification number? _____

3. Personal name subject heading? _____

4. How many pages? _____ Illustrated? _____

5. Publisher? _____

D.   LCCN 77-11689

1. Search key _____

2. Response display to the search key? _____

3. How many records in the display? _____

4. Which record was cataloged by LC? _____

When? _____ OCLC # _____

5. Main entry of LC record? _____

6. Publisher of paperback edition? _____

7. Does the LC record have more pages? _____

8. First topical subject heading on the LC record? _____

_____

E.   LCCN 76-29916

1. Search key _____

2. How many records were retrieved? _____

How many different authors? _____

3. Which record was cataloged by LC? _____

When? _____ OCLC # _____

4. What is the topical subject of the Smith work? _____

_____

5. Who published the Smith work? _____

6. Main entry of the work cataloged by the British Library? _____

_____

7. Original publisher of British work? _____

When was it originally published? _____

F. French Women of Letters

1. Search key _____

2. How many records were retrieved? _____

    How many different publishers? _____

3. Display the record cataloged by LC

    OCLC _____ Did LC input the record? __

4. LCCN? _____

5. LC Classification number? _____

    Book number? _____

6. Where was it published? _____ When? _____

7. What is the second subject? _____

    _____

G. The Earth Book of Stormgate

1. Search key _____

2. Initial display? _____ How many records? _____

3. Display the record cataloged by LC

    OCLC # _____ LCCN? _____

4. Topical subject heading? _____

    _____

5. ISBN? _____

6. Publisher? _____

    Distributor? _____

H. Kehde, Ned

1. Search key _____

2. Display the record cataloged by LC _____

    How many subjects are there? _____

3. Title proper? _____

4. LCCN? _____ OCLC # _____

5. LC assigned Dewey Classification number? _____

6. Publisher? _____

    Date of publication? _____

I. Rudkin, Ethel H.

1. Search key _____

2. Display the record cataloged by LC

    LCCN? _____ OCLC # _____

3. Pagination? _____

4. ISBN? _____

5. Edition of book? _____

    Reprinted from ed. of what year? _____

6. Geographic subject heading? _____

    _____

7. Topical subject heading? _____

    _____

EXERCISE 5

TAGGING EXERCISE

Transfer the cataloging records of the following three books onto workforms to simulate record preparation for original input into the Online Union Catalog. (Note that these full LC records are used here as examples only; they already exist as machine-readable records in OCLC.) Complete as many of the fixed field elements and variable fields as you can, using the abridged lists of fixed and variable fields in the Appendix for codes, tags, indicators, and subfields. Blank workforms follow. For this exercise use the default values provided on the workforms for tags 040 and 049.

A.

Jones, Gregory Philip.
   Government publications : a guide to Australian government publications in the Canberra College of Advanced Education Library / Gregory Jones, Colin Wills.—3rd ed.—Belconnen, A.C.T. : Canberra College of Advanced Education Library, 1981.
   i, 56 p. : ill. ; 26 cm.—(Library reference guides ; no. 2)
   Bibliography: p. 56.
   ISBN 0-85889-190-5 (pbk.) : $4.00
   1. Government publications—Australia—Bibliography—Catalogs. 2. Canberra College of Advanced Education. Library—Catalogs. I. Wills, Colin. II. Canberra College of Advanced Education. Library. III. Title. IV. Series.

Z4019.J66 1981   015.94—dc19   80-42054

B.

Special education index to parent materials.—1st ed.—Los Angeles, CA : National Information Center for Educational Media, University of Southern California, 1980.
   xvi, 214 p. ; 28 cm.
   An activity of the National Information Center for Special Education Materials.
   ISBN 0-89320-025-5 (pbk.)
   1. Handicapped children—Bibliography—Catalogs. 2. Handicapped children—Education—Bibliography—Catalogs. 3. Handicapped children—Education—Audio-visual aids—Bibliography—Catalogs. I. National Information Center for Educational Media. II. National Information Center for Special Education Materials.

Z6122.S64 1980   016.3719—dc19   79-84456

C.
International Conference on Cataloguing Principles (1961 : Paris, France)
   Report / International Conference on Cataloguing Principles, Paris, 9th-18th October, 1961 ; edited by A.H. Chaplin and Dorothy Anderson.—London : IFLA International Office for UBC, 1981.
   viii, 293 p. ; 21 cm.
   At head of title: International Federation of Library Associations and Institutions.
   Spine title: ICCP report.
   Includes bibliographical references and index.
   ISBN 0-903043-33-5 (pbk.)
   1. Cataloging—Congresses. I. Chaplin, Arthur Hugh, 1905- II. Anderson, Dorothy Pauline. III. International Federation of Library Associations and Institutions. IV. Title. V. Title: ICCP report. VI. Title: I.C.C.P. report.

Z693.A15I58   025.3—dc19   81-190444

     Upon completing the workforms, go to the terminal and input each bibliographic record. After final reformatting, get a printout of your work and then cancel your transaction. DO NOT INPUT INTO THE ONLINE UNION CATALOG—THIS IS AN EXERCISE ONLY. Remember to log on to the system in Limited Mode to prevent this from accidentally happening.

Books Tagging Form

OLUC

```
  OCLC:  NEW                    Rec stat:  n
  Entered:  19960919            Replaced:  19960919       Used:  19960919
▶ Type:  a        ELvl: ▮      Srce: ▮    Audn:        Ctrl:        Lang: ▮▮▮
  BLvl:            Form:        Conf:  0   Biog:        MRec:        Ctry: ▮▮▮
                   Cont:        GPub:      Fict:  0     Indx:  0
  Desc: ▮          Ills:        Fest:  0   DtSt: ▮      Dates: ▮▮▮▮,      ¶
▶    1    010          ¶
▶    2    040          ‡c IAY ¶
▶    3    020          ¶
▶    4    041 ▮        ‡h ‡b ¶
▶    5    050 ▮        ‡b ¶
▶    6    090          ‡b ¶
▶    7    049          IAYA ¶
▶    8    1▮▮ ▮        ¶
▶    9    245 ▮▮       ‡b ‡c ¶
▶   10    246 ▮▮       ¶
▶   11    250          ¶
▶   12    260          ‡b ‡c ¶
▶   13    300          ‡b ‡c ¶

▶   14    4▮▮ ▮▮       ‡v ¶
▶   15    5▮▮ ▮        ¶
▶   16    6▮▮ ▮▮       ¶
▶   17    6▮▮ ▮▮       ¶
▶   18    7▮▮ ▮        ¶
▶   19    8▮▮ ▮▮       ¶
```

Books Tagging Form

```
OLUC

  OCLC:  NEW                Rec stat:  n
  Entered:  19960919        Replaced:  19960919      Used:  19960919
▶ Type:  a      ELvl: ▇     Srce: ▇    Audn:        Ctrl:       Lang: ▇▇▇
  BLvl:          Form:      Conf:  0   Biog:        MRec:       Ctry: ▇▇▇
                 Cont:      GPub:      Fict:  0     Indx:  0
  Desc: ▇        Ills:      Fest:  0   DtSt: ▇      Dates: ▇▇▇▇,      ¶
▶    1    010        ¶
▶    2    040        ‡c IAY ¶
▶    3    020        ¶
▶    4    041 ▇      ‡h ‡b ¶
▶    5    050 ▇      ‡b ¶
▶    6    090        ‡b ¶
▶    7    049        IAYA ¶
▶    8    1▇▇ ▇      ¶
▶    9    245 ▇▇     ‡b ‡c ¶
▶   10    246 ▇▇     ¶
▶   11    250        ¶
▶   12    260        ‡b ‡c ¶
▶   13    300        ‡b ‡c ¶

▶   14    4▇▇ ▇▇     ‡v ¶
▶   15    5▇▇ ▇      ¶
▶   16    6▇▇ ▇▇     ¶
▶   17    6▇▇ ▇▇     ¶
▶   18    7▇▇ ▇      ¶
▶   19    8▇▇ ▇▇     ¶
```

Books Tagging Form

```
OLUC

  OCLC:  NEW                   Rec stat:  n
  Entered:  19960919           Replaced:  19960919      Used: 19960919
▶ Type: a      ELvl: ▮    Srce: ▮    Audn:       Ctrl:       Lang: ▮▮▮
  BLvl:        Form:      Conf: 0    Biog:       MRec:       Ctry: ▮▮▮
               Cont:      GPub:      Fict: 0     Indx:  0
  Desc: ▮      Ills:      Fest: 0    DtSt: ▮     Dates: ▮▮▮▮,      ¶
▶   1    010        ¶
▶   2    040        ‡c IAY ¶
▶   3    020        ¶
▶   4    041 ▮      ‡h ‡b ¶
▶   5    050 ▮      ‡b ¶
▶   6    090        ‡b ¶
▶   7    049        IAYA ¶
▶   8    1▮▮ ▮      ¶
▶   9    245 ▮▮     ‡b ‡c ¶
▶  10    246 ▮▮     ¶
▶  11    250        ¶
▶  12    260        ‡b ‡c ¶
▶  13    300        ‡b ‡c ¶

▶  14    4▮▮ ▮▮     ‡v ¶
▶  15    5▮▮ ▮      ¶
▶  16    6▮▮ ▮▮     ¶
▶  17    6▮▮ ▮▮     ¶
▶  18    7▮▮ ▮      ¶
▶  19    8▮▮ ▮▮     ¶
```

APPENDIX 1

SEARCH COMMANDS WITH INDEXED FIELDS AND SUBFIELDS

1. ONLINE UNION CATALOG

A. Search key searches

INDEX	SEARCH KEY FORMAT	COMMAND FORMAT	FIELDS INDEXED	SUBFIELDS INDEXED
LCCN	[LC control no.] including hyphen	fin ln [LC control no.] with or without hyphen	010	a,z
ISBN	[ISBN no.]	fin bn [ISBN no.]	020	a,z
ISSN	[ISSN no.] including hyphen	fin sn [ISSN no.] with or without hyphen	022	a,y,z
CODEN	cd:[CODEN no.]	fin cd [CODEN no.] or fin cd [cd:CODEN no.]	030	a,z
OCLC CONTROL NUMBER	#[Control no.] or *[Control no.]	fin an #[Control no.], fin an *[Control no.], or fin an [Control no.]	019	a
GOVERNMENT DOCUMENT NUMBER	gn:[Document no.] 1 or 2 letters followed by up to 10 digits	fin gn [Document no.] or fin gn [gn:Document no.] 1 or 2 letters, up to 10 digits; fin gn ["Document no."] or fin gn ["gn:Document no."] entire number	086	a,z
MUSIC PUBLISHER NUMBER	mn:[Publisher no.] 1 or 2 letters followed by up to 10 digits	fin mn [Publisher no.] or fin mn [mn:Publisher no.] 1 or 2 letters, up to 10 digits; fin mn ["Publisher no."] or fin mn ["mn:Publisher no."] entire number	028 262	a c

INDEX	SEARCH KEY FORMAT		COMMAND FORMAT	FIELDS INDEXED	SUBFIELDS INDEXED
PERSONAL NAME	4,3,1 4,2,1 4,1,1	4,3 4,2 4,1	fin dp 4,3,1 etc.	100 700	a a
CORPORATE NAME	=4,3,1 =4,2,1 =4,1,1	=4,3 =4,2 =4,1	fin dc =4,3,1 or fin dc 4,3,1 etc.	110 111 710 711	a,b a,b,n a,b a,b,n
NAME/TITLE	4,4 4,3 3,4 3,3	,4 ,3	fin da 4,4 etc.	1XX 240 243 245 246 740 7XX 245 240 245 only if no 1XX field	a,b,n & a a a a a; a,b,n & a; a & a
TITLE	3,2,2,1 3,2,1,1 3,1,2,1 3,1,1,1		fin dt 3,3,3,2 etc.	130 212 222 240 243 245 246 247 440 730 740 780 830	a,p a a a,p a,p a a a a a,p a t a,p

B. Keyword searches

INDEX	SEARCH COMMAND	FIELDS INDEXED	SUBFIELDS INDEXED	FIELDS INDEXED	SUBFIELDS INDEXED
AUTHOR	fin au	100	a,b,c,d,e,k,n,u,q	711	a,c,d,e,n,q
		110	a,b,c,d,e,k,n,u	770	a
		111	a,c,d,e,k,n,u,q	773	a
		400	a,b,c,d,e,q	780	a
		410	a,b,c,d,e,k,n,u	785	a
		411	a,b,c,d,e,n,q	787	a
		570	a	800	a,b,c,d,e,q,u
		700	a,b,c,d,e,q,u	810	a,b,c,d,e,n
		710	a,b,c,d,e,n	811	a,c,d,e,n,q
FREQUENCY/ REGULARITY	fin fq	310	a		
		315	a		
LANGUAGE	fin la	Fixed field	lang		
NOTES	fin nt	500	a	534	a,t
		501	a	536	a,b,c
		502	a	537	a
		504	a	538	a
		505	a,r,t	545	a
		508	a	582	a
		511	a	583	a,b,c,d,e,f h,i,j,k,l,3
		518	a		
		520	ab	753	a,b,c
		533	a,b,c,d,e,f		
PUBLISHER	fin pb	260	b,f		
		262	b		
PLACE OF PUBLICATION	fin pl	260	a		
		262	a		
		752	a,b,c,d		
REPORT NUMBER	fin rn	027	a,z		
		088	a		
		770	r,u		
		773	u		

INDEX	SEARCH COMMAND	FIELDS INDEXED	SUBFIELDS INDEXED	FIELDS INDEXED	SUBFIELDS INDEXED
SERIES	fin se	400	a,b,c,d,e,k,n p,q,t,u,v,x	762 800	a,q,s,t,x,y a,b,c,d,e,k
		410	a,b,c,d,e,k n,p,t,u,v,x	810	n,p,q,t,u,v a,b,c,d,e,k
		411	a,c,d,e,k,n p,q,t,u,v,x	811	n,p,s,t,v a,c,d,e,k,n
		440	a,b,n,p,v,x		p,q,s,t,v
		490	a,v,x	830	a,d,k,n,p,s,t,v
		760	a,q,s,t,x,y		
SUBJECT/ TITLE/ CONTENTS	fin st	034	a,b,d,e,f,g	610	a,b,c,d,e,k n,t,x,y,z
		130	a,d,g,k,n,p,s,t	611	a,c,d,e,n,q,x,y,z
		211	a	630	a,d,k,n,p,s,t,x,y,z
		212	a	650	a,b,x,y,z
		214	a	651	a,b,x,y,z
		222	a,b	652	a,x,y,z
		240	a,d,f,g,k,n,p,s	653	a
		242	a,b,n,p	700	t
		243	a,d,f,g,k,n,p,s	710	t
		245	a,b	711	t
		246	a,b,n,p	730	a,d,g,k,n,p,s,t
		247	a,b,n,p	740	a,n,p
		255	a,b,c,d,e	770	q,s,t
		400	n,p,t	773	p,s,t
		410	n,p,t	780	q,s,t
		411	n,p,t	785	q,s,t
		440	a,b,p,v	787	q,s,t
		490	a,v	800	n,p,t
		501	a	810	n,p,t
		505	a,r,t	811	p,t
		600	a,b,c,d,e,k p,q,t,x,y,z	830	a,d,k,n,p,s,t,v
SUBJECT	fin su	600	a,b,c,d,e,k p,q,t,x,y,z	630 650	a,d,k,n,p,s,t,x,y,z a,b,x,y,z
		610	a,b,c,d,e,k n,t,x,y,z	651 652	a,b,x,y,z a,x,y,z
		611	a,c,d,e,n,q,x,y,z	653	a

INDEX	SEARCH COMMAND	FIELDS INDEXED	SUBFIELDS INDEXED	FIELDS INDEXED	SUBFIELDS INDEXED
TITLE	fin ti	130	a,d,g,k,n,p,s,t	490	a,v
		211	a	700	t
		212	a	710	t
		214	a	711	t
		222	a,b	730	a,d,g,k,n,p,s,t
		240	a,d,f,g,k,n,p,s	740	a,n,p
		242	a,b,n,p	770	a,q,s,t
		243	a,d,f,g,k,n,p,s	773	p,s,t
		245	a,b,n,p	780	q,s,t
		246	a,b,n,p	785	q,s,t
		247	a,b,n,p,w	787	q,s,t
		400	n,p,t	800	n,p,t
		410	p,t	810	n,p,t
		411	p,t	811	p,t
		440	a,b,n,p,v	830	a,d,k,n,p,s,t,v
UNIFORM TITLE		130	a,d,g,k,n,p,s,t	243	a,d,f,g,k,n,o,p,r,s
		240	a,d,f,g,k,n,o,p,r,s	730	a,d,g,k,n,p,s,t
		242	a,b,n,p		

C. Phrase searches

INDEX	SEARCH COMMAND	FIELDS INDEXED	SUBFIELDS INDEXED
TITLE	sca ti	130	a,d,g,k,n,p,s,t
		240	a,d,f,g,k,n,p,s
		245	a,b,f,g,k,n,p
		246	a,b,n,p
		247	a,b,n,p
		730	a,d,g,k,n,p,s,t
		740	a,n,p

2. AUTHORITY FILE

A. Search key searches

INDEX	SEARCH KEY FORMAT	COMMAND FORMAT	FIELDS INDEXED	SUBFIELDS INDEXED
AUTHORITY RECORD CONTROL NUMBER	[[Control no.]	fin ln [Control no.]	010	a,z
ISBN	[[ISBN no.]	fin bn [ISBN no.]	020	a,z
ISSN	[[ISSN no.]	fin sn [ISSN no.]	022	a,y,z
NAME	[4,3,1	fin dn 4,3,1	100 110 111 151 400 410 411 451 500 510 511 551	a a,b a,b,n a,x,y,z a a,b a,b,n a,x,y,z a a,b a,b,n a,x,y,z
UNIFORM TITLE	[3,2,2,1	fin dt 3,2,2,1	130 430 530	a,d,g,k n,p,s,t a,d,g,k n,p,s,t a,d,g,k n,p,s,t
TOPICAL SUBJECT	[5,3	fin ds 5,3	150 450 550	a,b,x,y,z a,b,x,y,z a,b,x,y,z

B. Phrase searches

INDEX	SEARCH COMMAND	FIELDS INDEXED	ROOT INDEX	EXPANDED INDEX
PERSONAL NAME	sca pn	100,400,500	a,b,c,d,e,q	f,g,k,l,m,n, o,p,r,s,t
CORPORATE NAME	sca co	110,410,510	a,b,c,d,e,n	f,g,k,l,m, o,p,r,s,t
		151,451,551	a,b	
CONFERENCE NAME	sca cn	111,451,551	a,b,c,d,e,n,q	f,g,k,l,p,s,t
TITLE	sca ti	100,400,500	f,g,k,l,m,n o,p,r,s,t	a,b,c,d,e,q
		110,410,510	f,g,k,l,m,o p,r,s,t	a,b,c,d,e,n
		111,411,511	f,g,k,l,p,s,t	a,b,c,d,e,n,q
		130,430,530	a,d,f,g,k,l,m n,o,p,r,s,t	
SUBJECT	sca su	100,400,500	a,b,c,d,e,f,g,k l,m,n,o,p,q,r,s,t	x,y,z
		110,410,510	a,b,c,d,e,f,g,k l,m,n,o,p,r,s,t	x,y,z
		111,451,551	a,b,c,d,e,f,g,k l,n,p,q,s,t	x,y,z
		130,430,530	a,d,f,g,k,l,m,n o,p,r,s,t	x,y,z
		150,450,550	a,b	x,y,z
		151,451,551	a,b	x,y,z

APPENDIX 2

SEARCH DISPLAYS AND NAVIGATION COMMANDS

1. SEARCH DISPLAYS

Online Union Catalog	
Group display	100-1500 records organized by material and year
Truncated display	6-99 records with one line descriptions
Brief display	2-5 records with, generally, 2 to 6 lines of description
Single record display	1 full bibliographic record

Authority File	
Quickview display	101-600 records with selected one line descriptions. A compressed version of the truncated display
Truncated display	26-100 records with one line descriptions
Brief display	2-25 records with one line descriptions
Single record display	1 full authority record

2. SEARCH NAVIGATION COMMMANDS

NAVIGATION COMMAND	DESCRIPTION
DIS [number(s)]	Display record or group of records selected from search list
FOR	Move forward one screen in a list, or go to the next record in a set of records
BAC	Move back one screen in a list, or go to the previous record in a set of records
PDN	Move forward one screen in a list, or go to the next screen in a bibliographic record
PUP	Move back one screen in a list, or go to the previous screen in a bibliographic record
<HOME>	Move to the first screen of a list or bibliographic record
<END>	Move to the last screen of a list or bibliographic record
GOB	Move back to the search screen next highest in the display hierarchy

NAVIGATION COMMAND	DESCRIPTION
GOB GR	Move back to previous group display
GOB TR	Move back to previous truncated display
GOB BR	Move back to previous brief display
GOB BI	Move back to previous phrase index
DH	Display default locations records
DHA	Display all locations records
DHR	Display regional locations records
DHS	Display state locations records
BIB	Return to bibliographic record from location record

3. CATALOGING NAVIGATION COMMANDS

NAVIGATION COMMAND	DESCRIPTION
Cursor	Move left, right, up, or down one key at a time, or by holding the key down, more rapidly
PUP	Move back one screen
PDN	Move forward one screen
<HOME>	Return cursor to the home position
<END>	Move cursor to bottom right corner of screen
<CTRL><→>	Move cursor to first letter of word to right
<CTRL><←>	Move cursor to first letter of previous word to left
<TAB>	Move cursor one tab to the right
<SHIFT><TAB>	Move cursor one tab to the left
<CTRL> <END>	Move cursor to end of same line
<CTRL> <HOME>	Move cursor to beginning of same line
<ENTER>	Move cursor to beginning of next line
TAG	Move to screen containing selected tag no.
LINE	Move to screen containing selected line no.

APPENDIX 3

SELECTED OCLC-MARC FIELDS WITH INDICATORS AND SELECTED SUBFIELDS

This listing of selected OCLC-MARC fields is not intended in any way to be exhaustive. It is merely intended to provide a introductory guide to the most commonly encountered fields and subfields. Consult OCLC's *Bibliographic Formats and Standards* for a complete list of OCLC-MARC fields.

Fixed fields

BLvl   Bibliographic level
> m: Monograph
> s: Serial

Biog   Biography
> a: Individual autobiography
> b: Individual biography

Conf   Conference publication
> 0: Item is not a conference publication
> 1: Item is a conference publication

Cont   Nature of entire work or nature of contents
> b: Bibliographies
> c: Catalogs
> d: Dictionaries
> l: Legislation
> r: Directories
> s: Statistics

Ctry   Country, or state, of publication
> OCLC-MARC code for place
> e.g. nyu: New York State

Dates   Date or dates of publication

Desc   Descriptive cataloging form
> a: AACR2
> blank: Non-ISBD

DtSt   Type of date/Publication status

> m: Multiple date of publication
> r: Reprint
> s: Single date of publication
> t: Publication date and copyright date both listed

ELvl   Encoding level

> blank: Full-level LC, BL, NLC, NLA, or NLM cataloging
> 8: CIP cataloging
> I: Full-level cataloging by member of OCLC
> K: Less-than full cataloging by member of OCLC

Fict   Fiction

> 0: Item is not fiction
> 1: Item is fiction

GPub   Government publication

> blank: Not a government publication
> f: Federal
> i: International
> l: Local
> s: State

Ills   Illustrations

> a: General illustrations
> b: Maps
> c: Portraits

Indx   Index

> 0: Item does not contain an index
> 1: Item does contain an index

Lang   Language of work

> OCLC-MARC code for language
> e.g. eng: English

Srce   Cataloging source

> blank: Library of Congress
> d: Non-Library of Congress cataloging

Type   Type of record

> a: Printed material
> c: Music
> e: Maps
> g: Projected media
> j: Sound recordings
> m: Computer files

Variable fields

010 Library of Congress Control Number

      Indicators: None
      Subfields: a: Library of Congress control number
                     z: Canceled or invalid LCCN

040 Symbols for cataloging, inputting, and modifying institutions

      Indicators: None
      Subfields: a: Original source of cataloging
                     c: Inputting library
                     d: Modifying institution

020 ISBN

      Indicators: None
      Subfields: a: ISBN
                     z: Canceled or invalid ISBN

041 Language codes

      Indicators: 1st indicator: 0: Item is not and does not include a translation
                                   1: Item is or includes a translation
      Subfields   a: Language(s) of text
                     b: Language(s) of summaries or abstracts
                     h: Original language(s) of text

043 Geographic area code

      Indicators: None
      Subfields: a: Geographic area code

050 LC class number

      Indicators: 1st indicator: 0: Item is in LC
                                     1: Item is not in LC
                 2nd indicator: 0: Call number assigned by LC
                                   4: Call number assigned by other library
      Subfields: a: LC classification number
                     b: Item number

082 DDC class number

      Indicators: 1st indicator: 0: Full edition
                                     1: Abridged edition
                 2nd indicator: 0: Call number assigned by LC
                                   4: Call number assigned by other library
      Subfields: a: Dewey classification number
                     b: Item number
                     2: Source

090 Locally assigned LC-type class number
  Indicators: None
  Subfields: a: LC classification number
               b: item number

092 Locally assigned DDC class number
  Indicators: 1st indicator: 0: Full edition
                                1: Abridged edition
  Subfields: a: Dewey classification number
               b: Item number
               2: Source

049 Local holdings
  Indicators: None
  Subfields: c: Copy statement

100 Personal name main entry
  Indicators: 1st indicator: 0: Forename entry
                                1: Single surname
                                2: Compound surname
  Subfields: a: Personal name
               q: Fuller form of name
               b: Numeral used in name heading
               c: Term of address used in name heading
               d: Dates

110 Corporate name main entry
  Indicators: 1st indicator: 1: Place or place plus name
                                2: Name entered in direct order
  Subfields: a: Name of corporate body
               b: Subordinate body

111 Conference name main entry
  Indicators: 1st indicator: 1: Place or place plus name
                                2: Name entered in direct order
  Subfields: a: Name of conference
               n: Number of conference
               d: Date of conference
               c: Place of conference

130 Uniform title main entry
  Indicators: 1st indicator: Number of nonfiling characters
  Subfields: a: Uniform title
               n: Number of part of work
               p: Name of part of work
               l: Language of work

240 Uniform title

Indicators:	1st indicator:	1: Printed on cards
	2nd indicator:	Number of nonfiling characters
Subfields:	a: Uniform title	
	n: Number of part of work	
	p: Name of part of work	
	l: Language of work	

245 Title statement

Indicators:	1st indicator:	0: No title added entry
	2nd indicator:	1: Title added entry
	Number of nonfiling characters	
Subfields:	a: Title proper	
	n: Number of part of work	
	p: Name of part of work	
	h: General material designation	
	b: Remainder of title	
	c: Remainder of title page transcription	

246 Added title entry

Indicators:	1st indicator:	0: Note, no title added entry
		1: Note, title added entry
		2: No note, no title added entry
		3: No note, title added entry
	2nd indicator:	Blank: Variant doesn't appear on work
		0: Portion of title
		1: Parallel title
		4: Cover title
Subfields:	a: Title	
	i: Display text	

250 Edition statement

Indicators:	None
Subfields:	a: Edition statement
	b: Additional information following edition statement

260 Imprint

Indicators:	None
Subfields:	a: Place of publication
	b: Publisher
	c: Date of publication

300 Physical description

Indicators:	None
Subfields:	a: Extent of an item
	b: Illustrations
	c: Dimensions
	e: Accompanying material

440 Series statement

    Indicators: 2nd indicator: Number of nonfiling characters
    Subfields: a: Series statement
                  n: Number of part of series
                  p: Name of part of series
                  x: ISSN
                  v: Series number

490 Series statement not traced or traced differently

    Indicators: 1st indicator: 0: Series not traced
                                1: Series traced differently
    Subfields: a: Series statement
                  x: ISSN
                  v: Series number

500 General note

    Indicators: None
    Subfields: a: General note

502 Dissertation note

    Indicators: None
    Subfields: Dissertation note

504 Bibliography note

    Indicators: None
    Subfields: Bibliography, etc. note

505 Formatted contents note

    Indicators: 1st indicator: 0: Complete contents
                                1: Incomplete contents
                                2: Partial contents
    Subfields: a: Formatted contents note
                  t: Titles of contents
                  r: Statement of responsibility of contents
                  g: Miscellaneous information

520 Summary note

    Indicators: None
    Subfields: a: summary, etc. note

538 System requirements

    Indicators: None
    Subfields: a: system details note

600 Personal name subject added entry

    Indicators: 1st indicator: 0: Forename
                                  1: Single Surname
                                2: Compound surname

2nd indicator:0: LC subject heading

Subfields: a: Name
q: Fuller form of name
b: Numeral used in name heading
c: Term of address used in name heading
d: Dates
x: General subdivision

610 Corporate name subject added entry

Indicators: 1st indicator: 1: Place or place plus name
2: Name entered in direct order
2nd indicator   0: LC subject heading

Subfields: a: Name of corporate body
b: Subordinate unit
x: General subdivision

611 Conference name added entry

Indicators: 1st indicator: 1: Place or place plus name
2: Name entered in direct order
2nd indicator: 0: LC subject heading

Subfields: a: Name of conference
n: Number of conference
d: Date of conference
c: Place of conference
x: General subdivision

630 Uniform title subject added entry

Indicators: 1st indicator: Number of nonfiling characters
2nd indicator: 0: LC subject heading

Subfields: n: Number of part of work
p: Name of part of work
l: Language of work
x: General subdivision

650 Topical subject added entry

Indicators: 2nd indicator: 0: LC subject heading
Subfields: a: Topical subject heading
x: General subdivision
y: Period subdivision
z: Place subdivision

651 Geographic subject added entry

Indicators: 2nd indicator: 0: LC subject heading
Subfields: a: Topical subject heading
x: General subdivision
y: Period subdivision
z: Place subdivision

700 Personal name added entry

        Indicators: 1st indicator: 0: Forename entry
                                        1: Single surname
                                        2: Compound surname
                   2nd indicator:2: Analytical entry
        Subfields: a: Personal name
                              q: Fuller form of name
                              b: Numeral used in name heading
                              c: Term of address used in name heading
                              d: Dates
                              t: Title of work used as a subheading

710 Corporate name added entry

        Indicators: 1st indicator: 0: Forename entry
                                          1: Single surname
                                        2: Compound surname
                   2nd indicator:2: Analytical entry
        Subfields: a: Name of corporate body
                              b: Subordinate body
                              t: Title of work used as a subheading

711 Conference name added entry

        Indicators: 1st indicator: 1: Place or place plus name
                                          2: Name entered in direct order
                   2nd indicator:2: Analytical entry
        Subfields: a: Name of conference
                              n: Number of conference
                              d: Date of conference
                              c: Place of conference
                              t: Title of work used as a subheading

730 Uniform title added entry

        Indicators: 1st indicator: Number of nonfiling characters
                   2nd indicator:2: Analytical entry
        Subfields: a: Uniform title
                              n: Number of part of work
                              p: Name of part of work
                              l: Language of work
                              t: Title of work used as a subheading

830 Series uniform title added entry

        Indicators: 2nd indicator: Number of nonfiling characters
        Subfields: a: Series uniform title
                              n: Number of part of series
                              p: Name of part of series
                              v: Series number

APPENDIX 4

OCLC PUBLICATIONS DEALING WITH TECHNICAL SERVICES

Authorities User Guide, 2nd ed., 1994.

Bibliographic Formats and Standards, 2nd Ed., 1996. Published following the implementation of format integration, part 1, this single volume replaced separate standards books for each format.

Cataloging User Guide, 1993.

Concise Input Standards, 2nd ed., 1993. A listing of those guidelines that must be followed in inputting records into OCLC. Includes standards for both I and K level records.

Diacritics and special characters, 2nd ed., 1991.

Guide to Searching the Online Union Catalog, 2nd ed., 1992.

OCLC-MARC code lists, 2nd ed., 1993.

OCLC Participating Institutions, Arranged by Institution Name, published every July.

OCLC Participating Institutions, Arranged by OCLC Symbol, published every January, supplemented in July.

Passport Software User Guide, 4th ed., 1994.

Technical bulletins. Published irregularly, OCLC uses the technical bulletins to announce changes and enhancements in the OCLC system. Until these changes are incorporated into the above manuals, this is the only source for the most current information.

Several of the above publications, along with much other valuable information, are also available at OCLC's web site: http://www.oclc.org.

GLOSSARY

Archive record: Record maintained permanently within the OCLC system on which is stored an individual institution's use of a master record.

Authority File: File within OCLC where records containing the authorized bibliographic forms of names are stored. The Authority File should always be consulted before creating a heading in OCLC.

Authorization number: A unique number which, accompanied by a password, entitles the owner to a specific set of privileges within the OCLC system.

Bibliographic format: Within OCLC there are eight bibliographic formats that are used to distinguish between different types of library materials, such as computer files or video recordings. Until format integration each of the eight had markedly different looking records with fields defined differently or only for certain formats. Format integration has markedly diminished the difference between the different formats.

Brief display: Default display format for any search that retrieves between 2 and 5 matches within the Online Union Catalog or between 2 and 25 within the Authority File.

Cataloging level: Catalog records are assigned a cataloging level based on the completeness of the bibliographic information they contain. OCLC records are essentially divided between full-level bibliographic records and minimal-level bibliographic records. The distinction is important for the kind of editing to the master record that is allowed to each mode of authorization.

Constant Data: A labor saving device by means of which large amounts of frequently used data may be saved within a Constant Data record and applied to records whenever needed.

Constant Data Information List: A list of all the Constant Data records currently stored by an institution.

Copy Display: Secondary display area within OCLC in which records can be stored temporarily and viewed while another record remains in the Main display.

Derived search key: Search key that searches for author's names or titles according to a specific format of punctuation and characters.

Encoding level: Fixed field element that indicates the level of cataloging that has been applied to a bibliographic record.

End-of-message symbol: Symbol that defines the ending of a line within the OCLC system. When a command is executed, everything within the line to the left of the end-of-message symbol will be processed.

Enhance mode: Mode in which it is possible to modify most full-level master records. OCLC grants enhance mode, by format, only to those institutions that pass an examination on cataloging within that format.

Expanded index display: Expanded view of the same headings present in a root index display of a phrase index search. In this display, multiple occurrences of a heading are broken out into separate subheading entries.

Final actions: To complete processing on an OCLC record and to use it to create a local catalog record. There are two different final actions: Update and produce.

Fixed field: The first field within an OCLC record. The field consists of a set collection of elements determined by the format of the record. The fixed field is devoted mostly to data usable by online systems for record retrieval.

Format integration: Before format integration, great differences existed in tagging and coding between the various bibliographic formats. In three stages, the last of which was instituted by OCLC in March, 1996, tagging and coding of bibliographic records has been made consistent across all formats. The eight bibliographic formats recognized by OCLC still exist, but the differences between them are far fewer than before.

Full-screen editing: Option available within PRISM by means of which an entire screen of edited data on a record can be sent to the system with one command.

Group display: Default display format within the Online Union Catalog for any search that retrieves between 100 and 1,500 matches.

Home position: Left corner of the line immediately below the status line. The cursor will return to this position automatically after every command. It is from this position that most commands are executed.

Index label: Specific two-letter code that instructs the system which search is being requested (e.g. 'fin dt' for a title search).

Keyword search: Search type available only in the Online Union Catalog in which the system can be searched by individual words rather than by a specific format of characters.

Line: Within OCLC, line refers to an entire variable field that has been labeled with a specific line number. An OCLC line may consist of a number of actual lines of text.

Locations record display: Display accompanying a bibliographic record that lists those institutions that have placed holdings on the item within OCLC.

Lock and replace: Procedure by means of which the master record is edited. The mode of operation necessary to be permitted to lock and replace differs according to the specific situation.

Main display: The principal display area within OCLC. Most of the time that a record is displayed it is in the Main display.

MARC: Machine readable cataloging records that conform to automation standards that make them readily usable within many different automated systems. The basis of the OCLC Online Union Catalog.

Mark for transfer: To mark the fixed field or individual variable fields on a record in order that they may be carried over into a new workform.

Masking characters: Characters (there are two within OCLC, the ? and the #) which allow the system to match multiple words from a single search term.

Master record: Record maintained permanently within the OCLC system. Not to be confused with the Working copy that is displayed on an individual institution's terminal.

Message of the day: Message visible after signing on to OCLC. May contain information of changes to the system, notices of system problems or product announcements.

Mode of operation: Level of privileges within the OCLC system assigned to an authorization number.

Moving a record: To move a record from the Main Display into the Copy Display.

Numeric search keys: Search key that searches for standard numbers contained within a record according to a specific format.

OCLC-MARC: OCLC's implentation of the MARC standard.

Online Union Catalog: OCLC database containing over 35,000,000 bibliographic records as of the middle of 1996.

PASSPORT: Software package available from OCLC that is expressly designed to maximize efficiency in accessing their online services, including PRISM.

Phrase index search: Search type that places the searcher within an area of an index rather than retrieving specific matches. A phrase index search will always produce some result. There are a variety of different phrase index searches available within the Authority File, but it is valid only for titles within the Online Union Catalog.

PRISM: Interactive, online access to a variety of technical service and reference functions available from OCLC.

PRISM help: Help file available within PRISM with guidelines on the operation of most aspects of the system.

Produce: A final action by means of which a local catalog record is created and the institution's holdings placed within the OCLC system.

Qualifiers: A series of codes by means of which search keys can be rendered more specific. With qualifiers, searches can be limited by format, date of publication, cataloging source, and whether or not the work is a microform.

Quickview display: Default display format within the Authority File for any search that retrieves between 101 and 600 matches.

Root index display: The display that is initially presented by a phrase index search within the Authority File. It can be expanded into an expanded index display.

Save File Information List: A listing of all records currently in an institution's save file. The Save File Information List also contains other useful information about the records contained in the save file.

Search history: A list of the ten most recent searches executed in the Online Union Catalog and a separate list of the ten most recent searches executed in the Authority File. The list is accessible online at any time within a session

Search key search: The oldest search type. Search key searches follow very specific formats involving punctuation and length of data (e.g. '3,2,2,1' for a title search).

Segmented field: Field that is longer than the maximum allowable length within OCLC for an individual line. The system breaks the field into multiple segments each of which retains the basic line number but which also possess an individual segment number as well.

Start-of-message symbol: Symbol that defines the beginning of a line within the OCLC system. When a command is executed everything to the right of the start-of-message symbol within the line will be processed.

Stoplist: List of words that the OCLC system is programmed to disregard when constructing index files. Examples include articles. You must take the stoplist into consideration when constructing a search key.

Tag: Three-digit code by which a field in OCLC is identified.

Tag group: Collection of variable fields that share the same first digit and that convey similar but not identical types of information within OCLC records.

Truncated display: Default display format for any search that retrieves between six and 99 matches within the Online Union Catalog or between 26 and 100 within the Authority File.

Update: A final action by means of which a local catalog record is created and the institution's holdings placed within the OCLC system.

Validation: A procedure where the OCLC system checks a record for possible errors in inputting before allowing any final action to be taken on it. It can be requested or, in some cases, the system applies it automatically.

Variable fields: Collection of fields of variable length that follow the fixed field in an OCLC record. Each variable field is identified by a tag number that identifies the variety of information that it contains.

Workform: A blank template to assist in the inputting of new records. Workforms contain a representative collection of empty variable fields that can be filled in to create a new record.

Working copy: The version of the master record that is accessed when an institution retrieves a record. Unless saved, it is maintained by the system only during the current session.

ANSWERS

EXERCISE 1

SEARCH KEY	INITIAL DISPLAY 100 AUTHOR 245 TITLE CONTROL NUMBER
syke,chr,/1975	Brief display Sykes, Christopher, 1907- Evelyn Waugh : a biography #1876012
boo,an,pr,/1963	Brief display Bennett, Paul A., 1897-1966 Books and printing : a treasure for typophiles #20040977
jou,of,ar,e/ser/1932-9	Single record display No 100 field Journal of architecture, engineering, and industry #11320353
stei,legw/rec/-1972	Single record display Steig, Jeremy "Legwork" #7570190
kese,one^/rec	Brief display Kesey, Ken One flew over the cuckoo's nest #14514696
stei,joh,/mf/191?	Truncated display Steinbach, Johannes, 1881- Apologetisches Tendenzen in Lotzes Philosophieren #13607219
smit,w^,e/1934-51	Single record display Smith, W. Eugene, 1918- Spanish village #3545970
goul,ste,j,/-1969	Truncated display Gould, Stephen Jay An evolutionary microcosm #270328

chri,agat/-1944   Truncated display
Christie, Agatha, 1890-1976
An Agatha Christie omnibus
#8919575

twai,inno/????   Single record display
Twain, Mark, 1835-1910
The innocents at home
#7144018

EXERCISE 2

	SEARCH KEY		**RECORDS IN SET**
A.	personal name:	defo,dan,	exceeded system limit
	title:	jou,of,th,p	exceeded system limit
	name/title:	defo,jour	151
	combined:	fin dp defo,dan and dt jou,of,th,p	exceeded system limit
	title phrase:	sca ti journal of the plague year	9 — 59
B.	personal name:	hugo,vic,	exceeded system limit
	title:	mis,,,	exceeded system limit
	name/title:	hugo,mise	745
	combined:	fin dp hugo,vic, and dt mis,,,	exceeded system limit
	title phrase:	sca ti miserables	9 — 566
C:	personal name:	wool,vir,	1252
	title:	to,th,li,	143
	name/title:	wool,to	115
	combined:	fin dp wool,vir, and dt to,th,li,	100
	title phrase:	sca ti to the lighthouse	9 — 86
D.	personal name:	gord,nad,	368
	title:	jul,pe,,	48
	name/title:	gord,july	24
	combined:	fin dp gord,nad, and dt jul,pe,,	23
	title phrase:	sca ti july's people	9 — 11
E.	personal name:	jame,hen,	exceeded system limit
	title:	por,of,a,l	265
	name/title:	jame,port	220
	combined:	fin dp jame,hen, and dt por,of,a,l	149
	title phrase:	sca ti portrait of a lady	171

EXERCISE 3

UNQUALIFIED SEARCH	QUALIFIED SEARCH
A. Search key: flem,ian, Outcome: 1. Group display 2. Collective display 3. #175241	Search key: flem,ian,^/bks/1964 Outcome: 1. Collective display 2. #175241
B. Search key: twai,inno Outcome: 1. Group display 2. Collective display 3. Collective display 4. Collective display 5. Collective display 6. Collective display 7. #7390171	Search key: twai,inno/bks/1924 Outcome: 1. #7390171
C. Search key: cou,of,mo,c Outcome: 1. Group display 2. Collective display 3. #20602571	Search key: cou,of,mo,c/1986/vis Outcome: 1. Truncated display 2. #20602571
D. Search key: red,ba,of,c Outcome: 1. Group display 2. Collective display 3. Collective display 4. #28495776	Search key: red,ba,of,c/bks/1992 Outcome: 1. Truncated display 2. #28495776
E. Search key: cric,jura Outcome: 1. Collective display 2. Collective display 3. Collective display 4. #24010496	Search key: cric,jura/bks/1991 Outcome: 1. Truncated display 2. #24010496

EXERCISE 4

A. ISBN 0-688-03076-9
    1. 0688030769 / 2284086
    2. [100] Dayan, Moshe, ‡d 1915-1981.
    3. Uniform title
    4. [500] Story of my life
    5. [651] Israel ‡x Armed Forces ‡x Biography.

B. ISBN 0-679-50697-7
    1. 0679506977 / 2725081
    2. [040 ‡c] DLC (Library of Congress)
    3. [082] 946.081
    4. [245] The Distant drum
    5. [020 ‡c] $9.95
    6. [700] Toynbee, Philip.

C. ISBN 0-440-09343-0
    1. 0440093430 / 3072550
    2. [050 ‡a] PS3572.O5
    3. [600] Vonnegut, Kurt.
    4. [300 ‡a] xv, 304 p. / [300 ‡b] yes
    5. [260 ‡b] Delacorte Press/S. Lawrence

D. LCCN 77-11689
    1. ^77-11689 or RET / 77-11689
    2. Brief display
    3. Two
    4. Second / 19770816 (Aug. 16, 1977) / 3240824
    5. [100] Christie, Agatha, ‡d 1890-1976.
    6. [260 ‡b] Ballantine Books
    7. No
    8. [650] Women authors, English ‡y 20th century ‡x Biography.

E. LCCN 76-29916
   1. ^76-29916 or RET / 76-29916
   2. Three / two
   3. Third / 19761013 (Oct. 13, 1976) / 2823554
   4. [650] Terrorists ‡x Biography.
   5. [260 ‡b] Holt, Rinehart and Winston
   6. [100] Edwardes, Michael, ‡d 1923-
   7. [500] Hamilton / [500] 1973

F. French Women of Letters
   1. fre,wo,of,l
   2. Three / two
   3. 2883604 / [040 ‡c] no
   4. [010] 13-22969
   5. [050 ‡a] PQ149 / [050 ‡b] .K2
   6. [260 ‡a] London / [260 ‡c] 1862
   7. [650] Women novelists, French.

G. The Earth Book of Stormgate
   1. ear,bo,of,s
   2. Truncated / seven
   3. 3608983 / [010] 77-28774
   4. [650] Science fiction, American.
   5. [020] 0399121447
   6. [260 ‡b] Berkley Pub. Corp. / [260 ‡b] Putnam

H. Kehde, Ned
   1. kehd,ned,^ or kehd,ned,
   2. Four
   3. [245 ‡a] The American left, 1955-1970
   4. [010] 76-8002 / 2119449
   5. [082] 016.3205/13/0973
   6. [260 ‡b] Greenwood Press / [260 ‡c] 1976

I. Rudkin, Ethel H.
    1. rudk,eth,h
    2. [010] 74-196723//r894 / 1242718
    3. [300 ‡a] xvi, 7-102 p., [4] leaves of plates
    4. [020] 0854099921
    5. [250] 1st ed. reprinted / [500] 1936
    6. [651] Lincolnshire (England) ‡x Social life and customs.
    7. [650] Folklore ‡z England ‡z Lincolnshire.

EXERCISE 5

A.

```
▶ Type:  a    Elvl:  I    Srce:       Audn:      Ctrl:      Lang:  eng
  BLvl:  m    Form:       Conf:  0    Biog:      MRec:      Ctry:  at
              Cont:  bc   GPub:       Fict:  0   Indx:  0
  Desc:  a    Ills:  a    Fest:  0    DtSt:  s   Dates:  1981,  ¶
▶    1    010        80-42054 ¶
▶    2    040        DLC ‡c IAY ¶
▶    3    020        0858891905 (pbk.) : ‡c $4.00 ¶
▶    4    050 00     Z4019‡b .J66 1981 ¶
▶    7    082 00     015.94 B2 19 ¶
▶    8    090        ‡b ¶
▶    9    049        IAYA ¶
▶   10    100 1      Jones, Gregory Philip. ¶
▶   11    245 10     Government publications : ‡b a guide to Austra-
lian government publications in the Canberra College of Advanced
Education Library / ‡c Gregory Jones, Colin Wills. ¶
▶   12    250        3rd ed. ¶
▶   13    260        Belconnen, A.C.T. : ‡b Canberra College of Ad-
vanced Education Library, ‡c 1981. ¶
▶   14    300        i, 56 p. : ‡b ill. ; ‡c 26 cm. ¶
▶   15    440 0      Library reference guides ; ‡v no. 2 ¶
▶   16    504        Bibliography: p. 56. ¶
▶   17    650 0      Government publications ‡z Australia ‡x Bibliog-
raphy ‡x Catalogs. ¶
▶   18    610 20     Canberra College of Advanced Education. †b Li-
brary ‡x Catalogs. ¶
▶   19    700 1      Wills, Colin. ¶
▶   20    710 2      Canberra Collge of Advanced Education. ‡b Library. ¶
```

B.

```
▶ Type:  a    Elvl:  I    Srce:        Audn:        Ctrl:        Lang:  eng
  BLvl:  m    Form:       Conf:  0     Biog:        MRec:        Ctry:  cau
              Cont:  bc   GPub:        Fict:  0     Indx:  0
  Desc:  a    Ills:       Fest:  0     DtSt:  s     Dates:  1980,  ¶
▶  1    010         79-84456 ¶
▶  2    040         DLC ǂc IAY ¶
▶  3    020         0893200255 (pbk.) ¶
▶  4    050 00      Z6122 ǂb .S64 1980 ¶
▶  5    082 00      016.3719 ǂ2 19 ¶
▶  6    090         ǂb ¶
▶  7    049         IAYA ¶
▶  8    245 00      Special education index to parent materials. ¶
▶  9    250         1st ed. ¶
▶  10   260         Los Angeles, CA : ǂb National Information Center
for Educational Media, University of Southern California, ǂc 1980. ¶
▶  11   300         xiv, 214 p. ; ǂc 28 cm. ¶
▶  12   500         An activity of the National Information Center for
Special Education Materials. ¶
▶  13   650 0       Handicapped children ǂx Bibliography ǂx Catalogs. ¶
▶  14   650 0       Handicapped children ǂx Education ǂx Bibliography
ǂx Catalogs. ¶
▶  15   650 0       Handicapped children ǂx Education ǂx Audio-visual
aids ǂx Bibliography ǂx Catalogs. ¶
▶  16   710 2       National Information Center for Educational Media. ¶
▶  17   710 2       National Information Center for Special Education
Materials. ¶
```

C.

```
▶ Type:  a    Elvl:  I    Srce:       Audn:        Ctrl:       Lang:  eng
  BLvl:  m    Form:       Conf:  1    Biog:        MRec:       Ctry:  enk
              Cont:  b    GPub:       Fict:  0     Indx:  1
  Desc:  a    Ills:       Fest:  0    DtSt:  s     Dates:  1981,  ¶
▶    1   010        81-190444 ¶
▶    2   040        DLC ‡c IAY ¶
▶    3   020        0903043335 (pbk.) ¶
▶    4   050 00     Z693.A15 ‡b .IS8 1961 ¶
▶    5   082 00     025.3 ‡2 19 ¶
▶    6   090        ‡b ¶
▶    7   049        IAYA ¶
▶    8   111 2      International conference on Cataloguing Principles
‡d (1961 : ‡c Paris, France) ¶
▶    9   245 10     Report / ‡c International Conference on Cataloguing
Principles, Paris, 9th-18th October, 1961 ; edited by A.H. Chaplin
and Dorothy Anderson. ¶
▶   10   246 18     ICCP report ¶
▶   11   246 3      I.C.C.P. report ¶
▶   12   260        London : ‡b IFLA International Office for UBC, ‡c
1981. ¶
▶   13   650 0      viii, 293 p. ; ‡c 21 cm.  ¶
▶   14   650 0      At head of title: International Federation of Library
Associations and Institutions. ¶
▶   15   650 0      Includes bibliographical references and index. ¶
    16   710 2      Cataloging ‡x Congresses. ¶
▶   17   700 1      Chaplin, Arthur Hugh, ‡d 1905- ¶
▶   18   700 1      Anderson, Dorothy Pauline. ¶
▶   18   710 2      International Federation of Library Associations
and Institutions. ¶
```

ABOUT THE AUTHORS

Robert T. Warwick is Bibliographic Information Specialist, Technical and Automated Services, Rutgers University Libraries, New Brunswick, New Jersey.

Kenneth Carlborg has been a cataloger for over thirteen years. While at the University of Urbana-Champaign, he oversaw U.S. Department of Education Title II-C grants to catalog materials in the areas of foreign law and agriculture. He is currently Principal Cataloger for the University of Illinois at Chicago.